T0341623

FROM THE STUDY TO THE PULPIT

"I am always on the lookout for a good 'how-to' book on preaching the Old Testament. Moseley's *From the Study to the Pulpit* is one of the best books on the subject I have seen. His 8-step method for sermon preparation is clear, concise, and serviceable for any preacher. Moseley covers all the bases: genre, context, word studies, determining the theme, how to connect the text to Christ, and application. I especially appreciate his commitment to stressing the importance of the use of Hebrew in sermon preparation. This book is a must read for every preacher. I will be using it in my preaching classes and in my preaching of the Old Testament!"

—DAVID L. ALLEN, Dean, School of Preaching,
Southwestern Baptist Theological Seminary

"In this book Moseley offers eight strategic questions that will help the preacher or teacher take an Old Testament text and move from the written page to spoken presentation. A long-time pastor and excellent preacher, now an Old Testament professor, Moseley offers wonderful insights into understanding an ancient text and then communicating the truth of that text to a modern audience. This is a book that will be helpful to both novice and veteran preachers—and is likely to spark any number of great sermon ideas."

—MICHAEL DUDUIT, Executive Editor, *Preaching* magazine;
and Dean, Clamp Divinity School, Anderson University, Anderson, SC

"In this insightful volume, Moseley has drawn from a rich experience of more than thirty years of teaching and preaching the Old Testament and provided a theologically and exegetically sound guidebook for the pastor, teacher, and student of God's Word. His 8-step method takes the reader/expositor from the foundation of a careful hermeneutic in reading and interpreting Scripture to the prudent and practical proclamation of the Word to our contemporary church and world settings. In his methodology Moseley also provides a Christological lens through which to filter some of the difficult areas of Old Testament interpretation."

—R. DENNIS COLE, Professor of Old Testament Hebrew and
Archaeology, New Orleans Baptist Theological Seminary

"How to preach the Old Testament has been a problem in Christian history ever since Marcion rejected the whole thing back in the second century. Now, Moseley, a distinguished scholar and pastor, gives clear guidance on this perennial issue. His perspective honors the Old Testament as Christian Scripture and helps us to teach and preach it through a Christological lens. A book of theological depth and practical wisdom."

—TIMOTHY GEORGE, Dean, Beeson Divinity School of Samford University;
general editor of The Reformation Commentary on Scripture

"*From the Study to the Pulpit* is a gift to everyone who preaches or teaches or for anyone who seriously wants to understand and study the Old Testament. The writing is so accessible that the PhD in the seminary and the layperson in the church will both benefit from this work. This 8-step method for learning how to do exegesis/exposition of the text is an excellent guide for how to approach God's Word. Moseley provides a tool that will help teachers and students of Scripture discover how all the

Scriptures are profitable for believers today. The approach is Christ-centered and emphasizes prayer in the process. It truly is a must read for anyone wanting to responsibly comprehend, apply, and proclaim God's Word."

—T. J. BETTS, Professor of Old Testament Interpretation,
The Southern Baptist Theological Seminary

"With this carefully developed 8-step approach, Allan Moseley has provided a wonderful treasure for students, teachers, and pastors. Those who take time to read and reflect upon the wise insights found in *From the Study to the Pulpit* will be better prepared and equipped to understand and communicate the Old Testament message with greater faithfulness and effectiveness. I am genuinely delighted to recommend this thoughtful and helpful resource."

—DAVID S. DOCKERY, President, Trinity International University/
Trinity Evangelical Divinity School

"I wish I had had this book when I first began my preaching ministry. *From the Study to the Pulpit* provides an excellence guide for preparing to preach the Old Testament. The eight steps spelled out give clear and straightforward instruction for handling faithfully the Old Testament text. The chapter on pointing people to Jesus through the Old Testament was especially helpful."

—KENNETH KEATHLEY, Senior Professor of Theology,
Southeastern Baptist Theological Seminary

"What do you get when an Old Testament expert and master preacher writes a book on how to preach and teach from the Old Testament? You get Allan Moseley's *From the Study to the Pulpit*. Moseley's 8-step method is smart, accessible, and relevant to a broad range of interests, including Old Testament, preaching, and hermeneutics. Highly recommended."

—BRUCE ASHFORD, Provost, Professor of Theology and Culture,
Southeastern Baptist Theological Seminary

"Moseley combines his decades of pastoral preaching experience with a scholarly understanding of the Old Testament to give us a clear path from text to sermon. In addition to using solid principles of hermeneutics and exposition along the way, the author shows us how to get to Jesus with integrity from any Old Testament text. Pastors and preachers, get this book and keep it close. I promise that you'll use it often!"

—JIM SHADDIX, W. A. Criswell Professor of Expository Preaching,
Director, Center for Preaching and Pastoral Leadership,
Southeastern Baptist Theological Seminary

FROM THE STUDY TO THE PULPIT

An 8-Step Method for Preaching and Teaching the Old Testament

Allan Moseley

LEXHAM PRESS

From the Study to the Pulpit: An 8-Step Method for Preaching and Teaching the Old Testament

Copyright 2017 by Allan Moseley

Lexham Press, 1313 Commercial St., Bellingham, WA 98225
LexhamPress.com

First edition by Weaver Book Company.

Print ISBN 9781683592143
Digital ISBN 9781683592150

Cover design: Frank Gutbrod
Interior Design: Nicholas Richardson

24 v / UK

Printed and bound by CPI Group (UK) Ltd, Croydon, CR0 4YY

For my mother,
Adine Horn Moseley,
with much love and gratitude

CONTENTS

INTRODUCTION

"**P**reaching from the Old Testament is hard for me, so most of the time I don't attempt it." Over the years I have heard no small number of seminary students and pastors speak words like that. The purpose of this book is to help all of us preach and teach the Old Testament more faithfully and effectively. To that end, in the following pages I offer an 8-step method that I hope will be understandable and workable. In presenting this method I have attempted to strike a balance. On the one hand, I want to set the bar high and challenge readers to grow in exegetical proficiency. On the other hand, I hope to provide a simple, usable process that teachers can put to work right away.

Definitions and Presuppositions

This book is about exegesis, or exposition. It would be helpful to define exactly what we mean by those two terms. First, exegesis is the process of determining what a text says and what it means, getting out of the text what is in it. Darrell Bock points out that exegesis has its roots in a Greek term that means "to lead out of," and "so it means to 'read out' the meaning of the text. It is to explain or interpret a text." Bock further states that exegesis involves working with the text's original language, using sound interpretation principles and moving to application.[1]

Teachers of the Bible sometimes differ concerning how to use the terms exegesis and exposition. For example, Douglas Stuart writes that exegesis is not complete without application and proclamation.[2] Robert

---

1. Darrell L. Bock, "Opening Questions," in *Interpreting the New Testament Text: Introduction to the Art and Science of Exegesis,* ed. Darrell L. Bock and Buist M. Fanning (Wheaton, IL, Crossway, 2006), 23–26.

2. Douglas Stuart, *Old Testament Exegesis: A Handbook for Students and Pastors,* 4th ed. (Louisville: Westminster John Knox, 2009), 59–60.

Chisholm, on the other hand, separates exegesis from exposition. For him, exegesis refers strictly to our personal study of the text as we mine the meaning intended by the original author. Exposition, he maintains, refers to what happens after exegesis—the application of the meaning of the text to life and our presentation of its meaning and application to others.[3]

In this book I will use exegesis as Chisholm uses it, but unlike Chisholm I will use exposition to refer to both the process of study and the presentation of the results of that study. I define exposition as "the acquired skill of understanding and communicating the meaning of biblical texts, with the help of the Holy Spirit." In a book on pastoral leadership, I provide a more detailed definition of expository preaching, and it may be helpful to say it here: "A pastor preaches an expository sermon when he explains the meaning of a text of Scripture in the power of the Holy Spirit, follows the form of the text, applies the message of the text to the lives of hearers, affirms that Jesus is the fulfillment of the passage and the only Savior, and preaches for the purpose of changed lives to the glory of God."[4]

Two principal presuppositions guide the writing of this book. First, the author believes in the divine inspiration and therefore the perfection of the Bible. I affirm the Chicago Statement of Biblical Inerrancy, which states in part, "We affirm that Scripture in its entirety is inerrant, being free from all falsehood, fraud, or deceit."[5] Second, the author believes that it is important to teach and preach the Old Testament. We will see in this book that Jesus affirmed the authority of the Old Testament and he referred to it regularly. The early church used the Old Testament in its preaching and writing. For the apostle Paul, Scripture was what we call the Old Testament, and he wrote that "all Scripture is breathed out by God and profitable for teaching, for reproof, for correction, and for training in righteousness" (2 Tim. 3:16). That verse expresses the two presuppositions of

---

3. Robert Chisholm, *From Exegesis to Exposition: A Practical Guide to Using Biblical Hebrew* (Grand Rapids: Baker, 1998), 11.

4. Allan Moseley, "Preaching Expository Sermons," in *Entrusted to the Faithful: An Introduction to Pastoral Leadership*, ed. Ken Coley (Spring Hill, TN: Rainer, 2017), 51.

5. "The Chicago Statement on Biblical Inerrancy," 5, http://www.etsjets.org/files/documents/Chicago_Statement.pdf.

this author: the Old Testament is inspired by God, and it is profitable for the church.

Plan of the Book

The eight steps of the method of exposition described in this book constitute the eight chapters. The first two steps, translation and text criticism, are in chapter 1. The third step requires more space, so chapters 2 and 3 are devoted to genre interpretation. Then chapters 4 through 8 relate to steps four through eight: exploring the context, defining important words, identifying the big idea, making connections to Jesus, and applying the message.

Rather than provide my own translations, and for the sake of familiarity and consistency, I have elected to use the English Standard Version unless otherwise indicated. I hope readers will also use my footnotes as guides for further study, since in my presentation of numerous issues I touch only the tip of the proverbial iceberg. On the day I finished my final edit I received in the mail a copy of John Goldingay's *Reading Jesus's Bible: How the New Testament Helps Us Understand the Old Testament.*[6] I mention it here as a further resource that will surely be helpful to readers interested in the subject of this book, a resource I doubtless would have used and referred to had it been released earlier.

Audience and Purpose

The intended audience for this book is the great group of people who teach and preach the Old Testament. I hope this book will help pastors in their weekly preparation of sermons. I served as a pastor for fifteen years before serving as a full-time professor of Old Testament and Hebrew. Later I served as a pastor for ten more years while continuing to teach full-time. As a result, I have experienced the pressures of preparing to feed the flock God's Word every week, which a pastor friend calls "the relentless return of the Sabbath."

However, this book is not addressed exclusively to preachers. I also have in mind teachers who may teach the Old Testament in a small

---

6. John Goldingay, *Reading Jesus's Bible: How the New Testament Helps Us Understand the Old Testament* (Grand Rapids: Eerdmans, 2017).

group Bible study, a mission setting, a children's Sunday school class, or in some other context. We need not draw the line between preaching and teaching so boldly. In actual practice, preachers teach and teachers preach. For years I have taught graduate courses in hermeneutics, Hebrew, and the Old Testament to people who were preparing for all sorts of ministries in all sorts of places. I have also taught doctoral seminars in preaching the Old Testament in which the students were primarily pastors. In writing this book, I have had all of those students (past, present, and future) in mind. My hope is that this book will help them and others teach the Old Testament in their varied ministries and avoid some of the mistakes I have made in my own preaching and teaching through the years.

At the risk of being reductionist, people who teach and preach the Old Testament need help in three areas, the first of which is having an intentional process of exposition to follow. In Haddon Robinson's landmark book *Biblical Preaching*, he writes, "Clear, relevant biblical exposition does not take place Sunday after Sunday by either intuition or accident. Good expositors have methods for their study."[7]

This book is an effort to provide such a process to preachers and teachers of the Old Testament. Some books in this genre are written by authors who do not preach, or they preach only occasionally. Such books tend to be heavy on theory and light on practical help for weekly sermon or lesson preparation. In this book I attempt to provide some practical help. In some parts of the book I address hermeneutical issues, but I have attempted to do so only at points where knowledge of such matters is absolutely necessary to become an excellent expositor. I also illustrate principles of exposition that originate with my own teaching and preaching over the decades.

Second, teachers of the Old Testament need the skills to put an expositional process into practice. Other skills, like the ability to translate biblical Hebrew, will be learned elsewhere. Also, expositors grow in that skill as we follow the best practices of exposition every week. As much as we may learn from others' experience and ideas, we will learn some lessons only from our own experience.

---

7. Haddon W. Robinson, *Biblical Preaching: The Development and Delivery of Expository Messages*, 3rd ed. (Grand Rapids, Baker, 2014), 28.

Third, becoming excellent expositors of the Old Testament requires God's help. The Old Testament prophets spoke because God called them to speak and gave them words to say. As the apostle Peter expressed it, "Men spoke from God as they were carried along by the Holy Spirit" (2 Peter 1:21). As we apply our gifts and labor to the task of exegeting and teaching the Old Testament, may we do so praying that we will speak "from God" and that we will be "carried along by the Holy Spirit." We need God's help.

In Psalm 119, the psalmist asked God to help him see God's truth in his Word. He prayed, "Open my eyes, that I may behold wondrous things out of your law" (Ps. 119:18).[8] The truth God reveals in his Word is indeed "wondrous." A repeated Old Testament confession regarding God's knowledge is that it is "too wonderful for me" (Job 42:3; Ps. 139:6; Prov. 30:18). God, precisely because he is God, knows what we cannot know. Yet his revealed truth is accessible to us. God told his people in the wilderness that his law is "not too hard for you, neither is it far off" (Deut. 30:11). Michael Fishbane points out that in Psalm 119 the psalmist was living between those two poles: the assertion of tradents in the wisdom tradition that God's knowledge is beyond us, and the Deuteronomic affirmation that God's revelation is understandable.[9] Between those two poles, the psalmist asked God to open his eyes so that he could see God's truth in his Word. Such a prayer is necessary for us too. For that reason, the description of each of the eight steps in this book will include a call to prayer. Since our spiritual eyes are clouded by sin and ignorance, we need God to open them to behold the wonders of his revelation.

The psalmist's prayer in Psalm 119:18 reflects the humility we need as we approach God's eternal truth. In one of the hymns among the Dead Sea Scrolls, a member of the Qumran community contemplated God's revealed word and wrote, "How shall I behold [these things] unless Thou open my eyes?"[10] Today, we stand between the same two poles:

---

8. Such a prayer was not an isolated request, since this psalmist also asked God for help in understanding his revealed word in verses 12, 27, 33, 64, 66, 68, 73, 108, 124, and 135.

9. Michael Fishbane, *Biblical Interpretation in Ancient Israel* (Oxford: Oxford University Press, 1985), 539–42.

10. Geza Vermes, *The Complete Dead Sea Scrolls in English* (New York: Penguin, 1997), 293.

affirming that God's Word has wonders, yet believing that they are wonders that are accessible to us through prayerful exegesis. So we repeat the prayer of the psalmist, "Open my eyes, that I may behold wondrous things out of your law." Clara H. Scott expressed the same sentiment in the nineteenth century in her poem that was later set to music:

> Open my eyes, that I may see
> Glimpses of truth Thou hast for me;
> Place in my hands the wonderful key
> That shall unclasp and set me free.
>
> Open my ears, that I may hear
> Voices of truth Thou sendest clear;
> And while the wave notes fall on my ear,
> Everything false will disappear.
>
> Open my mouth, and let me bear,
> Gladly the warm truth everywhere;
> Open my heart and let me prepare
> Love with Thy children thus to share.
>
> Silently now I wait for Thee,
> Ready my God, Thy will to see,
> Open my eyes, illumine me,
> Spirit divine![11]

---

11. Clara H. Scott, "Open My Eyes, That I May See," in *The Hymnal for Worship and Celebration* (Nashville: Word Music, 1986), 381.

Chapter 1

WHAT DOES THE TEXT SAY?

8-STEP METHOD

STEP 1	Translating the text
STEP 2	Considering text criticism
STEP 3	Interpreting the genre
STEP 4	Exploring the context
STEP 5	Defining important words
STEP 6	Identifying the big idea
STEP 7	Connecting to Jesus
STEP 8	Applying the text to contemporary people

The first of our eight steps of exposition is translation, and the second step is textual criticism. Both those steps are addressed in this chapter, and both answer the question, what does the text say? To some people, asking what the text says may seem unnecessary, even absurd. They think, "It says what it says! What the text says is perfectly clear to anyone who just takes the time to read it!" But it's not that simple. How often do we read emails, texts, or messages on social media and we ask, "What is he saying?" or "What does that mean?" Those messages are in English and often from someone we know personally.

Old Testament texts were written by authors we do not know personally, and they lived thousands of years ago in cultures that were vastly different from ours. Also, they wrote in Hebrew, and sometimes it's tricky to find the right English word or phrase to convey the meaning of a word in another language. Furthermore, sometimes the ancient Hebrew texts or the ancient translations differ from one another, so we have to determine which reading is the original. Therefore, answering the question what does the text say is not that easy after all.[1] We are more likely to answer it well, though, if we acquire as much knowledge as possible about translation and text criticism, and if we apply that knowledge with discernment and dependence on the guidance of the Holy Spirit who inspired the text. And as soon as we possess the desire to depend on the Holy Spirit, we will be compelled to pray, asking for the Spirit's help.

Pray

Walter Kaiser concludes his *Toward an Exegetical Theology* with a chapter titled "The Exegete/Pastor and the Power of God." After eleven chapters of helpful instruction regarding the nature, history, and method of biblical exegesis, Kaiser emphasizes the need of the exegete/pastor for God's power. To have God's power, Kaiser says, we must pray. Preaching and teaching with God's power requires "abundant and Spirit-led prayer."[2]

Some books on Bible study, like Kaiser's book, reserve the emphasis on the necessity of prayer until the end. Other books emphasize prayer at the beginning. Unfortunately, some do not include the necessity of prayer at all. The present work features a section on prayer in every chapter. This arrangement is intended as a reminder that we who teach and preach God's Word should ask for God's help throughout every step of preparation. As Charles Spurgeon expressed it, "We ministers ought never to be many minutes without actually lifting up our hearts in prayer." Spurgeon called such prayer "a habit of the new nature for

---

1. Hermeneutics texts sometimes refer to such difficulties as gaps between the text and the reader, and between the world of the text and the world of the reader. The goal is to bridge the gaps. See, for example, Graeme Goldsworthy, *Gospel-Centered Hermeneutics* (Downers Grove, IL: InterVarsity Press, 2006), 28–32; and Henry A. Virkler and Karelynne Gerber Ayayo, *Hermeneutics*, 2nd ed. (Grand Rapids: Baker, 2007), 19–20.

2. Walter C. Kaiser Jr., *Toward an Exegetical Theology: Biblical Exegesis for Preaching and Teaching* (Grand Rapids: Baker, 1981), 240.

which we claim no more credit than a babe does for crying after its mother."[3] That's how Spurgeon portrayed his prayer in preparation to preach—a baby crying for his mother's help.

Spurgeon's preaching ability is legendary. The following is an excerpt from a biography written by George Lorimer that was published only months after Spurgeon's death. Perhaps with a bit of eulogizing hyperbole, Lorimer wrote that Spurgeon "achieved for himself a throne beyond that of earthly dignities, and won for himself a scepter that has brought more hope to human minds, and joy and peace to human hearts, than any that has been grasped during these later centuries either by kings or cardinals."[4] As if that wasn't enough, Lorimer went on to compare Spurgeon favorably with writers like Byron and Goethe, philosophers like Plato and Kant, and preachers like Chrysostom and Luther. He then wrote, "Among these names as lustrous as the brightest, and yet shining with a radiance all its own, gleams that of Charles Haddon Spurgeon, the greatest of modern Puritan preachers."[5]

It's hard to imagine higher praise for a human being. But how did Spurgeon see himself? On his knees in prayer like a crying baby—helpless, hungry, and in need of God's help. Maybe Spurgeon was a great Bible preacher because he realized that without God's help he was not great at all. If someone so gifted and committed was in such need of God's help, surely we too need God's help. We, like Spurgeon, are children, and children can say something great only if their parents tell them what to say. Our heavenly Father shows us what to say when we look in his Word, and his Holy Spirit helps us to understand his Word (1 Cor. 2:12–16). We access his help by asking for it in prayer.

Determine the Best Translation

In the children's book *The Phantom TollBooth*, a child named Milo, the central character, travels by means of a toll both to a fantasy kingdom ruled by two men, Azaz the Unabridged and his brother the Mathemagician. Azaz believes words are more important than

---

3. C. H. Spurgeon, *Lectures to My Students* (Peabody, MA: Hendrickson, 2010), 208.

4. George C. Lorimer, *Charles Haddon Spurgeon* (Boston: James H. Earle, 1892), 8.

5. Ibid., 11.

numbers, and the Mathemagician believes numbers are more important than words. They turn to their sisters, Rhyme and Reason, to settle the dispute, and the sisters decide that words and numbers are equally important. Their decision equally infuriates Azaz and the Mathemagician, so the two brothers ban their sisters from the kingdom. Milo arrives in the kingdom after Rhyme and Reason have been banished, so naturally he encounters quite a bit of confusion. The Mathemagician insists that he has attempted reconciliation with Azaz by writing a letter to him, but Azaz did not even answer it. When Milo sees the letter, though, it's just a conglomeration of numbers. The letter makes perfect sense to the Mathemagician, but Azaz was not able to translate it.[6]

People communicate differently, and they even think differently. What makes perfect sense to one person is unintelligible to someone else. Obviously that is the case when people communicate in different languages, but understanding can be a problem even when people speak the same language. The Old Testament was written in Hebrew, with some passages in Aramaic. Hence, its message must be translated to be understood, and it should be translated into words and sentences people understand. Our explanations of the translation should also be understandable to the persons to whom we speak, or we will find ourselves in the same situation as Azaz the Unabridged and the Mathemagician. And especially since the Bible is God's truth to humanity, we had better make sure we get it right. People who preach and teach the Bible are motivated to do their work faithfully and effectively. They want to grow in their knowledge of the Bible and their ability to communicate its message. This chapter is an effort to contribute to that growth. It is written to help people who will spend time learning Hebrew and doing their own translation, and to help people who will do all their exposition in English.

Why Study the Old Testament in Hebrew?

Anyone who has studied a language other than their native language knows that something is lost in translation. The old Italian proverb is *traduttore traditore*, meaning "translator, traitor." The proverb expresses

---

6. Norton Juster, *The Phantom Tollbooth* (New York: Random House, 1961), 195–99.

a truism: all translators are traitors in some way because they inevitably betray certain qualities of texts in the process of translation. Subtle nuances, emphases, or even basic meanings are often missed by those who are not fluent in a language. Translation difficulties increase exponentially when a language was part of a culture that existed thousands of years ago. Such is the case with biblical Hebrew. On the other hand, the more proficient we are in a language, the more we understand all the nuances of what is said and written in that language. In this section, I want to make a case for learning and using Hebrew in Old Testament exposition. For the sake of readers for whom study of Hebrew is not possible, I will try to make the case as quickly and painlessly as possible, and maybe even occasionally interesting.

First, reading texts in their original language helps us to understand them more clearly. When I was in college I completed two years of Greek study and one year of Hebrew study, and in seminary I continued to study the languages. While I was in seminary, a pastor friend who had not studied the languages told me that he saw no need to do so. He commented sarcastically, "The only reason I can think of to learn Greek is to impress people when I preach." I was astonished. I said nothing because I did not want to show any disrespect, but my thought was, "The only reason I can think of to learn Greek and Hebrew is to understand the Bible!" Decades have passed since that conversation, and my thought at that moment has proven to be more accurate than I could have known then. I have been able to learn and teach so many truths from the Bible more accurately because of my study of the languages, and the more I have studied them the more helpful they have been.

Bible teachers often tell their students that reading the Bible in English is like watching a black-and-white television program. Reading the Bible in the original languages is like watching a color television in high definition. For example, Ruth 4 describes Boaz's redemption of Ruth in preparation to marry her. He went to the gate of the city to find the nearest relative who had the first right of redemption. In the providence of God, that very man walked by the gate. Boaz said to him, "Turn aside, friend; sit down here" (v. 1). Actually, Boaz did not use the Hebrew word for friend. Boaz used two Hebrew words that referred to something that was to remain unnamed. David used the same two words when he went to the town of

Nob. Ahimelech the priest expressed surprise that David was in Nob alone. David replied that he was going to meet his men at "such and such a place" (1 Sam. 21:1–2). David was keeping the location of his men a secret, so he used two Hebrew words that meant something like "such and such," or "whatever." Boaz used the same two Hebrew words to refer to the guy who had the right of redemption, so he was saying, "Hey, So and So, come over here and sit down." In fact, the man's name is not found at all in the book of Ruth, so we don't know his name. Since he failed to step up and redeem poor Ruth and her mother-in-law, it's likely that either the writer decided not to use his name to save his family embarrassment, or the writer did not include his name because he didn't *deserve* for his name to be recorded. Thus, the writer opted to refer to him as "So and So," or "What's His Face." However, the major modern English translations have "friend" (ESV, NASB, NIV, NRSV). HCSB even has "Boaz called him by name," though the CSB has the translation note, "Or said, 'Come here Mr. So-and-so.'" The KJV has "Ho, such a one!" Only when we identify the Hebrew word and note the way it is used elsewhere can we begin to understand Boaz's greeting. It's black and white versus high definition.

Examples like Ruth 4:1 may give the impression that every verse in the Old Testament will read differently when we read the text in Hebrew. That is not the case. Most of the time translators can render the meaning of Hebrew words into English with such a high degree of precision that the meaning is clear whether reading in Hebrew or English. Still, reading the text in its original language makes a difference. Moisés Silva expresses this understanding well:

> The value of studying the biblical languages does not reside in its potential for displaying exegetical razzle-dazzle. In fact, striking interpretations that lean too heavily, sometimes exclusively, on subtle grammatical distinctions are seldom worth considering. On the other hand, genuine familiarity with Greek (and Hebrew!) develops sensitivity and maturity in the interpreter and allows his or her decisions to be built on a much broader base of information. More often than not, the fruit of language learning is intangible; it remains in the

background, providing the right perspective for responsible exegesis.[7]

In other words, facility in Hebrew can improve our interpretation of a passage. But even when ability to read Hebrew "remains in the background," it increases our knowledge base and sharpens our perspective for all our interpretive decisions.

Second, major English translations are produced by committees, and committees tend to preserve traditional renderings, even when those renderings may not be the most accurate translations. Proverbs 22:6 is a case in point. It reads, "Train up a child in the way he should go, even when he is old he will not depart from it" (NASB). However, the Hebrew text does not read "the way he should go." Notably missing is the word "should." A more literal translation is, "Train a child according to his way." What is "his way"? That's open to interpretation. Every child is different, so maybe the point is to teach each child according to the way he or she learns best—his own way. The content of the teaching, given the context in Proverbs and in the Old Testament, would be how to fear God and live wisely. On the other hand, maybe "his way" should be interpreted *in contrast to* God's way of wisdom. Taken that way, the point of the verse would be that if parents train children according to their natural inclinations (i.e., their own way), then they will stay on that path into adulthood because that is the only way of living they have been taught. So in Proverbs 22:6 we are faced with two possible interpretations, neither of which are available to us until we read the verse in Hebrew. But if that's the way the verse reads in Hebrew, why don't the English translations reflect that? We cannot be certain, but the traditional translation dates back centuries and many Christians have claimed it as a promise for their families. It's likely that more recent translation committees decided not to deprive Bible readers of that promise, thus preserving a traditional rendering even though it is not the most faithful translation. However, teachers and preachers of the Old Testament want to teach

---

7. Moisés Silva, *Has the Church Misread the Bible? The History of Interpretation in Light of Current Issues*, Foundations of Contemporary Interpretation (Grand Rapids: Zondervan, 1987), 13.

and preach it faithfully, and the way to accomplish that is to read it in its original language.

Third, language changes. The English of the Middle Ages was quite different from the English of the twenty-first century. Just read Chaucer's *Canterbury Tales* as it was originally written, if you can.

One evening I was teaching from the book of Proverbs in a church. After the Bible study, a lady who was a new Christian and new to the Bible approached me and asked, "Why does God say scuba diving is a sin?" She was utterly sincere, and I tried to assure her that to my knowledge God has not said that scuba diving is a sin. Then she pointed out Proverbs 20:10, which reads in the King James Version, "Divers weights, and divers measures, both of them are alike abomination to the LORD." Then I attempted to explain to her that the King James Version was translated in 1611, and "divers" was an older English word that today would be spelled "diverse" and it means "different." So Proverbs 20:10 says that God does not approve of using different weights in buying and selling goods to deceive customers, and it says nothing about scuba diving. Her confusion was caused by the fact that the English language has changed.

Today, language is changing even more quickly. Only a decade or two after an English translation is produced, the nuances of some words will have changed. The New International Version was first published in 1978. It translates the prayer in Psalm 139:24 as, "See if there is any offensive way in me." In 1978, "offensive" could carry ideas like moral disgust or moral revulsion. In the decades since, however, people in Western culture seem "offended" over virtually everything and virtually nothing. "You wrote 'he and she' instead of 'she and he.' That's offensive to me." Okay, maybe your way of writing is better, but it seems unlikely that my choice of word order rises to the level of moral disgust. Thus, by the way "offensive" is being used, its meaning has been downgraded, or at least altered. But the Hebrew word translated "offensive" communicates the idea of emotional or physical pain. It can be rendered with words like "hurt," "anxious toil," "agony," or "hardship."[8] Its first use is in Genesis 3:16 to refer to Eve's pain in

---

8. Ludwig Koehler and Walter Baumgartner, *The Hebrew and Aramaic Lexicon of the Old Testament*, trans. M. E. J. Richardson (Leiden: Brill, 2001), 1:865.

childbirth that was God's punishment for her sin. In Isaiah 63:10 it refers to the pain in God's Spirit that results from the rebellion of his people and that leads to his punishment. It seems better, therefore, to use an English equivalent that is stronger than "offensive," since today that word that can refer to a minor misstep. The meaning of the word has shifted since 1978.

Fourth, dialects of English differ from place to place. English translations are produced potentially for the entire English-speaking world. Certain words may have specific nuances in one area but not another. When Bible teachers stand to teach or preach the Old Testament, they are not speaking to the entire English-speaking world. They are speaking to one group of people in one area at one moment in time. Hopefully they know those people, at least they probably know them better than the people who produced their English Bible translation. That knowledge makes them capable of being better translators for that group of people, if they are reading the text in Hebrew.

Fifth, reading texts in their original language encourages careful analysis. For English speakers, reading classical Hebrew is obviously harder than reading English. The difficulty of reading Hebrew inevitably slows down readers and forces them to pay more careful attention to the details of the text. But when we read the text in English, we usually recognize it immediately. We remember reading it before, and often we even remember the way a Bible teacher or pastor taught the text in the past. Thus, before we pay attention to the state of verbs, the appearance of unique terms, or contextual issues, we have already deferred to certain ideas about the text's meaning and application. At its best, reading the Bible in that way is less than careful analysis; at its worse it is prejudicial and lazy.

Sixth, some expressions are not translatable without explanation. Translators for published English Bibles deserve our sympathy. They are not allowed to explain the meaning of a term or clause. They are permitted only to select an English word or two to represent a Hebrew word or expression, and they know that frequently Bible readers cannot appreciate the full meaning without further explanation. In Hosea 14:1, for example, Hosea preaches, "Return, O Israel, to the LORD your God." In verse 2, he repeats, "Return to the LORD." In verse 4, as a result of the repentance of the people the

Lord says, "I will heal their apostasy" (ESV, NASB). Instead of "apostasy," other translations have "waywardness" (NIV), "backsliding" (KJV), or "disloyalty" (NRSV). The Hebrew word, though, is the same word translated "return" in verses 1 and 2. In verse 4, the word refers to turning *away* from God instead of turning *to* him. So God said that when they turned *to* him, he was going to heal their turning *away*.

Then in the second part of verse 4, God said, "My anger has turned from them" (ESV). "Turned" translates the same Hebrew word again, but here it refers to God's anger turning away from repentant sinners. Then verse 7 says, "Those who live in his shadow will again raise grain" (NASB). "Again" translates the same Hebrew word Hosea used four times earlier in these verses. Verse 7 says that prosperity, or fertility, will return to God's people. By means of five uses of the same Hebrew word, Hosea used wordplay to highlight what spiritual renewal looks like. We return to God, and then his anger turns from us. Also, he heals our turning hearts and his blessing returns to us. Hosea called us to notice that four kinds of turning occur in a renewed relationship with God. But it's hard for people to notice the repetition of turning when they don't read the text in Hebrew. They need someone to read the Hebrew text and explain it to them, and that's what preachers and teachers want to do well for the church.

Seventh, accurate exposition is the most important task for Bible teachers and preachers. People in ministry, whether vocational or voluntary, have numerous demands on their time. They counsel the hurting, visit the sick and bereaved, pursue people outside the faith, serve the needy, struggle for time to pray, attend to seemingly endless administrative tasks, and at the end of most days they feel like they have not done enough. In the morning they share euphoric celebration over the birth of a child to a formerly barren couple. In the afternoon they feel soul-crushing grief over the death of a young mother with cancer. They fight for a fragile sense of order in the pandemonium while also doing daily battle with demonic forces and the laziness of the flesh. In the attempt to manage that whirlwind of a life, preparing to teach and preach the Bible can seem like one more item on the to-do list. It is not. Bible exposition is both the most important task for church leaders like pastors and the foundational task for all others.[9] Bible teaching and preaching is the church's protection from doctrinal aberration.[10] The Bible shows the way to know God in Christ, it shows Christ-followers how to behave, and it gives the church its structure, mission, priorities, and authority. Christians are "people of the Book," but we cannot know what the Book says without accurate exposition. We who teach dare not get it wrong. We dare not give it less than our best.

Some local churches recognize the primacy of faithful Bible teaching arising from careful exposition, and others do not. Preachers and teachers *must* recognize its primacy, because they bear the responsibility before God to teach his Word accurately. Pastors, especially, cannot delegate the feeding of their sheep to a committee, a staff member, or authors of commentaries. God intends for his sheep to be fed by their shepherds. Therefore, faithful shepherds devote themselves to the tedious, glorious work of careful exposition.

Eighth, the ability to translate Hebrew gives Bible teachers and preachers the ability to help people choose the best Bible translations. "Which Bible translation should I use?" is a common question people ask Bible teachers. When expositors have experience doing their own translation, comparing the Hebrew text with the various English translations week after week, they will have enough knowledge to make informed recommendations to people interested in the Bible. Years ago, a pastor was called a "parson." The word arose from the fact that people in a community considered him the "person" they could go to in order to ask important questions about life and God. As *the* person, the parson was the embodiment of the work of the church in a community and a reliable guide to the truth the church teaches. Of course, we live in

---

9. For a fuller explanation of the importance of expository preaching, see the author's chapter, "The Pastor and Expository Preaching" in *Entrusted to the Faithful: An Introduction to Pastoral Leadership*, ed. Ken Coley (Spring Hill, TN: Rainer, 2017), 47–49.

10. "The more a theologian detaches himself from the basic Hebrew and Greek text of Holy Scripture, the more he detaches himself from the source of real theology! And real theology is the foundation of a fruitful and blessed ministry." Heinrich Bitzer, ed., *Light on the Path: Daily Scripture Readings in Hebrew and Greek* (Grand Rapids: Baker, 1982), 10, cited in John Piper, *Brothers, We Are Not Professionals: A Plea to Pastors for Radical Ministry* (Nashville: B&H, 2002), 81.

the "information age," so there will always be people who know more about a particular subject than any of us as individuals. Still, which Bible translation is best is a question any pastor or informed Bible teacher should be able to answer from his or her own translation experience. The alternative is to give an answer that is limited to personal opinion and not very helpful, like, "The New International Version flows really well when I read it, so I recommend that translation." We can do better. Another inadequate answer is to defer to other teachers who can read Hebrew. "My college/seminary professor said the New American Standard Bible is the translation that is closest to the Hebrew, so I recommend that version." But has God called that college or seminary professor to lead the people who hear you teach the Bible? We dare not delegate spiritually crucial matters to an "authority" we may not even know personally and who has no connection to the lives of people we teach.[11] Nothing will prepare Bible teachers to answer questions about the various English translations as well as their own experience in translating the text for themselves.

Learning a language and wrangling with it week by week is hard work. Faithful exegesis is hardly ever convenient. Sometimes it even seems like drudgery, but it is also necessary and worth it. In the story about Milo's conversation with the Mathemagician, at one point Milo laments that everything he is encountering is too difficult for him. The Mathemagician gently replied, "You'll find . . . that the only thing you can do easily is be wrong, and that's hardly worth the effort."[12]

What Makes a Good Translation?

"Isn't one's choice about a Bible translation a matter of personal preference?" Some people think of the issue that way, but actually it's more complicated. Publishers produce translations of the Bible for specific reasons, and they produce them according to particular translation philosophies. Furthermore, opinions about Bible translation philosophies vary rather widely, which at times has made the field of Bible

---

11 John Piper passionately argues this point as related to pastors. "When we fail to stress the use of Greek and Hebrew as valuable in the pastoral office, we . . . surrender to the seminaries and universities essential dimensions of our responsibility as elders and overseers of the churches." Piper, *Brothers, We Are Not Professionals*, 84–85.

12. Juster, *The Phantom Tollbooth*, 198.

translation surprisingly contentious. Far from being merely an issue of personal preference, Bible translation is a biblical and even an ethical issue. It's a biblical issue because one's approach to Bible translation should match what the Bible says about itself, and the Bible says some things that seem relevant to the way we should go about translating it. Bible translation is an ethical issue because people who read or hear one's translation trust that the translation accurately represents what the source text says.

The goal of this section is not to articulate an exhaustive translation philosophy, though what I write reflects a particular philosophy that will be identifiable to those familiar with the issues. The goal is to offer help in the exposition of the Old Testament to those who use the English Bible and to those who use both the English and Hebrew texts. I have recommended doing one's own translation, but many Bible teachers use only English translations. For such teachers and preachers, accurate exposition requires awareness of translation issues and some knowledge of why translators translate the way they do. The Bible students we teach read different translations, and each translation contains footnotes that refer to alternate translations. Which translation is best, and why did the translator choose one word or phrase instead of another? The aim of this section is to increase the ability of Bible teachers and preachers to answer such questions. To accomplish that I will provide some definitions of terms that are necessary to have a conversation about translation. Next, I will offer a description of a desired translation, interacting along the way with various voices in the translation debate. I hope this section will also help expositors who read the Hebrew text, since we will think through what a good translation will look like.

Definitions

The original language in which a text is written is typically called "the native language." In the case of the Old Testament, the native language is Hebrew (except for Ezra 4:8–6:18; Ezra 7:12–26; Jer. 10:11; and Dan. 2:4b–7:28, which are in Aramaic). "The receptor language" is the language into which a text is translated. In the case of readers of this book, the receptor language is English.

As for translation philosophies, two philosophies dominate the current practice of Bible translation, with the result that

virtually all translations adhere more or less to one of these philosophies. "Paraphrases" are not considered in these definitions because
they are not the same as translation. For example, Kenneth Taylor
produced The Living Bible by paraphrasing an English text, not by
translating the Hebrew and Greek into English. Some translations depart from the native language more freely in an effort to communicate its ideas into the receptor language in a fresh and striking way.
Paraphrases are so free in this regard that they are no longer properly
referred to as translations.

 "Essentially literal translations" are sometimes referred to as "literal,"
or "word for word" translations. While perhaps helpful, such descriptions are not technically accurate. "Essentially literal translators" readily
admit that a truly literal, or word-for-word translation is impossible,
or if it was produced it wouldn't make must sense. For example, when
Joseph's brothers came to him in Egypt the second time, Joseph asked
them about the welfare of their father (Gen. 43:27). If we translated
Joseph's words literally, the result would be something like, "And he
asked them for peace. 'Is it peace with your father?'" The word translated "peace" is the familiar word *shalom*. While one of the basic meanings for *shalom* is "peace," that term was also used in other ways. One
way it was used was as a general greeting. Essentially, asking someone
about "peace" was a way of saying "how's it going?" (cf. Exod. 18:7;
Judg. 18:15; 2 Sam. 11:7). It was a colloquial expression in the same
way "how's it going?" is colloquial, since we don't mean to imply by
that question that anything is going anywhere. So an essentially literal translation renders Genesis 43:27 as, "And he inquired about their
welfare and said, 'Is your father well?'" (ESV). So when opponents of
an essentially literal translation philosophy state that translating literally is impossible because of factors like idiomatic expressions, they are
stating what all translators already know. The important point is that a
translator who works to produce an essentially literal translation "strives
to find the English word or combination of words that most accurately corresponds to the words of the original text."[13] The focus is on

---

13. Leland Ryken, "Five Myths about Essentially Literal Bible Translation,"
in *Translating Truth: The Case for Essentially Literal Bible Translation* (Wheaton, IL:
Crossway, 2005), 58.

accurately representing the Hebrew text, attempting "to represent *the meaning of every word* in the original in some way or other in the resulting translation."[14] The motto of the essentially literal translators of the Revised Standard Version was "as literal as possible, as free as necessary."[15] The goal is to be as literal as possible while still understandable and clear.

Essentially literal translation has also been referred to as "formal correspondence translation." The forms of the text in the native language are translated into corresponding forms in the receptor language. For example, if the form of a Hebrew verb and its context indicate that the action is in past tense, then it is translated into past tense in English.[16] If a verb is reflexive, referring to something the subject of the verb does to or for himself, then the verb should be translated as reflexive in English. The title "formal correspondence" is not used as commonly anymore because of the recognition that in so many cases it is impossible to reproduce the forms of Hebrew in understandable English. Word order, for example, is different in Hebrew sentences than in English sentences and sometimes can be quite confusing to English readers. Therefore, translators do not reproduce the Hebrew word order "literally," or "word for word," because to do so would make little sense in the receptor language. Still, the goal of an essentially literal translation is to represent *as much as possible* every Hebrew word by an equivalent English word and every Hebrew phrase by an equivalent English phrase. Excellent examples of essentially literal translations are the English Standard Version and the updated New American Standard Bible. The King James Version is also an example of this translation philosophy, though it is dated. Its language issues, but not necessarily text critical issues (discussed later in this chapter), have been improved in the New King James Version.

---

14. Wayne Grudem, "Are Only Some Words of Scripture Breathed Out by God?" in *Translating Truth: The Case for Essentially Literal Bible Translation* (Wheaton, IL: Crossway, 2005), 20. Emphasis in original.

15. Ibid., 24.

16. Technically, Hebrew verbs do not have *tense*. Hebrew grammarians refer instead to the *state* of verbal action as complete or incomplete. However, referring to tense is the most convenient way to refer to verbal action. Moreover, the *idea* of tense must have been present in Hebrew.

Dynamic equivalence translations are less word-for-word translations and more thought-for-thought translations. Such translations are sometimes referred to as "meaning based" or "meaning driven." The latter title seems less helpful since every responsible translation is driven by the desire to translate the meaning of the original. Gordon Fee and Mark Strauss refer to this philosophy as "functional equivalence." Instead of aiming at reproducing the *forms* of the native language, as with formal equivalence, the emphasis is on determining the *function* of the words and phrases and reproducing those functions in English. Advocates of dynamic equivalence "stress that the translation should sound as clear and natural to the contemporary reader as the original text sounded to the original readers."[17] Translators who follow a dynamic equivalence philosophy also usually ask whether a potential translation will have the same effect on contemporary readers as the Hebrew text had on the original readers. Eugene Nida, the "father" of dynamic equivalence translation, and Charles Taber wrote exactly that in their book describing their approach to translation. "To measure dynamic equivalence we can only rightly compare the equivalence of response, rather than the degree of agreement between the original source and the later receptors. . . . Dynamic equivalence is therefore to be defined in terms of the degree to which the receptors of the message in the receptor language respond to it in substantially the same manner as the receptors in the source language."[18]

The dynamic equivalence approach to translation has raised questions among people who are interested primarily in accuracy in translation.[19] First, unless the text actually tells us, which is rare, how can we know the way the original receptors of the message responded to it? Isn't our hypothesis about their response an imprecise standard by which to measure the accuracy of our translation? Second, since dynamic equivalence is a thought-for-thought translation, how can we

---

17. Gordon Fee and Mark Strauss, *How to Choose a Translation for All Its Worth* (Grand Rapids: Zondervan, 2007), 26.

18. Eugene Nida and Charles Taber, *The Theory and Practice of Translation* (Leiden: Brill, 1969), 23–24.

19. Some have gone further to suggest that the approach of dynamic equivalence is more a system of hermeneutics than translation. See, for example, Robert L. Thomas, *Evangelical Hermeneutics: The New Versus the Old* (Grand Rapids: Kregel, 2002), 81–112.

be sure we have arrived at the "thought" of the original text unless we aim at representing every word of the original text as literally as possible?

Recommendations

Some Bible teachers will produce their own translation as part of their study. Others will study the text in English translations. But even preachers and teachers who study the Hebrew text for themselves will teach people who read only the English text. Therefore every teacher of the Old Testament will have to select a translation to use for teaching and to recommend to people. Consider three recommendations concerning the selection of a translation for preaching and teaching the Old Testament.

First, use a translation that attempts to represent every word of the original as far as possible, not just the ideas of the text. Eugene Peterson, who produced the The Message, described his translation philosophy this way: "The most important question is not, 'What does it say?' but 'What does it mean?'"[20] But how can we know what it means if we do not know what it says? Isn't meaning derived from the words that are used? In the preface of the New International Version, the translators state that the goal is to get at "the thought of the biblical writers."[21] How is it possible to know the thoughts of the biblical writers? The only access to their thoughts is through their words. We do not know what they were thinking as they wrote; we only know what they wrote. Also, the doctrine of divine inspiration refers specifically to God's inspiration of the words they wrote, not what they were thinking as they wrote. All of this suggests that every word of the original text is important, not just the ideas or thoughts.

An example will illustrate the difference between rendering every word into English and reproducing the ideas of the original text. Proponents of dynamic equivalence translation and a proponent of essentially literal translation refer to 1 Kings 2:10. The English Standard

---

20. Peterson, *Eat This Book: A Conversation in the Art of Spiritual Reading* (Grand Rapids: Eerdmans, 2006), 175–76.
21. "Preface," in *The Holy Bible, New International Version* (Nashville: Holman, 1986), viii.

Version seeks to represent every word of the Hebrew text in the translation, "Then David slept with his fathers and was buried in the city of David." However, Gordon Fee and Mark Strauss, both of whom are advocates of dynamic equivalence translation, state that such a translation presents two problems. "First, in English the idiom 'slept with' commonly refers to sexual intercourse; second, 'fathers' is an archaic way to refer to ancestors."[22] The translators of the New Living Translation agree, and they translate the verse, "Then David died and was buried in the city of David." In the introduction to their translation they explain, "The New Living Translation clearly translates the real meaning of the Hebrew idiom 'slept with his fathers' into contemporary English."[23] Thus, while all the words of the text are not represented, the idea of the words is expressed in a way that modern readers would express it today.

Wayne Grudem, a proponent of essentially literal translation, objects that some ideas are missing in this thought-for-thought translation. One missing idea is the concept of sleeping "as a rich metaphor for death, a metaphor in which there is a veiled hint of someday awakening from that sleep to a new life." The metaphor of sleeping also evokes the idea of the cessation of earthly labor. Modern readers will not confuse the metaphor with sexual intercourse because of the clear meaning of the broader context, which has the statement "when David's time to die drew near" (1 Kings 2:1). Furthermore, the language of sleep to refer to death is carried over into the New Testament (e.g., 1 Cor. 15:6), so dropping the metaphor results in the loss of this terminological concordance between the testaments and the theological continuity it implies.

Second, the idea of David's corporate identity with his ancestors the patriarchs is expressed in the phrase "with his fathers," but that is also missing in the New Living Translation.[24] The New Living Translation and advocates of dynamic equivalence translation argue for translating the main idea into equivalent English. But what about each subordinate idea, even if it is, as Grudem states, only a "hint"? Aren't the

---

22. Fee and Strauss, *How to Choose a Translation for All Its Worth*, 92.

23. "Introduction," in *Holy Bible: New Living Translation* (Wheaton, IL: Tyndale, 1996), A12.

24. Grudem, "Are Only Some Words of Scripture Breathed Out by God?," 21–22.

subordinate ideas inspired by God and important? But they are seen by English readers only in a translation that attempts to represent every word.

Another example of the deficiency of dynamic equivalence translations is the wording of the New International Version in Micah 4:9–5:4. The Hebrew word typically translated "now" occurs five times in these verses. It's an important word in this passage because it serves as a temporal marker; it signals that a shift in time is taking place. In these verses, Micah jumps from one era to another rather abruptly and "now" signals each new era. The first appearance of "now" is in 4:9, and the time period is the lifetime of Micah, that is, the eighth century BC. The second "now" is in 4:10, and the time period is the Babylonian invasion of Jerusalem, when the Babylonians conquered Jerusalem and carried its inhabitants into exile in the early sixth century BC. Next, in 4:11 Micah shifts to the period a few decades from his time of writing, when the Assyrians besieged Jerusalem in 701 BC. Again, Micah signals the shift with "now" and prophesies the fall of the Assyrians and their mercenaries. In 5:1 Micah uses "now" again to shift the time period to another occasion of defeat. Perhaps the specific occasion is the Roman conquest of the area of Judah because Micah quickly enters the first century with a prophecy that the Messiah will be born in Bethlehem and will shepherd his flock. The final "now" is in 5:4 and introduces a brief description of the messianic age that is still future for us. Such sudden shifts in time are not unusual in the prophetic literature, but imagine how difficult it would be to interpret Micah 4 and 5 correctly without the temporal marker "now." Yet the New International Version has "now" twice (4:10 and 4:11), translates "now" as "then" once (5:4), and in two cases leaves "now" completely untranslated (4:9; 5:1). Thus the repetition of the Hebrew word is lost, and deciphering Micah's meaning is made more difficult. One wonders why the translators did not choose to consistently represent the word that is in the text. Teachers and preachers of the Old Testament should use a translation that does.

Second, use a translation that accurately represents the world of the original writers. The goal of exposition is to determine the meaning of the text in its original context and then explain and apply that meaning to people today. Leland Ryken correctly expresses that process as a two-way journey. "First we journey to the world of the biblical text.

. . . Then we make a return journey to our own world and apply the principles and experiences of the biblical text to our lives." So what the text meant in its original context is important, because as is often said, a text cannot mean what it never meant. What a text meant in its original context is what Ryken calls "the first leg of this two-way journey."[25] But what if the original context, or world, of the text is obscured by translators who wish to contemporize the text?

An example of contemporizing the words of the Bible is the decision by the translators of the New International Version to render "Lord of hosts" and "God of hosts" as "the Lord Almighty" and "God Almighty." The translators explain that they made that decision "because for most readers today the phrases 'the Lord of hosts' and 'God of hosts' have little meaning."[26] In the world of the Old Testament, the "hosts" in "Lord of hosts" referred to the armies of Israel, the planets and stars (the heavenly host), and the angels (the angelic host). Portraying God as the Lord of the hosts was a Hebrew way of expressing God's greatness and his rule over every part of his vast creation. The decision to erase the word "hosts" because it is not used commonly by most readers today is unfortunate. It erases the "otherness" of the text and insists that we read the Old Testament with modern, Western conceptions. But the Old Testament is neither modern nor Western. Since the Old Testament is an ancient book, shouldn't it read like an ancient book?

God chose to reveal his word in a particular place at a particular time to a particular people. To obscure that place, time, and people diminishes the importance of God's choice while increasing the importance of Western modes of expression. Perhaps what should happen is something like the opposite. Instead of transforming the Old Testament to fit modern Western society, perhaps the modern West should be confronted with the words and world of the Old Testament so that it can be transformed. Such confrontation is dulled when a translation obscures the world of the Old Testament so that we do not encounter its difference. We need to bridge the gap between the ancient world of the text and modern Bible students but that is the role of exposition, not

25. Leland Ryken, *The Word of God in English: Criteria for Excellence in Bible Translation* (Wheaton, IL: Crossway, 2002), 175.

26. "Preface," *New International Version*, ix.

translation. The translation we use should be understandable, of course, but it should give us what the Bible actually says.

Third, use a translation that reproduces the literary form of the original text. The Old Testament is filled with poetic parallelism and metaphorical language. Such rhetorical techniques communicate powerfully. Sometimes when translators aim to communicate the meaning of the text without reflecting the actual words of the original, the force of the poetic language is lost.

For example, Psalm 34:8 says, "Taste and see that the LORD is good" (ESV). "Taste" is poetic language that compares putting one's faith in the Lord to a common human experience. Almost everyone has tried food that we did not think we would like, but when we tasted it we were surprised by how delicious it was. The Good News Bible, however, does not represent every word of the original and makes the clause prosaic with its translation, "Find out for yourself how good the LORD is." Such a dynamic equivalence translation eliminates the poetic language. Hence, the verse no longer appeals to the reader's imagination and its impact is weakened.

Sometimes dynamic equivalence translations can retain metaphorical language but change the biblical metaphor. In Amos 4:6 the Lord refers to the famine he sent with these words: "I gave you also cleanness of teeth in all your cities" (NASB). However, the New International Version has "empty stomachs" instead of "cleanness of teeth," evidently thinking that the biblical metaphor was not clear enough. Bible readers are not informed that they are reading a different metaphor than the metaphor in the original text, but they are.

Determine the Best Text

The first step in faithful exposition is translation. We determine what the text says. The second step is similar to the first. Still looking at the Hebrew text or to resources that refer to the Hebrew text, we establish whether the wording of our passage may vary in any of the ancient Hebrew texts or ancient translations. This work is referred to as text criticism, or textual criticism. To some people textual criticism sounds like the practice of making disparaging remarks about a text. But in biblical studies textual criticism refers to the effort to determine as closely as possible the original text. I define textual criticism as follows:

the scientific system of comparing the different readings of imperfect copies, or variants, using standard principles for the purpose of determining the reading that is most probably the original. The task of translation is to render the original Hebrew text in equivalent English. The task of textual criticism is to determine what the original Hebrew text says.

Let's begin our consideration of the important subject of determining the best text by acknowledging two fundamental facts about the text. First, we do not possess the original manuscripts of the Old Testament. The original manuscripts are referred to as the autographs, or the autographa. Second, the manuscripts that we possess vary from one another. For centuries, scribes preserved the Old Testament by copying Hebrew manuscripts by hand. The evidence indicates that those scribes were highly committed to their work, put "fail safes" in place to guard against error, and regarded the text they were copying as sacred and inviolable. It is clear that they did their work with a high degree of accuracy. For example, the Isaiah Scroll from the Dead Sea Scrolls dates to about 100 BC. When compared with the text of Isaiah in the standard Hebrew text dating to about AD 1008, "only three words exhibiting a different spelling were found for a book that runs about one hundred pages and sixty-six chapters in our English texts." Such a state of purity is, as Walter Kaiser puts it, "nothing short of spectacular."[27]

Still, from time to time scribes made mistakes. Some Hebrew letters look a lot alike, and sometimes scribes wrote the wrong letter. Some Hebrew words sound alike, and a few times it appears that scribes wrote the wrong word. Sometimes they mistakenly skipped a word or letter, or inverted letters within words.

When it appears that scribes made a copying error in the Hebrew text, scholars place a footnote at the bottom of the page calling attention to the problem and offering a solution. About one word in every ten words has a footnote.[28] Therefore, about 90 percent of the Hebrew text is without variation. But where variation, or a "variant" occurs,

---

27. Walter C. Kaiser Jr., *The Old Testament Documents: Are They Reliable and Relevant?* (Downers Grove, IL: InterVarsity Press, 2001), 45–46.

28. Ellis R. Brotzman and Eric J. Tully, *Old Testament Textual Criticism: A Practical Introduction*, 2nd ed. (Grand Rapids: Baker, 2016), 3–4.

how do we determine which reading is the original? We do so by the practice of textual criticism.

Preachers and teachers of the Old Testament will inevitably encounter textual variants, or uncertainty about the original reading. When they find such difficulties, they will have to make decisions regarding how to handle them. When I was preaching through the book of Malachi, I arrived at Malachi 2:15 and had great difficulty translating the verse. I noticed that the verse has four textual footnotes, meaning that textual scholars have made at least four suggestions regarding how to correct alleged corruptions in the verse. One suggestion in the footnotes suggests that the entire verse was likely added. Another note suggests that possibly a clause or multiple clauses have dropped out somehow. Two additional notes provide alternate readings in ancient translations.[29] In the English text, the English Standard Version provides four footnotes with alternate translations. Frankly, the meaning of none of them is really clear. The New American Standard Bible has three translation footnotes. I sought help in the commentaries. One commentator states, "It is impossible to make sense of the Hebrew as it stands."[30] Another refers to "the likelihood of textual corruption" and adds "any interpretation and translation must be understood to be tentative."[31] Others make similar comments.

In such a situation, expository preachers have two options. First, we can spend valuable teaching time attempting to unravel the tangle of textual and syntactical problems in the verse. Second, we can make the point that we think is the big idea of the verse without showing our hearers the details of how we arrived at our conclusions. Sometimes I choose the former. In this case, I chose the latter because other verses in the context address the sanctity of marriage as does verse 15, though I cannot be sure what it adds to the topic. Presumably because of textual corruption, the meaning of the verse is just not clear.

---

29. *Biblia Hebraica Stuttgartensia*, 2nd ed., ed. K. Elliger and W. Rudolph (Stuttgart: Deutsche Bibelgesellschaft, 1983), 1084.

30. Pieter A. Verhoef, *The Books of Haggai and Malachi*, The New International Commentary on the Old Testament (Grand Rapids: Eerdmans, 1987), 275.

31. E. Ray Clendenen, *Malachi*, The New American Commentary (Nashville: Broadman & Holman, 2004), 349–50.

Textual criticism is a specialized academic field. Becoming a skilled textual critic takes a tremendous amount of knowledge, experience, and formal study—more than most teachers of the Old Testament will acquire. Still it's crucial that preachers and teachers know what the original text says. Also, our hearers are reading English translations that have footnotes in the text, like "some ancient manuscripts have another reading." How will we explain such footnotes to our people? How will we reach a high degree of confidence that we are teaching the original text? I recommend five paths to an adequate level of knowledge about text critical issues for the purpose of preaching and teaching the Old Testament accurately. Every teacher and preacher of the Old Testament should aim at following at least three or four of these paths in order to acquire proficiency in textual criticism.

1. Educate yourself about the reliability of the text.

If the text of the Old Testament has accumulated so many scribal errors over the centuries, how can we be sure that what we read today is what authors wrote in the autographa? We can be sure. First, remember that about one word in every ten has a textual footnote. That means 90 percent of the text is without variation. Given the number of centuries the Old Testament was copied by hand, that's bordering on miraculous. Second, almost all the textual complications or errors can be identified and corrected. So much is that the case that textual critics make rather bold statements about their confidence in the condition of the text of the Old Testament. For example, Douglas Stuart writes, "It is fair to say that the verses, chapters, and books of the Bible would read largely the same, and would leave the same impression with the reader, even if one adopted virtually every possible *alternative* reading to those now serving as the basis for current English translations."[32] In other words, Stuart says that if we made every possible change to the text at every point where we think there has been a mistake, still the Old Testament would read essentially the same and readers would receive the same messages.

Another text critic, Shemaryahu Talmon, writes, "The scope of variation within all these textual traditions is relatively restricted.

---

32. Douglas Stuart, "Inerrancy and Textual Criticism," in *Inerrancy and Common Sense*, ed. Roger R. Nicole and J. Ramsey Michaels (Grand Rapids: Baker, 1980), 98.

Major divergences which intrinsically affect the sense are extremely rare."[33] Ellis Brotzman uses an analogy to illustrate the condition of the Old Testament text. Modern texts like letters and articles contain typographical errors all the time. Almost without exception the errors can be identified and corrected by the reader, and the errors do not decrease the value of the message conveyed by the words. Similarly, in the Old Testament, "the vast majority of the differences between manuscripts are quite minor. Many reflect insignificant pronunciations . . . or spelling differences."[34] Furthermore, "The discipline of textual criticism gives us the tools to correct manuscripts and establish the original text."[35] Laird Harris provides another analogy. He writes that if the standard yard at the Smithsonian Institution was lost or destroyed it would not really affect the accuracy of our measurements. There are many copies of the standard yard, and comparing and using those would lead us to something so close to the original that we would never know the difference.[36] Similarly, we do not have the original text of the Old Testament, but Harris's point is that our copies are so close to one another that we can determine the message of the original so closely that the absence of the original doesn't make any difference.

It is even possible to use the term "inerrancy" in a meaningful way with reference to the Old Testament while at the same time being aware of textual variants. The classic statement of inerrancy to which evangelicals typically refer is the Chicago Statement on Biblical Inerrancy, written in 1978. That document refers explicitly to scribal errors in Article X:

> We affirm that inspiration, strictly speaking, applies only to the autographic text of Scripture, which in the providence of God can be ascertained from available manuscripts with great accuracy. We further affirm that copies and translations of Scripture

---

33. Shemaryahu Talmon, "The Textual Study of the Bible: A New Outlook," in *Qumran and the History of the Biblical Text*, ed. Frank Moore Cross and Shemaryahu Talmon (Cambridge, MA: Harvard University Press, 1975), 326.

34. Brotzman and Tully, *Old Testament Textual Criticism*, 3.

35. Ibid., 4.

36. R. Laird Harris, *Inspiration and Canonicity of the Bible: An Historical and Exegetical Study* (Grand Rapids: Zondervan, 1957), 88–89.

are the Word of God to the extent that they faithfully represent the original.

We deny that any essential element of the Christian faith is affected by the absence of the autographs. We further deny that this absence renders the assertion of Biblical inerrancy invalid or irrelevant.[37]

Sooner or later the people we teach will ask us about the footnotes they read in the Old Testament. We should be able to answer their questions and give them titles of sources in which they can find further information. I recommend that teachers and preachers of the Old Testament read and refer to at least a few of the following resources as part of their effort to educate themselves and those they teach:

Blomberg, Craig L. *Can We Still Believe the Bible? An Evangelical Engagement with Contemporary Issues*, 13–41. Grand Rapids: Brazos, 2014.

Kaiser, Walter C., Jr. *The Old Testament Documents: Are They Reliable and Relevant?* Downers Grove, IL: InterVarsity Press, 2001.

Wegner, Paul D. "Has the Old Testament Text Been Hopelessly Corrupted?" in *In Defense of the Bible: A Comprehensive Apologetic for the Authority of Scripture*, edited by Steven B. Cowan and Terry L. Wilder, 119–38. Nashville: Broadman & Holman, 2013.

2. Learn how to read the Hebrew text and the footnotes in the Hebrew text.

This path is the longest and hardest. However, the ability to read the footnotes in the Hebrew text also gives the teacher additional knowledge and authority. Such expertise gives the people we teach access to knowledge they would not have otherwise. Only a few days before

---

37. "The Chicago Statement on Biblical Inerrancy," http://www.etsjets.org/files/documents/Chicago_Statement.pdf.

writing these words, some friends contacted me to ask about an editorial in a prominent newspaper that made extraordinary and spurious claims about some verses in the Hebrew Bible. Through checking the Hebrew text and the textual footnotes for myself, I was able to debunk the editorial's claims as fallacious. In the past I had served as the pastor of these friends, and to be able to continue helping them in their faith gave me great joy.

The ability to read the Hebrew text and to interpret the textual footnotes is a powerful tool in a teacher's toolbox. As far as I know, this tool can be developed only through formal study. It requires enrollment in courses in Hebrew grammar, syntax, and exegesis. In the latter courses, students begin to read the textual footnotes and interpret them. Some academic institutions also offer a course specifically dedicated to Old Testament textual criticism. Though longer and harder, this path is the most rewarding for teachers and preachers of the Old Testament.

3. Study at least one good book in the field of textual criticism.

Such study would necessarily be a part of step 2, but even when teachers do not take that path they can study books on textual criticism for themselves. In that way they will educate themselves in the issues at least in an introductory way. Through studying the contents of only one or two good sources they will learn enough to be able to answer many questions for the people they teach and to increase their confidence in the reliability of the text of the Old Testament. In addition to the books cited above, some of the most helpful resources are listed below. Wegner's book is particularly valuable. It is written for non-specialists and it addresses text critical issues for both testaments.

Brotzman, Ellis R., and Eric J. Tully. *Old Testament Textual Criticism: A Practical Introduction.* 2nd edition. Grand Rapids: Baker, 2016.

Wegner, Paul D. *A Student's Guide to Textual Criticism of the Bible: Its History, Methods, and Results.* Downers Grove, IL: InterVarsity Press, 2006.

Wurthwein, Ernst. *The Text of the Old Testament: An Introduction to the Biblia Hebraica*. 4th edition. Grand Rapids: Eerdmans, 1979.

4. Become familiar with the relevant "witnesses" to the text of the Old Testament.

Witnesses to the text are ancient Hebrew texts or ancient translations that "witness" to the way the text read at the point when they were copied. Textual critics compare such texts in their efforts to determine the reading that is most likely to be original. People who teach and preach the Bible should know the identity and significance of such texts. When they read that the Septuagint, for example, has a different reading than the Hebrew text, they should know what that means. For this path, the books by Wegner and Wurthwein cited above are invaluable. A brief review of most of the major witnesses is also provided below.

The Masoretic Text. The Masoretes were Jewish scribes who copied manuscripts of the Hebrew Bible for centuries. They also added vowel points to the consonantal Hebrew text to aid pronunciation. The Masoretic Text refers to the Hebrew text that was authoritative for the Masoretes and was copied and transmitted by them from one generation to another. The Masoretic Text is attested among the Dead Sea Scrolls, and the oldest complete Masoretic Hebrew Bible dates to AD 1008. This Hebrew text is commonly used as the standard Hebrew Bible today. Virtually every school that teaches Hebrew and the Hebrew Bible uses this text.

The Dead Sea Scrolls. These are scrolls that date to about 200–100 BC. Among the scrolls are documents that relate to the religious life of the Essenes, the community that apparently produced the scrolls or at least preserved and hid them. Also, the Dead Sea Scrolls include prophecies about the future and commentaries on some books of the Old Testament. Most important, every book of the Old Testament except the book of Esther is represented among the Dead Sea Scrolls in whole or in part. The reason the Dead Sea Scrolls are so significant is that before their discovery the earliest copy of the entire Hebrew Bible dated to AD 1008. Since the Dead Sea Scrolls date to the second century BC, they moved back our knowledge of the text of the Old Testament by over a thousand years.

The Septuagint. The Septuagint is the most important version/translation for textual criticism because of its early date and general reliability. It was probably translated over a period of years, perhaps from as early as 300 BC to 150 BC. The Old Testament was translated from Hebrew into Greek because of the large number of Jews who spoke Greek during that period. A large Greek-speaking community of Jews lived in Alexandria, where the Septuagint was produced. Hebrew was becoming a dead language, and the Jews wanted a Bible they could read in their own language. "Septuagint" means "70," and the Septuagint is often abbreviated by the Roman numeral LXX. The number 70 comes from the "Letter of Aristeas," which includes a story about 72 scholars producing the Septuagint in 72 days. Today that story is not regarded as accurate, but the name of the translation remains. The quality of the translation of the various Old Testament books varies, since different translators produced the translations of the books. Still the Septuagint is a valuable witness to the text of the Old Testament since it often seems to represent a different Hebrew text than the one from which the Masoretes copied.

The Aramaic Targums. The word "targum" means "interpretation." During the exile in Babylon, the Jewish people increasingly spoke Aramaic. The priests and scribes continued to read their Bible in Hebrew, but they would often explain the message by paraphrasing in Aramaic to aid understanding. For an example of such explanation, see Nehemiah 8:7–8. Originally oral, this interpretation was eventually reduced to writing, and the recorded interpretations became the Targums. Tradition states that the oral Targums began in the time of Ezra, about 450 BC, but most of the written Targums were not recorded until about AD 200.

The Samaritan Pentateuch. This is the text of the Pentateuch used by the Samaritans. The Samaritans are mentioned in the New Testament, but their origins date to the exile after the fall of the northern kingdom of Israel. The Samaritans had Jewish roots, but they also had several theological characteristics that distinguished them from the Jews. For one thing, they regarded only the Pentateuch as canonical, not the entire Old Testament. Therefore, the Samaritan Pentateuch was the Samaritan Bible. It assumed definite form probably about 100 BC. At that point, and possibly before, it had a textual history that was independent of the

Masoretic Text used by the Jews. It was written in Samaritan script, which resembles Paleo-Hebrew, and it does not have the vowel points added later by the Masoretes. How close is the Samaritan Pentateuch to the Hebrew text that became standard for the Jews? The Samaritan Pentateuch differs from the Masoretic Text about 6,000 times, but most of the differences are spelling variations.

The Peshitta. The Peshitta is the Old Testament translated into Syriac, the native language of Syria. "Peshitta" means "the simple" or "the plain," but the reason this word was chosen as the title is unknown. It was translated in the first century AD. There are many similarities between the Peshitta and the Targums, so many that text critic Ernst Wurthwein wrote that it is likely that the Peshitta is directly dependent on an early Palestinian Targum.[38]

5. In preparation to teach an Old Testament passage, use at least one critical commentary.

In this case, "critical" refers to commentaries that provide a thorough consideration of exegetical details, including matters related to translation and text criticism. Preachers and teachers of the Old Testament are sometimes quick to use commentaries that provide contemporary application and illustration. Such commentaries are helpful, but before Bible teachers apply and illustrate they need to know *what* to apply and illustrate. What is the original text (textual criticism) and what does the text say (translation)? For Bible teachers who do not translate the Hebrew and read the textual footnotes for themselves, critical commentaries that supply such information are even more important. The quality and helpfulness of commentaries varies from volume to volume and from series to series. However, some commentary series that typically provide information related to translation and textual criticism are as follows:

- Apollos Old Testament Commentary (InterVarsity Press)
- New American Commentary (Broadman & Holman)
- Revised Expositor's Commentary (Zondervan)

---

38. Ernst Wurthwein, *The Text of the Old Testament: An Introduction to the Biblia Hebraica*, 4th ed. (Grand Rapids: Eerdmans, 1979), 80.

- The Anchor Bible (Doubleday)
- The New International Commentary on the Old Testament (Eerdmans)
- The Old Testament Library (Westminster)
- Word Biblical Commentary (Thomas Nelson)

Readers should note three caveats regarding such commentaries. First, sometimes the text-critical information in commentaries requires a knowledge of abbreviations and other technical information in order to understand the comments about textual variants. Second, information about Hebrew words sometimes assumes a knowledge of basic Hebrew grammar. Hence, at times readers may find it difficult to follow the commentators' argumentation. Third, commentary series more or less reflect the theological perspectives of the publishers and editors, and the series cited above vary in that regard. Still this path to learning about the condition of a text under consideration can help expositors. Teachers and preachers of the Old Testament will usually exegete texts more accurately when they follow this path regularly.

In conclusion, what should expositors say about text-critical issues to the people they are teaching? They should take into consideration the group of people to whom they are speaking. Speaking to a group of teenagers or new Christians will involve an approach that is significantly different from what a teacher may say to a group of graduate divinity students. It seems best to assume the people want to know the truth, but the way we communicate the information or how much information we communicate may vary widely. Certainly we will want to be sensitive to the potential consequences of our comments. We can talk about the variant in such a way that we build the faith of our hearers and provide a defense against unbelievers who attack the integrity of the Bible. On the other hand, if we handle a textual variant in the wrong way, the people we are teaching may think more about the variant than the certain message in the text. Our goal, after all, is to present the truth of the Bible to the people who hear us teach and preach. Translation and textual criticism are only the first two steps in our preparation to reach that goal.

Chapter 2

WHAT IS THE TEXT'S GENRE?
(PART 1)

8-STEP METHOD

A few weeks before writing this chapter I wrote a review of a new book for a theological journal. Last Sunday I preached a sermon in a local church. Today I wrote a personal, newsy letter to one of my sons. If I had stood before the church and read my book review, it would have been inappropriate. Sometimes I mention books when I preach, but spending time in a sermon to offer a detailed critique of the relative merits of a new book would be out of place in a sermon. It would have also been inappropriate if I had written my son a letter with the same form and content as my sermon. He would wonder why I had written a sermon to him, and he may have called a mental health professional to submit my name for an overdue evaluation.

A critical book review, a sermon, and a personal letter are different forms of communication. They follow different rules of grammar and syntax, and the form inevitably affects the selection of words. The form also creates certain expectations on the part of the reader. When readers turn to the book review section of a theological journal, they don't expect to read a sermon, however much they might be helped by one. When a pastor stands to preach, people in the congregation expect a certain form of speech, not a book review or a newsy family note, for example.

Such forms of communication are called genres. Every act of communication is expressed by means of some genre. Magazine articles, novels, blog entries, tweets, textbooks, junk mail, editorials, Facebook posts, poems, and biographies are all different genres. Every day we encounter such genres, without even thinking about it we classify messages according to genre, and we have certain expectations based on genre. We don't have to think about it because we know the rules of all the genres that are common in our everyday lives. For example, we don't expect junk mail to provide thoughtful cultural commentary, but we expect exactly that when we read an editorial.

The first chapter was devoted to the first two steps of our 8-step process of Old Testament exposition: translation and textual criticism. The next two chapters will be devoted to the third step: genre interpretation. This step requires more space because the goal is to provide some help in understanding and interpreting each of the major Old Testament genres. Along the way, I hope readers will be convinced of the importance of considering a text's genre as a part of their process of exposition.

All the sentences in the Old Testament were written in specific genres. However, the genres in the Old Testament are in a different language and they arose in a different time and culture. They are ancient and Near Eastern, not modern and Western. Therefore, when we read a passage in the Old Testament, we have to be intentional about genre classification and we have to learn the rules of the genres in order to know how to interpret them.[1] The genres in the Old Testament are narrative, law, poetry, proverbs, and prophecy. Some scholars would refer to wisdom literature as a separate genre, based on the wisdom

---

1. Robert Stein based his book on interpreting the Bible on following the "rules"

themes addressed in books like Job, Proverbs, and Ecclesiastes. Also, some of the genres can be further divided into subgenres. For example, prophecy is often subdivided into salvation oracles, judgment oracles, lawsuits, dirges, vision reports, disputations, and apocalyptic. The poetry of Psalms is usually subdivided into thematic categories like praise psalms, laments, thanksgiving psalms, nature psalms, national and royal psalms, imprecatory psalms, wisdom psalms, penitential psalms, and psalms of confidence/faith. In this chapter we will consider how to preach and teach from passages that are classified as narrative and proverbs. In chapter 3 we will see how to handle law, prophecy, and poetry when we prepare to preach and teach.

Regrettably, some Christians seem to think that considering the literary features of a text, like genre, is somehow less spiritual. We should answer the question Clyde Kilby asks: "Did God inspire the form or only the content of the Bible? Is its form only a man-made incidental?"[2] For people who believe that the words of the Old Testament are inspired by God, the answer to that question should be easy. Hebrew poetry is based on parallel words. The poetic form arises from the words of the text. If we believe that God inspired the words, then necessarily we also believe that God inspired the poetic form that is tied to the choices of words. The proverbs in the Old Testament are also tied closely to word choice, as are all proverbs, and a stated purpose of the book of Proverbs is "to understand a proverb and a saying, the words of the wise and their riddles" (Prov. 1:6). My point here was expressed succinctly by C. S. Lewis, who writes, "There is a . . . sense in which the Bible, since it is after all literature, cannot properly be read except as literature; and the different parts of it as the different sorts of literature they are."[3]

In spite of the importance of literary form, failure to consider the effects of genre is a common mistake in interpreting Old Testament texts. And when preachers and teachers make interpretation mistakes,

---

of each genre. Robert H. Stein, *A Basic Guide to Interpreting the Bible: Playing by the Rules*, 2nd ed. (Grand Rapids: Baker, 2011).

2. Clyde S. Kilby, "The Bible as a Work of Imagination," in *The Christian Imagination: The Practice of Faith in Literature and Writing*, rev. ed., ed. Leland Ryken (Colorado Springs, CO: WaterBrook, 2002), 105.

3. C. S. Lewis, *Reflections on the Psalms* (New York: Harcourt, Brace, and World, 1958), 3.

they pass those mistakes along to the people they teach. They also apply the Bible to the lives of their hearers in ways not intended by the author. We should heed Haddon Robinson's warning when he was writing about misreading the genre of narrative: "There is no greater abuse of the Bible than to proclaim in God's name what God is not saying."[4] The point of this chapter and the next is that to determine what God is saying in a biblical text it is necessary to interpret properly its genre. First, however, it is necessary to pray.

Pray

In the Bible, God speaks. To exegete the Bible properly, our hearts must be ready to hear God. Steven Smith contends that the different genres of the Bible are God's different "voices." Sometimes God thunders commands, sometimes he tells a story, and sometimes he gives us words to whisper to him in prayer. Just as we communicate in different ways, so does God.[5] That should be expected, since we are made in his image. If we want to *teach* his Word like he spoke it, then we will have to *hear* it like he spoke it. As we begin to study God's Word, let us pray that our hearts will be captivated by God's voice. Only then will our teaching be captivating and faithful. If we want our teaching and preaching to make an impact, we must first be impacted by God in his Word.

The Bible is a spiritual book since God's Spirit inspired it, and to understand a spiritual book we have to read it in a spiritual way. Our ancestors called this *lectio divina*, "spiritual reading." It is reading that includes disciplines like meditation, asking God to transform us, reading with the church, and obedience. Before we do the work of interpreting the literary form of a text in the Bible, we bow our heads in prayer and ready our hearts for God's words to enter our souls and change us.

Teaching exactly what is in the text is our task, but exegetical accuracy is lifeless without the work of God's Spirit in us. We make our goal nothing less than encountering God himself in the text, hearing him speak to us, and transforming us as only he can. Such a goal requires

---

4. Haddon W. Robinson, "Foreword" in Steven D. Mathewson, *The Art of Preaching Old Testament Narrative* (Grand Rapids: Baker, 2002), 12.

5. Steven Smith, *Recapturing the Voice of God: Shaping Sermons like Scripture* (Nashville: Broadman & Holman, 2015), 5–6.

prayer. We speak to God and ask him to speak to us. He speaks to us and does his work in us through his Word. As Paul wrote to the Christians in Thessalonica, God's Word "is at work in you believers" (1 Thess. 2:13). But God works in us with his Word only if we open our hearts in prayer to God's work. Once God does his work in us in the prayer closet, we are ready to be his instruments to do his work in the lives of the people who will hear us preach and teach.

Preaching and Teaching Narratives

Stories are powerful and appealing. That's clear from the popularity of novels and movies. Judging from the prominence of stories in ancient literature, people have always loved stories. Evidently God has made us in such a way that we enjoy a good story. Preachers and teachers observe the heightened attentiveness of their hearers when they begin to tell a story. I once asked students in a seminar on preaching whether the people to whom they preach enjoy stories. One young pastor answered, "No. All my people want is theology." I don't know his people; perhaps he is correct and they are different from most everyone else in the history of the world. But the main problem with his answer is the apparent assumption that stories and theology are mutually exclusive. They are not. God inspired stories throughout the Bible to reveal himself and his truth. Stories account for at least 30 to 40 percent of the Old Testament.[6] God has ordained that one way we will get to know him is by means of stories.

We get to know other people the same way. On a first date, men and women don't usually learn about one another by exchanging their IQ numbers and their scores on the Myers-Briggs personality test. They tell stories about themselves. "When I saw *Finding Nemo*, I cried when they found Nemo." "When she wrote that mean message to me, I decided not to reply, and I invited her to the party anyway."

Similarly, in the Old Testament we get to know God by reading the stories about what he said and did in history. Furthermore, the entire Bible is one big story with many narratives combining to form a metanarrative. Contemporary theologians and Bible teachers regularly

---

6. Steven D. Mathewson, *The Art of Preaching Old Testament Narrative* (Grand Rapids: Baker, 2002), 20.

emphasize the necessity of seeing the Bible as one narrative and inter-preting it that way. Christopher Wright, for example, writes:

> In the Bible God has told us one single big story that spans the whole of space and time. That single big story is broken up into several mega-stories that take up whole chunks of history. And each of those mega-stories is constructed out of many small stories—the ones we usually have in mind when we talk about "Bible stories."

Wright, as others have done, proceeds to divide the Bible's one big story into segments—creation, fall, promise, gospel, mission, and new creation.[7] Clearly the story form is important in the Bible and we should not neglect stories in our preaching and teaching. How should we exegete stories? The following six practices of good exposition are essential.

1. Select a complete story.

In a genre like a New Testament epistle, a paragraph or less may be a complete unit of thought. In teaching Old Testament narratives, to teach a complete unit of thought we consider an entire story. Stories in the Bible have a point, and typically we don't see the point until we reach the end of the story. When we select a verse or two, or even a paragraph in a story, inevitably we will not honor the story form God inspired. Instead, we will preach an idea or two that appears in the story while neglecting the story itself. God gave us a story, so we read the entire story and teach the entire story.

How do we determine where one story ends and another begins? To locate transition points, we look for changes in place, changes in time, changes in major characters, or a change from narrative to poetry

---

7. Christopher J. H. Wright, *How to Preach the Old Testament for All Its Worth* (Grand Rapids: Zondervan, 2016), 33–36, 87. Other authors who show how the Bible is one story and urge us to read it that way are Craig G. Bartholomew and Michael W. Goheen, *The Drama of Scripture: Finding Our Place in the Biblical Story*, 2nd ed. (Grand Rapids: Baker, 2014); Gregory Koukl, *The Story of Reality* (Grand Rapids: Zondervan, 2017); and Vaughn Roberts, *God's Big Picture: Tracing the Storyline of the Bible* (Downers Grove, IL: InterVarsity Press, 2002).

or legislation. For example, the narratives in the book of Judges are easily divided according to the main character or judge. When the author records more than one story related to one person, as is the case with Gideon, Abimelech, and Samson, an entire story is one episode in their lives, and such episodes are clearly distinct from one another. The books of Kings and Chronicles are similar, in that new stories often begin with new kings or prophets. In the books of Ezra and Nehemiah, changes in location are significant, since whether the main characters are in Persia or Judah makes a big difference in the meaning of the story and the setting of the story in salvation history.

As an example, consider the first two chapters of Nehemiah. They can be divided into three stories by time and location. Chapter 1 opens on the first day of the Jewish month of Chislev. In that chapter, Nehemiah is in Persia and he hears about the condition of Jerusalem and prays. We should probably consider that chapter the first story. Chapter 2 opens on the first day of the month of Nisan, four months later, so a change in time signals that the story in chapter 1 has ended. In verse 9 of chapter 2, Nehemiah sets off for Jerusalem, so the first eight verses are set in Persia and should probably be considered a distinct story. From verse 9 to the end of the chapter, Nehemiah arrives in Jerusalem and encounters the walls, the people of Jerusalem, and his opposition. So we should probably consider verse 9 to the end of chapter 2 the third story in the book of Nehemiah.

2. Determine the main point of the story.

A young preacher asked a veteran pastor how many points the ideal sermon should have. The older pastor replied sarcastically, "At least one." Sermons should have a point. Even more important, the main point of the sermon should match the main point of the text. In many New Testament passages the main point is easier to identify. For example, Philippians 2:4–5 says, "Let each of you look not only to his own interests, but also to the interests of others. Have this mind among yourselves, which is yours in Christ Jesus." The verses that follow describe how Jesus gave himself for others. The main point of that passage of Scripture is not difficult to determine—Jesus gave himself for others and we are to adopt his way of thinking by making others more important than ourselves.

Often the main point is more difficult to identify in Old Testament narratives. First, Old Testament stories don't include a summarizing statement that expresses the moral of the story. They don't address imperatives to the reader, and the narrators did not write convenient statements like, "This is the main point I want to make!"

Second, sometimes we don't think of stories as having a point at all except to record historical information. But the authors (and the Author) of stories in the Old Testament did not record them merely to ensure that future generations would be aware of some historical information. The thousands of years in the Old Testament period contain millions of moments and events. Old Testament writers included a very small percentage of those moments and events in their histories. Why did they select those particular moments and events? They had a reason, a point. The goal of our exegesis is to discover that point.

How do expositors identify the main point of an Old Testament story? A few examples should help develop the skill of finding a story's big idea. In the narrative in the first chapter of Ruth, the scene changes from Bethlehem to Moab, then back to Bethlehem. The characters also change, since three of them (Naomi's husband and two sons) die in Moab, and two characters (the sons' Moabite wives) are added.

Still, instead of breaking up the narrative every time the location or characters change, it is best to regard the entire first chapter as one story. The point doesn't emerge until the end of the chapter, and chapter 2 heads in an entirely different direction—God's provision of a husband for Ruth. The plot of the story is a quick succession of events—a famine in Bethlehem, a move to Moab, two weddings, three deaths, Naomi's decision to return to Bethlehem, Ruth's decision to go "all in" with Naomi, and finally their arrival in Bethlehem. After all those events in Naomi's life, she provides a theological summary for the people of Bethlehem, and for us: "the Almighty has dealt very bitterly with me" (1:20).

Where's the main point in all that? The big idea has something to do with the answer to the question, "What does this story say about God?" In the case of Ruth 1, despite all the calamity that befell Naomi's family and despite her bitterness about it, she still affirmed God's sovereignty over the events of her life. In fact, she affirmed that truth five times (vv. 13, 20–21). It's hard to miss the point that the author wanted to emphasize. Even though Naomi's family apparently disobeyed God in moving away from the Promised Land, and even though Naomi and Ruth returned to Bethlehem with no husbands and no children, we still see the providential hand of God at work. That point seems confirmed by the conclusion of the book of Ruth. At the end of the book, Ruth is married to Boaz and has a child who will be the progenitor of King David and eventually Jesus the Messiah. The stories in the book seem to be a string of tragedies and coincidences, but God used them all as threads in his tapestry of salvation history. So to express the main point of Ruth 1 in one sentence, it is that the saving God is sovereign over the events of our lives, so we trust him no matter what happens. Of course, the story includes other themes, like the presence of suffering in this fallen world, Ruth's amazing expression of loyalty to Naomi and faith in God, and Naomi's bitterness. Teaching this story will surely include such themes, but the main point of our teaching or preaching should be the main point of the text. That's what we emphasize so that our hearers cannot miss it.

Determining the main point of the first chapter of Ruth involved at least four requirements. First, it required reading the story carefully. Before we can say that we have read a story carefully we will have to read it several times, preferably in Hebrew. When we read the story carefully, we will notice features like repetition, as in Naomi's fivefold statement that God was behind the circumstances of her life.

Second, arriving at the main point of the story required reading the entire book of Ruth carefully. Reading the entire book is a requirement for teaching a narrative passage in any Old Testament book. We read the entire book to know where our story begins and ends, to know how the book begins and ends, and to know how our story fits into the larger story and purpose of the book.

Third, identifying the big idea of the story requires knowing the story of the entire Bible that begins with creation, leads to redemption in Jesus the Savior, and ends with the final consummation. The book of Ruth, including the story in the first chapter, has a place in the Bible's story, but one must know the entire story to know how Ruth fits into the whole. Also, without knowing all the Bible, how would we know anything about the historical setting of the period of the judges, the meaning of moving to Moab, or the significance of a Moabite like Ruth becoming a worshiper of Yahweh?

Fourth, the process of arriving at the main idea of a story should involve asking a question like, "What does this story say about God, God's ways, and/or God's salvation?" The Bible is about God. All the stories in the Bible are somehow about God. Therefore, the main point of every story will be theological in that it will relate to God.

3. Get the facts right.

Understanding and teaching Old Testament narratives inevitably requires historical research. Suppose you are preaching the story in the first eight verses of Nehemiah 2. Who is Artaxerxes? When was his "twentieth year," and what was happening during that period of history? Why is the action of this story taking place in Persia instead of Judah? Nehemiah 1 records that Artaxerxes gave permission to Nehemiah to travel to Jerusalem and rebuild the city. Since the book of Ezra records Artaxerxes' earlier order to stop construction in Jerusalem (4:7–24), his permission in Nehemiah 2 comes as a surprise. But we will not know that unless we have all the historical information at hand. Also, what is the meaning of Artaxerxes' words to Nehemiah, "Why is your face sad, seeing you are not sick?" (Neh. 2:2). Evidently, Artaxerxes had already determined that Nehemiah was not sick. Whether or not Nehemiah was sick was highly important to Artaxerxes since Nehemiah was Artaxerxes' cupbearer. Royal cupbearers tested a king's food and drink before the king was exposed to it in order to make sure it wasn't poisoned. Without that historical information, we will not know the significance of the phrase "seeing you are not sick."

Verse 2 in Nehemiah 2 says that when the king asked Nehemiah what was wrong, Nehemiah "was very much afraid." Why would Nehemiah be "very much afraid" because of a simple question? To answer that question we need to know that servants in the courts of ancient Near Eastern monarchs were expected to please the king. Typically, kings in the ancient Near East did not tolerate disobedience or even sadness in their presence, and they imprisoned and executed courtesans on a whim. The book of Genesis records an example. Joseph was in prison with two of Pharaoh's servants. One of those servants was a cupbearer like Nehemiah, and Pharaoh had thrown him into jail because he was less than charming (Gen. 40). Nehemiah knew that if he displeased the king his life was in danger. He also knew that he was about to ask for something—the reconstruction of Jerusalem—that Artaxerxes had already denied. Such information helps us understand why Nehemiah was "very much afraid." Knowing that information requires some historical homework.

The emphasis on getting the facts right is a consequence of the belief that texts arise from contexts. The consideration of context will be addressed in a later chapter. My point here is to emphasize that if a text's context is important to correct interpretation, then accurate information about that context is essential. Teachers and preachers of the Old Testament make mistakes in interpretation and application because of misinformation or ignorance about historical contexts. How can such mistakes be prevented? For accurate exposition, expositors should study the historical, geographical, cultural, and religious background of each narrative. To do so they will need good resources. Passing mention of a historical fact in a devotional commentary is not adequate. Minimally, an expositor's needed resources will include a few volumes on the history of Israel, a substantive historical atlas, information on the people groups of the ancient Near East and their religions, a few critical commentaries on the Old Testament book they are teaching, and perhaps a few volumes on the history of the ancient Near East.

Two words of caution are in order regarding historical accuracy when teaching Old Testament narratives. First, eliminate speculation. A common mistake Bible students make is attempting to read facts into a story that are not in the text. We're curious about *why* a character did what he did or said what he said. We conclude that he must have said it for some reason that seems perfectly logical to us. We also wonder what *else* he did, so we start reading between the lines and we supply information that is not in the text. For example, a man once told me that Ruth must have been physically attractive, and in the past he had heard a Bible teacher state that. When I asked how we know what Ruth looked like, he explained that Boaz singled her out from all the women who were gleaning in his field, so she must have been especially pretty. Well, maybe. The problem is that our only source of information about Ruth is the book of Ruth, and the book supplies no information about her appearance.

The conclusion that Boaz singled her out because she was pretty is a guess. Perhaps he singled her out for help because she was the only young woman he did not know, or perhaps she was most in need of help.

We base our theological conclusions on our exposition, and if we include speculation in our exposition, we are in danger of basing our theology on speculation, not the assertions of God's Word. Exposition is not strengthened by speculation. If we believe in the divine inspiration of the Bible, we should be confident that God has given us in Scripture the information he intends for us to know. The point of our exposition will be based on that revealed information, not our speculation.

A second word of caution is to remember the purpose of teaching narrative texts. Our aim is not to convey historical information or to entertain people with a good story. The purpose is to lead people to know the God who has revealed himself in the story and in Christ. As Bible teachers and preachers, our goal is theology, not history. Therefore, we study the historical background enough to get the facts right and to understand the story. Then we aim at grasping the main point of the story, which will be about God, his ways, and how we respond to him.

4. Allow the story form to affect the exposition.

Some expositors teach narrative texts the same way they teach epistles or psalms—that is, they find some main themes in the text and teach them by means of a list that they give to their hearers. If every theme arises directly from the story, that approach is not a bad start. However, in Old Testament narratives God gave us stories, not lists of principles or propositions. In teaching stories, it seems best to find a way to honor the form God gave to us.

Honoring the narrative form begins with reading the entire story aloud to allow the people to experience its drama. Stories have plots, and plots typically have the following elements: a beginning that introduces the setting of the action; a conflict or crisis; a denouement, or climax of the crisis; a resolution of the crisis; and sometimes a concluding statement or two. Stories also include characters: the protagonist who leads the action, the antagonist who opposes the protagonist, and foils who stand in the background.[8] Reading the entire story introduces or re-introduces the hearers to the flow of the story's plot. They feel the temporal movement of the story, and they feel the tension of the crisis. They see what the characters in the story do, and they hear what the characters say. They begin to identify the heroes and villains.

After reading the entire story, how do we honor the narrative form in our exposition? Some people who teach exposition instruct preachers and teachers of the Old Testament to follow the story form in the presentation of their exposition. They say that our teaching of the story should be a re-telling of the story, and as we re-tell the story we add comments of explanation or exhortation along the way. Some books encourage expositors to reserve any "points" we may make until the end, delaying any resolution to allow hearers to feel the tension of the story.[9] A few teachers suggest that it is sometimes best for expositors not to state the main idea directly at all. Tell the story well and illustrate it well, and hearers will arrive at the big idea(s) on their own, they claim, and that may be more potent.[10]

But what if they *don't* arrive at the big idea on their own? What if my storytelling skills are not good enough? Pastors and other Bible teachers have the responsibilities to disciple the church and to speak God's truth clearly to people who have not yet come to faith in Jesus. In my view, such responsibilities call for preachers and teachers to make the point(s) of their teaching clear instead of leaving it to their hearers to get the point(s) on their own. Furthermore, if the reason for not giving the ending or the point(s) of the story is to retain the tension and suspense of the story, how much tension can our hearers

---

8. For more information about the elements of Old Testament stories and how they work, see Leland Ryken, *How Bible Stories Work: A Guided Study of Biblical Narrative* (Bellingham, WA: Lexham Press, 2015); Patricia Dutcher-Walls, *Reading the Historical Books: A Student's Guide to Engaging the Biblical Text* (Grand Rapids: Baker, 2014); and Richard L. Pratt Jr., *He Gave Us Stories: The Bible Student's Guide to Interpreting Old Testament Narratives* (Phillipsburg, NJ: P&R, 1990).

9. Mathewson, *The Art of Preaching Old Testament Narrative*, 113.

10. "Narratives are most effective when the audience hears the story and arrives at the speaker's ideas without the ideas being stated directly," Haddon W. Robinson, *Biblical Preaching: The Development and Delivery of Expository Messages*, 3rd ed. (Grand Rapids, Baker, 2014), 90–91.

feel if we have just read the entire story so that they already know how it ends?

Expositors can honor the narrative form by more than one method. Whether the exposition honors the story form or not depends more on the content of the exposition than the form. Earlier I referred to the fact that Nehemiah was "very much afraid" when Artaxerxes asked him why he looked sad (Neh. 2:2). In teaching that story, expositors should help hearers feel the tension of the moment when Nehemiah feared for his life in front of the most powerful man in the Near East. It is possible to emphasize Nehemiah's fear by means of a narrative form of exposition, telling the story dramatically. It is also possible to help readers experience the action of the story by making the point that faithfulness to God requires courage, then by explaining the text. First, Nehemiah was in danger because ancient Near Eastern kings did not often tolerate sadness in their presence. Second, Artaxerxes had already ordered the rebuilding of Jerusalem to stop. If Nehemiah stated that he wanted to rebuild Jerusalem, Artaxerxes could execute Nehemiah for disobedience or disloyalty. Spending some time explaining those facts goes beyond preaching a principle based on the story; it helps readers experience the story, thus honoring the form God inspired. We could also tell a contemporary story about someone's fear in the face of danger. The purpose of such a story would be to help our hearers contemplate further the words "very much afraid," enter into the drama of the moment, and even feel the fear Nehemiah felt.

5. Locate the narrative in redemption history.

An indelible part of my growing up years was hearing Paul Harvey on the radio. He would often read the news of the day, but the feature I remember best was "The Rest of the Story." In just a few minutes he would tell an interesting story, leaving out some key element of the story until the end. Often the key element was the name of a famous person. After relating little-known information about the person's life, he would then reveal the name and conclude with the line, "And now you know the *rest* of the story."

Exposition of Old Testament narratives should include "the rest of the story." A chapter in this book is devoted to showing how the Old Testament leads to Jesus. But at this point it is important to state that an exposition of a narrative text is not finished until we tell how the story ends in Jesus and his salvation. This is not to say that we preach or teach the entire story of the Bible in every exposition. We focus on the narrative we have identified as our text, and we preach or teach that text. However, somewhere in the exposition we should state that this story is one part of God's longer, larger story of calling the people of the world to himself. An account of the full scope of redemption history can occur at the beginning of the exposition, even in the introduction. We can also reserve our description until the end. Our explanation of redemption history may or may not consume a lot of time, but Bible expositors can and should help people find and understand the redemption God offers. God offers redemption through faith in Jesus, not through believing Old Testament stories and behaving like the heroes of those stories. Therefore, we tell "the rest of the story."

How should expositors make a connection between an Old Testament narrative and redemption history that leads to Jesus? Let's return to the stories in Ruth 1 and in Nehemiah 2 as examples. The following is one way to transition from Ruth 1 to redemptive history.

Naomi didn't see it, but God was working in all the events in her life, even her suffering, for his good purpose to bring salvation to the nations. The result of her return to Bethlehem with Ruth would be that Ruth would marry a man named Boaz. Ruth and Boaz would have a son together. That son would be the grandfather of Israel's greatest king, King David. So that son would also be the forefather of Israel's eternal King, Jesus the Messiah and Savior. God had a plan for Naomi and Ruth. His plan was to use them in his redemptive purpose to offer salvation and eternal life to everybody in the world through Jesus. They could not have seen that far in the future, but they could have trusted God that he knew what he was doing even though they couldn't see it. We face the same choice in our suffering. We can bitterly believe in God's sovereignty and say, "God could have stopped this!" or we can say, "God, I have no idea why you allowed this suffering to enter my life, but I *do* know that you are good, loving, gracious, and merciful; and you know what you're doing. So I'll trust you to use this suffering for your good plan of redemption in my life, just as you used the suffering of Naomi and Ruth in your plan of redemption."

With regard to Nehemiah 2, the story calls attention to the fact that Nehemiah was afraid when Artaxerxes asked him why he looked sad. In spite of his fear, Nehemiah spoke up courageously. Consider the following transition to God's history of redemption at the end of an exposition of Nehemiah 2.

This story about Nehemiah occurred as one brief moment in history, but God was guiding the events of that moment. He continued to guide events so that his people did rebuild the walls of Jerusalem. He protected those who returned to the land and he preserved them as a people. In doing so, God was keeping his eternal promises to Abraham. God promised Abraham to give his descendants the land of promise, and it was to that land of promise that Nehemiah and his contemporaries returned. God also promised to bless the world through the seed of Abraham. The New Testament identifies that seed as Jesus, who was a descendant of those who returned to the land in the time of Nehemiah. Through Jesus God blesses the world by offering eternal life and abundant life in him. In Jesus the invisible God became visible. When we receive Jesus, he empowers us to be all God has called us to be and to do all God has called us to do. God has already told us what he wants us to do with Jesus. Put your faith in him, receive him as Savior, and be reconciled to God today.

These are just two examples from the many narratives in the Old Testament. In chapter 7 we will think more carefully about connecting every part of the Old Testament to Jesus.

6. Connect the narrative to contemporary hearers.

Old Testament narratives reflect a world that does not exist anymore. Of course in the Old Testament world and in today's world, God is the same, people are still sinners in need of reconciliation to God, and the created order still groans for salvation. Other than such enduring truths, things have changed. Contemporary people don't live in tents like the patriarchs, they don't go to war with slingshots and spears, they don't survive by planting their own crops by hand, they don't sit and watch sheep all day, and when they travel to another part of the country they don't get there by walking. In light of the foreignness of such details, entering Old Testament stories mentally, understanding the action, and sympathizing with the characters is sometimes challenging. How can expositors help their hearers overcome the foreignness of Old Testament stories so they can see the main point(s) more clearly? Let's consider four methods.

One way to draw hearers into the story to enhance understanding and application is *identification.* Expositors can help hearers to identify with the characters in the narrative. When that happens, hearers immediately sense the relevance of the story. Characterization in English novels often includes lengthy descriptions of the appearance and personality of characters. For example, in Charles Dickens' novel *Oliver Twist,* Dickens describes Mr. Sowerberry the undertaker as "a tall, gaunt, large-jointed man, attired in a suit of thread-bare black, with darned cotton stockings of the same colour, and shoes to answer. His features were not naturally intended to wear a smiling aspect, but . . . his face betokened inward pleasantry."[11]

Such detailed characterization is sparse, usually altogether missing, in Old Testament stories. Typically readers of Old Testament narratives get to know the characters by what the characters do and say. The relative scarcity of character details, however, can remove impediments to our identification with Old Testament characters. We are less likely to conclude, "I can't really identify with that character because I'm not handsome/pretty," or "The story says she was 'gregarious,' and I'm just not like that." Whereas lengthy character descriptions could hinder identification with the characters, we *can* identify with what characters do and say. We can have faith like Abraham. We can obey God's call like Moses. We can also deceive like Jacob and commit idolatry like Aaron.

To help hearers experience and apply the story we are teaching, we can ask them something like, "Who are you most like?" For example,

---

11. Charles Dickens, *Oliver Twist* (St. Louis: Thompson, n.d.), 23.

if we are teaching the story about David's encounter with Goliath, we could ask, "Are you most like King Saul, occupying a position of respect but disobeying God, clinging to the past while missing God's plan for the future? Are you most like young David, trusting God while rejected by the official structures of society, showing grace to the very people who vilify you? Or are you most like the unnamed Israelites on the sideline, watching the war between faith and rebellion from a safe distance, interested but passive?"

Identification is an effective method of teaching and applying Old Testament narratives. New Testament writers used characters in Old Testament stories as examples of godly behavior, and they exhorted followers of Jesus to follow their examples. Paul used the idolatry of the Hebrews in the wilderness as an example of negative behavior. To paraphrase Paul's point, he wrote, "They committed idolatry. Don't commit idolatry like them!" (see 1 Cor. 10:1–14). James used Abraham and Rahab as examples of exercising a faith that works. James exhorted Christians to be like them (see James 2:21–26). When calling Christians to pray, James' point was, "Elijah prayed. Be like Elijah and pray!" (see James 5:13–18). Likewise, Peter presented Sarah's obedience to Abraham as an example of submission for Christian wives (see 1 Peter 3:1–6).

Since God inspired New Testament writers to apply the characters of Old Testament narratives in this way, contemporary expositors are also justified in calling believers to behave like positive characters in the Old Testament and to refrain from behaving like negative characters. However, while identification is legitimate for those who preach the gospel of Jesus, moralization is not. Moralizing is exhorting hearers to behave differently—"do better" and "be better"—while not including the gospel. Challenging hearers to "behave like David did in this narrative" is legitimate, but such a challenge cannot be the end. Christian preachers and teachers should include the gospel in every exposition. The gospel teaches that despite our best efforts to "be like David," we have failed to do so and we will fail in the future, but we have forgiveness and reconciliation with God in Christ. Also, we will never be able to "be like David" in our own strength, but the gospel teaches that we are able to do all things through Christ who strengthens us (Phil. 4:13). Christian preachers and teachers preach Christ. It is not inappropriate for an Old Testament character to dominate our exposition if he or she is the central person in our text, but at some point we will show that trying to follow a moral example is not adequate. We need Jesus to forgive us and help us. And our ultimate goal is not to be like an Old Testament character, but to be like Jesus, and to be like the Old Testament character inasmuch as he or she was like Jesus.

A second way to connect contemporary people with Old Testament stories is through *explanation*. Typically, the world of Old Testament stories is foreign to modern people. Horns on altars, threshing floors, chariots, and Edomites are not part of our world. Preaching or teaching from stories that contain such details will require explaining what is unclear. Preachers and teachers can help the people they teach by developing the skill of using descriptive language, drawing pictures with their words to help people "see" the story. Once when preaching through Leviticus I arrived at chapter 8 where Aaron and his sons are consecrated and dressed in priestly garments. I explained the garments, but a garment with a breastpiece, an ephod, and a sash is difficult for contemporary people to visualize. So in that case I provided a verbal explanation and projected an artist's rendering on the big screen so people could get a visual conception of the appearance of the priests. Such drawings are helpful tools, but we should also be careful to check them for accuracy and to explain that it is an artist's rendition that falls short of the certainty of a photograph. We work to insure accuracy in our explanation.

Third, to connect a narrative to contemporary hearers, preachers and teachers may use *conversion*. We help hearers understand the narrative world of the Old Testament when we convert the details of a story into contemporary phenomena that correspond to phenomena in the story.

For example, think of Abram and Sarai leaving Abram's family to follow God's direction to the Promised Land. Abram was seventy-five years old (Gen. 12:4), and Sarai was sixty-five years old. What was it like for two senior adults to set out on a journey that was hundreds of miles, traveling on foot or donkey? In pioneer America, the call was "Go west, *young* man," not "Go west, *old* man." But there they go—Abram driving their Mesopotamian RV and Sarai holding the GPS and asking Abram to stop at all the Cracker Barrel exits. Most senior adults play golf, watch Bonanza re-runs, and knit for grandchildren. Not Abram and Sarai. They didn't have any grandchildren. In fact, they didn't have any children. They were waiting on the child God had promised while they were traveling to the land he promised. Sarah finally became pregnant at age 90. In childbirth class, all the young couples wondered why Abraham and Sarah were there, and they chuckled at the oldsters. After Isaac was born, when the parents at the PTA meeting found out that old Abe and Sarah were Isaac's parents, not his grandparents, they likely choked on their chicken fingers, and when they got home they choked because they were laughing so hard. They were doing what Sarah had predicted. She named her boy Isaac, which means "laughing," because, she said, "Everyone who hears will laugh over me" (Gen. 21:6).

Yes, Abraham and Sarah must have faced challenges as they traveled from Ur to Haran, then from Haran to Shechem. They also faced challenges when they became parents as senior adults. Converting their story into contemporary terms helps hearers to sympathize with those challenges and to share in the laughter. When using such an approach, expositors should make sure to communicate the circumstances of the ancient context at some point. Converting the details of that context into corresponding modern phenomena does not harm our hearers' appreciation of the original context. To the contrary, it enhances understanding and application. This type of cultural conversion does not belong in a Bible translation, but it is a helpful tool in a sermon or Bible study.

Another way we can help contemporary hearers experience the world of Old Testament stories is *narration,* telling the story in a dramatic way. By "dramatic" I'm not referring to displaying lots of emotion or "acting out" the story. I'm referring to telling the story well and including details in the text to help people "see" the characters and the action. As John Goldingay expressed it, "The skilled storyteller can bring to life the concreteness and thus the reality of a story by more subtle, low-key explanations of the meaning of this detail or that, in the course of the imaginative reconstruction of a significant scene."[12] Most biblical stories contain details that give depth, color, and movement to the story. Therefore, to communicate the narrative effectively we can simply tell the story in the same way we would tell an interesting illustration. Consider the following excerpt from James Montgomery

---

12. John Goldingay, *Models for Interpretation of Scripture* (Grand Rapids: Eerdmans, 1995), 77.

Boice's commentary on Hosea, in which he dramatically portrays the account of Hosea purchasing his wife in Hosea 3.

> Thus was Gomer put up for sale. Her clothes were removed, and the men of the city were there to see her nakedness and bid for her. God told Hosea to buy his wife back. One man started the bidding: "Twelve pieces of silver!" "Thirteen!" said Hosea. "Fourteen pieces of silver!" Hosea's bid was "Fifteen!" The low bidders were beginning to drop out, but one man continued bidding: "Fifteen pieces of silver and a bushel of barley!" Hosea said, "Fifteen pieces of silver and a bushel and a half of barley!" The auctioneer looked around and, seeing no more bids said, "Sold to Hosea for fifteen pieces of silver and a bushel and a half of barley." Now notice, at this point Hosea owned his wife. . . . Hosea could have killed Gomer if he had wanted to. Yet he did not. . . . Instead of seeking vengeance, he put Gomer's clothes on her, led her away into the anonymity of the crowd and claimed that love from her that was now his right. Moreover, as he did so he promised no less from himself. . . . Does God love like that? Yes, God loves like that! God steps into the marketplace of sin and buys us out of sin's bondage by the death of Christ.[13]

Producing a dramatic effect as we re-tell the story is valuable. The stories themselves are dramatic, with unparalleled events and unforgettable characters. Leading people to experience the drama is a worthy objective. Still, we dare not go beyond the facts of the story. What God has given us is sufficient. Our narrations are imperfect efforts at best, but the narratives in the Old Testament are inspired by God and therefore perfect.

Preaching and Teaching Proverbs

Over the years, preaching and teaching the book of Proverbs has been a great source of joy to me. I have never doubted that preaching the proverbs will help people, because they have helped me in so many

---

13. James Montgomery Boice, *The Minor Prophets*, 2 vols. (Grand Rapids: Baker 1996), 1:31.

ways. I began studying Proverbs as a young man and continued in doctoral work as I translated much of the book and was part of a seminar on Proverbs. Through the years I have studied the book further in preparation to teach, preach, and write on Proverbs.[14] What is the best way to approach preaching and teaching the proverbs? How do we help people to see God's wisdom and access it? Consider five suggestions.

1. Recognize that the book of Proverbs consists of two genres.

The first nine chapters of the book of Proverbs are usually referred to as the Instruction Literature. The Instruction Literature is primarily in the form of exhortations from a wise teacher/parent to a young person for the purpose of motivating the young person to seek and find wisdom. Derek Kidner calls them "miniature essays."[15] In the first chapters of Proverbs readers are urged repeatedly to acquire wisdom. A few of the exhortations are in a form close to narrative, like the sage's story about observing a loose woman and the foolish sucker who goes to her at night, and the description of wisdom shouting in the streets so people would not turn to her. Perhaps we could call Proverbs 1–9 extended exhortations with occasional narration.

Proverbs 10–31 is usually called the Sentence Literature. The Sentence Literature is in the form of proverbs—two-line sayings, aphorisms that cleverly communicate some truth about life. Ted Hildebrandt has defined a biblical proverb as "a short, salty, concrete, fixed, paradigmatic, poetically crafted saying."[16] John Russell's epigram is that a proverb contains "the wisdom of many and the wit of one."[17] In other words, many people are aware of the truth communicated by the proverb, but only one person expressed the truth in a concise, clever way so it could be eloquently communicated and

---

14 See Allan Moseley, *Living Well: God's Wisdom from the Book of Proverbs* (Bellingham, WA: Lexham, 2017).

15. Derek Kidner, *An Introduction to Wisdom Literature: The Wisdom of Proverbs, Job, and Ecclesiastes* (Downers Grove, IL: InterVarsity Press, 1985), 19.

16. Ted A. Hildebrandt, "Proverb," in *Cracking Old Testament Codes: A Guide to Interpreting the Literary Genres of the Old Testament* (Nashville: Broadman and Holman, 1995), 234.

17. Cited in Allan Moseley, *Living Well*, 12.

easily remembered.[18] Proverbs usually express a truism about life in a succinct way. As Cervantes, the sixteenth century novelist, put it, "Proverbs are short sentences, drawn from long experience."[19]

Preaching and teaching the book of Proverbs begins with the recognition of the two genres in Proverbs and the realization that both genres powerfully communicate truth. In the first nine chapters it is possible to select one passage to teach or preach, since several verses are often bound together as one exhortation or story. However, the verses in chapters 10-31 are not arranged thematically, with a few exceptions like 31:10–31. We cannot say that their order is random, since we believe the Holy Spirit ordered them. But abrupt shifts in theme from one verse to the next is the regular pattern for the Sentence Literature. Therefore, it is most likely best to preach or teach thematically, selecting verses from various places that relate to one theme.

2. Remember the implications of the genre of proverb for meaning.

We will make interpretation and application mistakes if we interpret proverbs as absolute promises. They are not. Proverbs present the typical consequences of wise or foolish behavior. A modern proverb is, The early bird gets the worm. The point is that if we want to have income, or anything, we can't sit around and wait for it to come to us. We have to go get it, and the quicker the better lest someone get it first and we lose the opportunity. That is generally true. However, that proverb is not an absolute promise. Sometimes we're diligent and prompt but still we miss an opportunity. Sometimes people show up late and blessings seem to fall into their laps. In a similar way, most of the biblical proverbs express general principles of life that prove true in most cases.

Consider an example. Proverbs 10:3 says, "The LORD does not let the righteous go hungry, / but he thwarts the craving of the wicked." That is generally true, especially in light of eternal rewards. God blesses righteousness and he opposes wickedness. However, many righteous

---

18. For further examination of the genre of proverbs, see Leland Ryken, *Short Sentences Long Remembered: A Guided Study of Proverbs and Other Wisdom Literature* (Bellingham, WA: Lexham Press, 2017).

19. Cited by Roy B. Zuck, *Learning from the Sages: Selected Studies on the Book of Proverbs* (Grand Rapids: Baker, 1995), 15.

people have suffered and even starved. Just think about Job. So Proverbs 10:3 is not an absolute promise; it is a proverb that expresses the way life generally works. Therefore, when we read any verse in the Sentence Literature we remember that its proverbial genre indicates that it expresses a general truth about life and we do not interpret it as an absolute promise.

3. Become adept at distinguishing the types of proverbs.

Some scholars have classified the proverbs, specifically the Sentence Literature, as to their form—that is, their means of expressing truth. I have done the same, and the exercise of thinking through these various forms has been helpful to me as I have preached from Proverbs. As we consider ten such forms, remember that the Holy Spirit inspired his Word to be expressed in these ways. That fact makes the means of expression important. Also, remember that the book of Proverbs states that one of its purposes is to help people understand eloquent speech (1:6). Studying the form of these beautiful sayings, memorizing them, and contemplating their meaning increases our wisdom in that we are developing the ability to express ideas elegantly and memorably.

The first form is a theological assertion. Proverbs that make a statement about God are common. For example, Proverbs 18:10 says, "The name of the LORD is a strong tower; / the righteous man runs into it and is safe." In the ancient Near East, towers were essential components of a city's defensive system. The metaphor of God as a tower communicates that God provides security. Proverbs 21:3 says, "To do righteousness and justice / is more acceptable to the LORD than sacrifice." This assertion about God tells us God's preference; he prefers righteousness and justice over religious rites.

A second proverbial form is a statement of fact. For example, Proverbs 19:6 says, "Many seek the favor of a generous man, / and everyone is a friend to a man who gives gifts." Such a proverb has no exhortation to right behavior and no comparison. It is simply a truism about life. If someone is known as a big gift-giver, he'll be invited to more birthday parties. That's the way life works. Proverbs 17:18 also states a fact: "One who lacks sense gives a pledge / and puts up security in the presence of his neighbor." The truth about life is that only someone lacking sense borrows money from his neighbor or pledges to pay someone else's debt to his neighbor. Notice that this statement of fact carries an implicit recommendation: if you want to act wisely, don't do that.

A third form of proverb is the comparison of two categories. "The glory of young men is their strength, / but the splendor of old men is their gray hair" is Proverbs 20:29; and 18:9 states, "Whoever is slack in his work / is a brother to him who destroys." Both proverbs are comparisons of categories. Such comparisons cause readers to contemplate the ways these kinds of people are alike and different, and as we think about the comparisons we learn something about life.

A fourth way proverbs communicate truth is by a description of a category/fact. Here's a good example: "A friend loves at all times, / and a brother is born for adversity" (17:17). That's a definition of a true friend: someone whose love is constant through good times and bad. A friend is also like a brother. Proverbs 18:2 defines the category of fool: "A fool takes no pleasure in understanding, / but only in expressing his opinion." Most of us know people like that. They possess an abiding conviction that the world would be a poorer place if it was deprived of their opinion on virtually every subject. But they do not love to learn, so what they say doesn't have much insight, and when we talk they don't listen very well. That's a description of the category fool.

The fifth category of proverbs is promise or prediction. One of the means of teaching wisdom was to predict blessing for those who live wisely and doom for those who live foolishly. For example, Proverbs 19:5 says, "A false witness will not go unpunished, / and he who breathes out lies will not escape"; and 17:2 says, "A servant who deals wisely will rule over a son who acts shamefully, / and will share the inheritance as one of the brothers." Both those verses predict likely outcomes resulting from specific kinds of behavior. However, as we interpret such promises we should remember that they are proverbs first. They exist to teach us how life usually works, not to make absolute promises about predetermined outcomes.

The sixth category of proverbial forms is adversative commentary. Adversative refers to the fact that the proverb expresses an antithesis. "Many a man proclaims his own steadfast love, / but a faithful man who can find? (20:6). That commentary contrasts professing loyalty with actual loyalty. A lot of people claim to be loyal, because it's easy to claim to be loyal. But it's a lot more difficult to find someone who will remain loyal when the winds of adversity begin to blow. Proverbs 16:9 is also an adversative commentary: "The heart of man plans his way, / but the LORD establishes his steps." Some people like to plan their life's direction. They have a ten-year plan, a twenty-year plan, not to mention annual goals. Planning is a good discipline, but this verse reminds us of the interfering sovereignty of God who at any time may disrupt our plans by introducing circumstances beyond our capacity to anticipate. We have a tendency to want to rule our own lives, but God has the tendency to overrule our ruling. That's adversative commentary.

The seventh form of proverbs is metaphor or analogy. The Hebrew word for proverb, *mashal*, refers to a comparison or analogy. In fact, the Hebrew title for the book of Proverbs is the plural form of *mashal*, so Proverbs is a book of comparisons. Not surprisingly, many proverbs are in this form. Proverbs provides many vivid analogies or metaphors that evoke real-life images and therefore aid in understanding. Proverbs 17:3 says, "The crucible is for silver, and the furnace is for gold, / and the LORD tests hearts." That proverb pictures a silversmith or goldsmith melting his molten silver or gold in the refining pot to make sure the dross is separated from the precious metal. That is the way the Lord tests our hearts, watching over the process of purification, separating the impurities from our hearts, which are as precious to him as gold or silver. Another analogy is in 16:24: "Gracious words are like a honeycomb, / sweetness to the soul and health to the body." Our gracious words are as pleasant as honey to those who hear them. The same pleasurable sensation we have on our tongues when we eat honey is the way we make people feel in their souls by speaking pleasant words.

The eighth form is a comparison of worth. This form is similar to the metaphor, but it is a specific kind of analogy; it is a comparison of relative worth—the worth of one thing relative to the worth of something else. For example, Proverbs 17:12 says, "Let a man meet a she-bear robbed of her cubs / rather than a fool in his folly." The wisdom teacher is saying that it is better to meet a mother bear filled with bloodthirsty rage than to meet a fool in his folly. The reader of that proverb surely gets the point—it's extremely important to avoid folly. Another comparison of worth is 16:8: "Better is a little with righteousness / than great income with injustice." Which is better? Living by a strict code of conduct with the result that in retirement we have limited income, or cutting a few ethical corners with the result that we amass enormous wealth? "Better is a little." This proverb does not predict that righteous living results in having a little. Elsewhere Proverbs predicts that righteousness results in prosperity. But 16:8 is a comparison of worth that forces us to evaluate what's most important.

A ninth form of proverb is the exhortation. Some proverbs are explicit instructions to follow a recommended course of action. They are similar to commands. Proverbs 19:18 reads, "Discipline your son, for there is hope; / do not set your heart on putting him to death." That's an exhortation to practice the kind of parenting that includes discipline. Another exhortation addresses how to relate to evil persons. "Be not envious of evil men, / nor desire to be with them" (24:1).

The tenth form of proverb is a statement of incongruence. Some proverbs claim that certain things do not go together. For example, "Fine speech is not becoming to a fool; / still less is false speech to a prince" (17:7). The category of excellent speech is incongruent with the category of fool. If a fool happened to utter such speech it would be odd. The opposite is true for leaders or princes. Saying things that are not true is incongruent with leadership. People who lie may hold a position of leadership, but they forfeit the opportunity to lead most people.

4. Categorize all the verses of Proverbs according to theme.

As a young man I read through the book of Proverbs several times, categorizing each verse according to its theme. At the conclusion of that exercise, I had several sheets of paper with lists of verse references that were grouped into over forty categories. I have returned to those categories many times to find God's wisdom for my life. As a young pastor, when I faced a difficult circumstance, I would look at categories like "relationships" or "speech" for help in how to relate to people and to access God's wisdom about how I should speak to them.

My own experience of learning and applying the book of Proverbs demonstrated to me how practical its contents are to so many life situations. The people we teach face the same situations. Why not teach and preach the book in the same way it helps us? Read through the book several times, categorizing the verses as to their themes, and then teach what Proverbs says about each theme. My own categories include themes such as possessions, speech, relationships, pride, relating to parents, anger, work, sexual purity, parenting, relating to authorities, old age, women, men, fearing and trusting God, sin, and listening to wisdom. Read and contemplate God's wisdom on the topics in Proverbs and allow their truth to become part of your thinking and living. Then add some application and illustration and the proverbs practically teach themselves.

5. Relate the exposition to God.

Among those who study ancient Near Eastern literature much has been made of the similarities between the book of Proverbs and the proverbs in Akkadian and Egyptian literature. The parallels are an established fact. For example, a few proverbs have been found in Akkadian letters that pre-date Solomon's reign by centuries, demonstrating that the genre of proverb was a part of ancient Near Eastern life. Akkadian documents that date to after Solomon include the "Counsels of Wisdom" (eight century BC) and "The Words of Ahiqar" (seventh century BC). These texts have no direct, or verbal, connections with Proverbs, but they address the same themes, like the use of speech, avoiding the harlot, being generous and not borrowing money, working hard, and not arguing with superiors.[20] Wisdom texts in Egypt addressed many of the same wisdom themes in documents like "The Instruction of Ptah-hotep," "The Instruction for King Meri-Ka-Re," and "The Instruction of Ani."[21] Each of these documents pre-date Solomon. More discussion has focused on the similarities between Proverbs and "The Instruction of Amenemope" since the parallels are not only thematic but verbal, especially with Proverbs 22:17–24:22. However, the conception of God in Proverbs differs markedly from Akkadian and Egyptian texts. First, Proverbs reflects a monotheistic understanding of God, which is unique in ancient Near Eastern documents. Plus, in Egyptian texts "god" sometimes refers to pharaoh, sometimes to a high god, and sometimes to

---

20. See the texts in James B. Pritchard, ed., *Ancient Near Eastern Texts Relating to the Old Testament,* 3rd ed. with supplement (Princeton, NJ: Princeton University Press, 1969), 425–26, 594.

21. Pritchard, *Ancient Near Eastern Texts,* 412–20.

an undefined force that is perhaps a personal or local deity. That is vastly different from Proverbs' consistent references to Yahweh. In fact, the word "Yahweh" occurs five times in Proverbs 22:17–24:22. For example, the reason the reader should "hear the words of the wise" (22:17) is "that your trust may be in the LORD" (22:19), and wise people don't rejoice when their enemies fall, "lest the LORD see it and be displeased" (24:18).

Unlike other ancient Near Eastern wisdom texts, then, the book of Proverbs is not mere pragmatism. It is practical, but its practical counsel is related to God repeatedly. Therefore, when we preach and teach it, our exposition should also relate to God. As I have written elsewhere,

> The book of Proverbs is more than a repository of "how to" principles for successful living. It is part of the grand narrative of God's past, present, and future work of salvation that is unveiled in Scripture. In many ways, the book of Proverbs demonstrates that wisdom can be accessed only in a relationship with God. Fearing God, or living in a right relationship with him, is the beginning of wisdom (Prov. 1:7; 9:10), and readers of Proverbs are exhorted to "trust in the LORD with all your heart" (3:5). We cannot have God's wisdom without God, because as Proverbs 2:6 says, "The LORD gives wisdom." In the old covenant period, the Lord gave wisdom to those who put their faith in him and thus became part of the covenant people (Gen. 15:6; Gal. 3:5–14).
>
> The New Testament also highlights that true wisdom is inextricably bound to relatedness to God. Paul emphasized that the "sacred writings" of the Old Testament are able to make us "wise for salvation through faith in Christ Jesus" (2 Tim. 3:15). First Corinthians 1:30 also says that God is the source of our life "in Christ Jesus, who became to us wisdom from God, righteousness and sanctification and redemption." . . . Both Proverbs and the balance of Scripture teach us that in order to acquire wisdom a relationship with God through Christ is necessary. So biblical wisdom has a thousand practical implications, but it begins with one spiritual reality—a relationship

with God through Christ. Once God accomplishes his saving work in our lives on the basis of our faith, we live in a way that is different, holy. The wisdom in the book of Proverbs shows us how to live that way.[22]

Proverbs is the book that exhorts us, "Trust in the LORD with all your heart, / and do not lean on your own understanding. In all your ways acknowledge him, / and he will make straight your paths" (3:5–6). If we heed that exhortation when we teach the book, we will consistently point people beyond human behavior to God himself who is the fount of all wisdom and the source of the power we need to live wisely.

---

22. Moseley, *Living Well*, 4–5. For an excellent, extended discussion of how the book of Proverbs points to Christ and is fulfilled in him, see Jonathan Akin, *Preaching Christ from Proverbs* (Spring Hill, TN: Rainer, 2014).

Chapter   3

WHAT IS THE TEXT'S GENRE?
(PART 2)

8-STEP METHOD

STEP 1	Translating the text
STEP 2	Considering text criticism
STEP 3	**Interpreting the genre**
STEP 4	Exploring the context
STEP 5	Defining important words
STEP 6	Identifying the big idea
STEP 7	Connecting to Jesus
STEP 8	Applying the text to contemporary people

The third step of our process of exposition is genre interpretation. It follows translation and textual criticism, both of which help to answer the question, what does the text say? In the last chapter we introduced the importance of identifying a text's genre as part of our exposition. Genre should affect our interpretation of any text, and since it affects our interpretation it will also affect the way we teach the text to other people. So far we have considered how to teach from narrative texts and proverbs. In this chapter we will continue a consideration of genre, specifically giving attention to the proper approach to teaching legal texts, prophecy, and the poetry of the book of Psalms. First, we'll give attention to prayer. Only after meeting with God in prayer will we be prepared to interpret any genre well. Since we will explore how to teach the poetry of Psalms in this chapter, we'll begin by considering how the psalms can help us grow in prayer.

Pray

In Dietrich Bonhoeffer's book *Psalms: The Prayer Book of the Bible*, he states that we learn to pray in the same way a child learns to speak. The child's parent speaks to the child, and the child repeats the words of the parent. Similarly, in the book of Psalms God our Father gives us the words of prayer, and we speak the words back to him. For Bonhoeffer, the fact that God has given us words to speak to him in prayer obligates us to use them in that way. He writes, "We ought to speak to God . . . not in the false and confused speech of our heart, but in the clear and pure speech which God has spoken to us."[1] Ronald Heine, in his volume on the interpretation of the Old Testament by the early church fathers, agrees. He maintains, "The psalms can become our instruction book in prayer, teaching us how to lay our souls bare before God in God's own words. They can also give a whole new agenda to our prayer life."[2] This agenda, Heine states, is not our agenda, but God's.

The "new agenda" for prayer about which Heine writes may be new to us, but it is not new. The prayers of the psalms are as old as King David, "the sweet psalmist of Israel" (2 Sam. 23:1). Throughout the ages, God's people have prayed the psalms. Heine reviews the importance of the psalms in the praying of the church fathers in the first five Christian centuries. He summarizes, "The early Christian mind was soaked with psalms. . . . The early Christians carried the psalms in their minds and in their hearts."[3] For example, Augustine delivered homilies to his congregation on each of the 150 psalms. In Augustine's comments on Psalm 35 (Psalm 34 in the Septuagint that Augustine used), he emphasized that true prayer seeks nothing but God himself. Our goal should be to desire God's presence more than we desire anything else. The psalmist wrote in Psalm 35:9, "My soul will rejoice in the LORD."

---

1. Dietrich Bonhoeffer, *Psalms: The Prayer Book of the Bible*, trans. James H. Burtness (Minneapolis: Augsburg, 1970), 11.

2. Ronald E. Heine, *Reading the Old Testament with the Ancient Church* (Grand Rapids: Baker, 2007), 174.

3. Ibid., 144.

Augustine exhorts us to ask ourselves whether we rejoice in the Lord or in something else. He cites Jesus' invitation for us to ask in prayer, and Augustine then bids us to contemplate what we might ask for.

> "Ask what you will!" If you are a lover of property, you will want to possess the whole earth. . . . And when you own the whole earth, what then? You will ask for the sea, in which, after all, you cannot live. . . . Go beyond that too, ask for the air as well, even though you cannot fly in it. . . . He who made them all has said: "Ask what you will"; and yet you will find nothing more precious, nothing more excellent than Himself who made them all. Ask for Him who made them, and in Him and from Him you will possess all He has made. . . . If you ask for anything else, you wrong Him and harm yourself, by preferring what He made before Him, whereas He, its Maker, desires to give you himself.[4]

When we pray, do we ask for God in prayer? Or do we ask God to be the dispenser of what we really want? The psalms will help us to grow in prayer if we will make them our prayer book and use them to seek God in prayer. Our prayer will be formed by Scripture when we allow the psalms into our thinking, our feeling, and our praying. Before we teach the psalms, we should pray them. Especially when we are preparing to teach from the book of Psalms, speaking the inspired words to God in prayer will prepare our hearts to understand, to feel, and to teach the words. In that way, our study and therefore our teaching will be more than academic; they will arise out of our fellowship with God in prayer.

Preaching and Teaching Old Testament Law

Many Christians have had the experience of committing themselves to read through the Bible. They begin by reading the dramatic narratives of Genesis and the spectacular miracles of Exodus. They're soaring high until they arrive at the lengthy list of laws in the Book of the

---

4. Augustine, *St. Augustine on the Psalms*, 2 vols., trans. Scholastica Hebgin and Felicitas Corrigan (Westminster, MD: Newman, 1961), 2:201–202.

Covenant after the Ten Commandments (Exod. 20:22–23:33). At that point the engine sputters and their excitement about reading through the Bible begins to lose altitude. By the time they reach Leviticus they have stopped soaring and started crawling. They read about sacrifices that are no longer offered, a priesthood that no longer exists, and laws they are not obligated to obey. All of that and more is described in tedious detail, so some people ask, "Why is this in the Bible?"

But contemporary Christians should know the contents of the legal sections of the Old Testament, and Christian preachers and teachers should teach it. As a pastor I spent about six months preaching through Leviticus, and the people were enthusiastic about studying that part of the Bible. People saw that the Old Testament law is not merely about rituals; it is about God. Preaching and teaching Old Testament law is challenging. However, teaching this part of the Old Testament can open the eyes of believers to the meaning of the law so that in the future when they read the law they will see powerful truths about God that will have profound effects on the way they think and live.

I have devoted more space to the genre of law for three reasons. First, emphasis is needed because so many teachers and preachers avoid teaching this part of the Bible. I want to show why it is important to teach it and how to do it well. Second, Western culture desperately needs significant exposure to God's law. We are in a freefall into moral anarchy. People are losing the very idea of divine law. Perhaps preaching and teaching God's law can impede our descent. Third, understanding the law is fundamental to appreciating the gospel. How can we grasp gospel concepts like the nature of our sin, the holiness of God, and the greatness of God's grace if we do not know the law?

Old Testament Law: A Theological Primer

According to one way of defining Old Testament law, it is identified as the Torah, or the Pentateuch, that is, the first five books of the Old Testament. However, since we are approaching the Old Testament according to genre, when I refer to preaching the law I am referring more specifically to those parts of the Torah that consist of lists of commands, case laws, and descriptions of all the aspects of Israel's worship rituals. To help us teach Old Testament law, I will offer eight recommendations. But first I want to offer a brief theological primer to the law. Such a theological introduction is the crucial foundation for interpreting the law correctly, and to teach a text correctly we have to interpret it correctly. We should have the following propositions in mind every time we prepare to teach a text in the Old Testament law. When we master the ideas of this primer, hopefully we will also see why and how we should teach and preach the law to contemporary believers.

Old Testament law is important because it is a revelation from God.

The book of Leviticus, for example, opens with the statement, "The Lord summoned Moses and spoke to him" (1:1). In fact, Leviticus states thirty-eight times that the Lord spoke to Moses and/or Aaron. Also, eighteen times the book records that the Lord "commanded" Moses, Aaron, and the people. Other legal sections of the Old Testament have similar statements. Since the law expresses the very words of God in direct speech, people who know and love God will value the law and will approach it with reverence. The law is God's speech to God's people.

God's law in the Old Testament is positive and good.

Some Christians seem to think that devotion to God's law necessarily leads to legalism. That is not so, and the Bible contains numerous expressions of the law's virtues. The psalmist said to God, "Your commandments are my delight" (Ps. 119:143). The apostle Paul wrote that "the law is holy, and the commandment is holy and righteous and good" (Rom. 7:12). Therefore, God's people should never approach the law with a negative attitude: "Oh, no! Not that boring stuff!" Instead, we should become committed students of the law, as were Jesus and Paul.

The old covenant law expresses God's character.

Consider Deuteronomy 22:6–8: "If you come across a bird's nest in any tree or on the ground, with young ones or eggs and the mother sitting on the young or on the eggs, you shall not take the mother with the young. You shall let the mother go. . . . When you build a new house, you shall make a parapet for your roof, that you may not bring the guilt of blood upon your house, if anyone should fall from it." Those two laws are no longer normative in the new covenant age. However, they reveal something about God. The law about birds limits the extent to which members of a particular animal species can be harmed, revealing that God cares about the perpetuation of species. The second law protects human life, revealing that God values life on this earth for each person. Thus, we approach every Old Testament law asking, "What does this reveal about God?" just as we approach every part of Scripture with that question.

Old Testament law addresses behavior and the condition of the heart.

Some people have created a false dichotomy between the Old Testament and the New Testament along these lines: The Old Testament is law the New Testament is grace; the Old Testament requires mere compliance to external legal standards but the New Testament calls for transformation of the heart. Such a dichotomy does not accurately reflect the contents of the Old Testament. Leviticus 19:17, 32, for example, state, "You shall not hate your brother in your heart. . . . You shall fear your God." Obviously loving someone in our hearts is not a matter of mere external compliance; it requires our hearts to be right. The law also commands us to love God (Deut. 6:1–6). When we teach Old Testament law, we always keep in mind that we cannot know God, worship God, or obey God rightly without hearts that are transformed by faith and trust in God (cf. Gen. 15:6; Prov. 3:5–6).

God gave his law in the old covenant period as part of his redemption plan.

The laws in the Old Testament are set in the literary context of a narrative. When we read the law, we should always read it as a part of the larger story in which it is set. The law is not the beginning of the story, and God never intended for it to be the end of the story. When we teach Old Testament law, we should set the law in its historical context. What occurred before the giving of the law, and what occurred after the giving of the law? When we ask such questions we are entering the story of the Bible, and the consistent theme of that story is God's redemption plan—the acts of God as part of his plan to call all peoples to himself.

When we consider all of salvation history we remember that God gave his law in a specific time period for specific reasons. God had already told Abraham that he would bless the nations through Abraham's progeny (Gen. 12:1–3). Israel's obedience to God's law would help fulfill God's purpose of blessing the nations. As other people groups saw the different way Israel lived, the way of obeying God's law, they would see what it is like to know and follow the one true God. They would also learn about the moral character of God by observing his laws at work. Thus, the law served a missionary purpose from the beginning. It was part of God's plan to draw the nations to faith in him. Readers of the Bible can see God's plan play out in numerous ways, since the Bible reveals God's work of redemption throughout history. The law is one part of that larger plan.

God gave his old covenant law because of sin.

In the beginning, God gave only one law to humanity. He told the first man and woman not to eat the fruit from one particular tree (Gen. 2:17). They transgressed that law, so God began adding laws to circumscribe the sinful behavior that continued to proliferate. Galatians 3:19 seems to make exactly that point: "Why then the law? It was added because of transgressions." As transgression multiplied, God added laws to reveal his displeasure with sin and to make plain his way of health and blessing.[5] God's gift of the law guided many people away from sin and into his way of life. We can only imagine how sin might have multiplied even further had it not been for the restraining force of God's law. God's law continues to restrain us from sin. Like the Israelites in the old covenant period, we too are sinners. God's law has a sanctifying effect in our lives.

Old Testament law is personal, to be obeyed in the context of a love relationship with God.

Typically we do not obey laws because of a personal relationship. For example, we don't stop our cars at stop signs because someone we love

---

5. John Sailhamer makes much of this point, emphasizing that the failure of the Hebrews to approach God at Mt. Sinai resulted in the multiplication of laws. Further, God gave the laws knowing the people would fail to keep them, proving the Pauline doctrine that living by faith like Abraham was the only valid way of salvation and that living by the law could never be efficacious. John Sailhamer, *The Meaning of the Pentateuch* (Downers Grove, IL: InterVarsity Press, 2009), 380–415.

wrote that traffic law and we don't want to do anything that might strain the relationship. To the contrary, we obey that law merely to avoid the consequences of a collision or a traffic citation. God's law is different. He gave his law to his people because he loved them (Deut. 7:6–13). God's people were to obey his law out of love for him (Deut. 6:1–6; John 14:15). God did not give his law to the world in general. He gave it to his people with whom he had established a covenant relationship. With respect to Old Testament law, first comes a covenant relationship with God, then comes the law.

We can view God's law, especially the sacrificial system, as God's invitation to his people to come into his presence. In the sacrificial system God was telling his people to draw near to him. The sacrificial system existed because human sin and God's love existed. God loved his people and wanted them to draw near to him. However, they had sinned and could not come into his presence without atonement for their sin. So God provided the sacrificial system to atone for sin so they could come near to him. Thus, the law contains the good news that even when we turn our backs on God and break his laws, he loves us and pursues us to reconcile us to himself. God invites us to his presence. Roy Gane refers to the descriptions of the various sacrifices in Leviticus as "God's altar calls."[6] Because God loves his people, his law contains invitations for his people to come to the altar to worship him.

God gave the old covenant law to his people as an act of grace and after his grace.

The Ten Commandments begin with an indicative verb, not an imperative. "I am the LORD your God, who brought you out of the land of Egypt, out of the house of slavery" (Exod. 20:2). God gave his law to his people *after* he had redeemed them, not before. First he saved them by his grace, then he commanded them how to live. The order is important, important enough for God to place a reminder of his redemption at the head of the Ten Commandments as a preamble to his law. Yes, God's creation laws apply to all people, redeemed and unredeemed. But God's covenant laws applied only to his covenant people,

---

6. Roy Gane, *Leviticus, Numbers*, The NIV Application Commentary (Grand Rapids: Zondervan, 2004), 25.

and he established that covenant by the gracious acts of his choice and his redemption.

The idea that a covenant with God by God's grace comes before his law is foundational to the gospel and has profound implications for the way we preach and teach the Bible today. First, we call people to the salvation God offers by his grace. Then after they receive God's grace and enter a covenant relationship with him, we train them how to live according to God's commands. Humans are not capable of obeying God's law without his enabling power in us, and we have that power only after God is in our lives through Christ. Also, his commands are further expressions of his grace since they show us the way to live a happy, fulfilled life. This has always been God's way—first, salvation by his grace that comes through exercising faith in him, and then a changed life that includes obedience to his commands. As John Frame writes, "The demand for obedience in both covenants is not a demand that people earn their salvation through meritorious works. . . . Rather, it calls upon the believer to obey God (by God's grace) as the appropriate response to redemption."[7]

Old Testament law includes promises of blessing for obedience.

In Leviticus 26 and Deuteronomy 27–28 God specified all the ways his people would suffer if they disobeyed his law and all the ways they would prosper if they obeyed. The promises of blessing sets God's law apart from the laws to which we are accustomed. We expect to suffer as a result of breaking laws. When we break a law we could be convicted of a crime and imprisoned, or worse. But we are not accustomed to experiencing blessings because of our obedience to law. In all my years of driving a car, an officer of the law has never pulled me over and told me, "Dr. Moseley, we have noticed your exemplary obedience to the traffic laws lately, so I'm pulling you over just to say thanks. Also, I have a little gift from all of us at the Highway Patrol Office that I would like to present to you as a small token of our appreciation." Such a scenario will never happen because that's not the way civil law works. However, it is the way God's law works. He promises to bless people who obey his

---

7. John Frame, *The Doctrine of the Christian Life* (Phillipsburg, NJ: P&R, 2008), 207.

law. Obeying God's commands is the way to enjoy the good life (Deut. 5:33; 8:1). God gave his law to help his people, not to hurt them.

God intended the old covenant legal system to be temporary.
To repeat Galatians 3:19: "Why then the law? It was added because of transgressions, until the offspring should come to whom the promise had been made." The "offspring" is literally the "seed," the seed of the woman who would bruise the serpent's head (Gen. 3:15), the seed of Abraham who would bless the nations (Gen. 22:18). The New Testament identifies Jesus as that seed (Gal. 3:13–16). God gave his law for a specific period of time to reveal his way of life until the time was right for the One to come who is "the way, and the truth, and the life" (John 14:6). Jesus fulfilled the law (Matt. 5:17), and the New Testament affirms that Jesus has made the old covenant and its stipulations obsolete (Eph. 2:11–15; Col. 2:16–17; Heb. 8:6–13). For a particular period of time God intended to reveal himself and his will through the old covenant that included a law code that addresses generally every area of life: work, sickness, wealth, clothes, diet, sex, birth and death, worship, and relationships with people outside the faith. Those laws served important purposes like revealing God's character, proscribing wickedness, outlining the shape of morality, preparing humanity for the coming of Christ, highlighting Christ's perfections, and teaching the nature of Christ's sacrifice. The period of time during which those old covenant laws were in effect has passed. Now that the old covenant and its laws are obsolete, how do Christians preach and teach from the law? Many of the laws in the Old Testament are not binding on God's people today. God gave them to his people in a specific place for a specific time. But they are in the Bible and therefore authoritative for us. So, what do we do with them? What do they mean to us today? How do we teach and preach from them?

Preaching and Teaching Old Testament Law: Eight Recommendations

The theological consideration of the law above should put us on the right path toward teaching the law to the contemporary church. Already we are thinking in terms of how the law relates to God, his saving work in history, and the New Testament. It is helpful to have the previous ten principles well in hand every time we prepare to preach from the law. Thinking theologically, historically, and canonically should constrain us from drifting toward allegorical thinking. I once read a sermon in which the preacher stated that the three sections of the tabernacle symbolize three parts of human nature: the outer court represents the body, the Holy Place represents the soul, and the Holy of Holies represents the spirit. Such an approach alters the nature of the law, turning it into an allegory. He went on to state that the table of bread symbolizes the emotions, the incense altar symbolizes the will, and the lampstand symbolizes the mind. Another pastor said the fact that the seven lamps were on one lampstand symbolizes the unity of churches today. Someone else wrote that the twelve loaves of bread on the table represent the unity and completeness of the church. Another pastor said the bread refers to the church's preachers.[8] Does the Bible say that those items are symbolic in such ways? It does not, so the symbolism originated in the minds of the preachers, not in God's revealed Word. That way of interpreting the Old Testament can lead to theological error since the interpretations and applications derive from the interpreter's mind, not from what the Bible asserts. More about allegory later, but I suggest that we refrain from allegorizing.

Clearly, a major challenge in teaching Old Testament law is learning to interpret it well. A way of interpreting Old Testament law that is explicitly Christian would be helpful. On the one hand, we need a way that will help us avoid the kind of fanciful allegorical interpretations cited above. On the other hand, we need a way that will help us avoid the kind of historicism that limits our study of the law to descriptions of what happened in Israel's history.[9]

My first recommendation is to affirm inspiration and helpfulness. Second Timothy 3:16 says, "All Scripture is breathed out by God and profitable for teaching, for reproof, for correction, and for training in righteousness." When the apostle Paul wrote that, the New Testament did not exist. He was writing about the Old Testament Scripture that includes the law, and he wrote "all Scripture is breathed out by God."

---

8. Mark W. Elliott, *Engaging Leviticus: Reading Leviticus Theologically with Its Past Interpreters* (Eugene, OR: Cascade, 2012), 255–56.

9. Essentially the same recommendations as those that follow here are described

"*All* Scripture," including the legal corpus. So, we affirm inspiration—God breathed out, inspired, the Old Testament laws.

Many Christians divide the laws into three categories: ceremonial laws, civil laws, and moral laws. Ceremonial laws have to do with rituals regarding worship, leadership of worship, and preparation for worship. Jesus made the Old Testament ceremonial system obsolete when he became our high priest and the final sacrifice for sin (Heb. 8:13; 9:11–10:18). Also, the civil laws no longer apply to us in the new covenant age, since their purpose was to govern the civil life of the nation of Israel during the period of the old covenant. However, the moral laws of the Old Testament still apply to us, since most or all of them are repeated in the New Testament.

Dividing Old Testament laws into three categories can be helpful. However, it falls short of constituting a satisfactory method of interpreting the laws. First, such categories are extraneous to the Bible. Further, even though new covenant believers are not required to obey old covenant ceremonial and civil laws, 2 Timothy 3:16 states that they are breathed out by God. God gave his laws to his people in a specific place for a specific time, but they are in the Bible and all the Bible remains authoritative. So we begin not by placing laws into man-made categories but by affirming their inspiration.

Also we affirm the helpfulness of the law. Second Timothy 3:16 states, "All Scripture is . . . profitable for teaching, for reproof, for correction, and for training in righteousness." So all Scripture is not only inspired, all of it is also helpful, profitable. In the new covenant period, the Old Testament ceremonial and civil laws are not law for us; our disobedience to individual laws is not punished as was the case in ancient Israel. However, they are profitable in that they teach us about God, his will, and how to live for him in today's world.[10] That is true of every verse in the law.

Second, affirm fulfillment in Jesus. People who have a lower view of the inspiration of Scripture argue that pointing to Jesus from the law

---

in Allan Moseley, *Exalting Jesus in Leviticus*, Christ-Centered Exposition Commentary (Nashville: B&H, 2015), 6–9.

10. To see another brief method of interpreting Old Testament law that also includes an affirmation of its inspiration, see George H. Guthrie, *Read the Bible for Life: Your Guide to Understanding and Living God's Word* (Nashville: B&H, 2011), 95–108.

is eisegesis, since Moses and the ancient Hebrews knew nothing about him. However, if indeed Scripture is "breathed out by God," then certainly when God gave his law to Moses and his people, he already knew of Jesus. Also, Jesus affirmed that the law is about him. After Jesus' resurrection he met with a few of his disciples in the little town of Emmaus. He said to them, "These are my words that I spoke to you while I was still with you, that everything written about me in the Law of Moses and the Prophets and the Psalms must be fulfilled" (Luke 24:44). Jesus fulfilled all the Old Testament, even the law. Jesus referred to "everything written about *me* in the Law of Moses." By "the Law of Moses" he meant the Torah, the first five books of the Old Testament. The laws we have been considering are found in the Torah, and Jesus said it is somehow about him. Therefore, if we intend to teach Old Testament law the way Jesus taught it, we will have to show how it is about Jesus.

Jesus also said, "Do not think that I have come to abolish the Law or the Prophets; I have not come to abolish them but to fulfill them" (Matt 5:17). Jesus stated that he came to fulfill the law. How does Jesus fulfill the law? Every Christian teacher and preacher should ask that question when teaching any legal text. The book of Hebrews provides an excellent answer, especially in chapters 7–9. I attempt to model how to preach about Jesus from the law in my book *Exalting Jesus in Leviticus.* The following is an example that was written to affirm that Jesus fulfills all the Levitical laws about sacrifices.

> Jesus is the fulfillment of all the sacrifices God commanded in Leviticus. All the sacrifices prepared people for the coming of Jesus—God the Son and humanity's Savior. The whole burnt offering was consumed completely on the altar; all of it was burned, nothing remained. Jesus also gave all of himself as a sacrifice, and Philippians 2 says that "he emptied himself . . . even to death on a cross" (vv. 7–8).
>
> The grain offering signified thanksgiving and dedication to God. Jesus expressed thanksgiving to God the Father (Luke 10:21; John 11:41), and he was completely dedicated to God. He said, "I have come down from heaven, not to do my own will, but the will of him who sent me" (John 6:38). The fellowship offering expressed peace with God. Jesus had and has perfect

fellowship with God the Father. In John 10:30 he said, "The Father and I are one." Jesus also made peace with God possible for us; Colossians 1:20 says he made "peace through the blood of his cross."

The sin offering was to make atonement for sin. God judges sin, and his penalty for sin is death. The sin offering satisfied the wrath of God against sin. Jesus was our sin offering when he died on the cross for our sins. The New Testament word for satisfying God's wrath against sin is "propitiation," and 1 John 4:10 says, "Love consists in this: not that we have loved God, but that he loved us and sent his Son to be the propitiation for our sins." The restitution offering was for the guilt of sin and involved making restitution for wrongs done, paying back debts owed because of sin. The death of Jesus on the cross also fulfilled the guilt offering. Colossians 2:13–14 says God has "forgiven us all our trespasses, by canceling the record of debt that stood against us with its legal demands. This he set aside, nailing it to the cross." Jesus paid our sin debt on the cross.

Jesus wasn't just the next step in God's plan. He was always God's plan, and he is the final, once-for-all sacrifice for sin. When Jesus died on the cross, every sin of every person was placed on him. God never meant the old covenant sacrificial system to be permanent; it existed to prepare for the sacrifice of Jesus on the cross and to explain the sacrifice of Jesus.[11]

Third, determine what the law/text meant in its original context. We study what happened originally. What does the Bible say about how a particular sacrifice was offered, or how the Day of Atonement was observed? The contemporary meaning is based on the original meaning, and contemporary applications are based on the original application. Since a biblical text cannot mean what it never meant, we ask, How would this passage have been understood and applied in its original setting? We base our interpretation on that.

Fourth, note the similarities with today's context. For example, Leviticus 11:7 commands God's people to refrain from eating pork. Of

---

11. Moseley, *Exalting Jesus in Leviticus*, 81–82.

course, in the new covenant the dietary laws no longer apply. Evidently some people were pressuring followers of Jesus in Colossae to follow the dietary laws of the old covenant. Paul wrote to them, "Let no one pass judgment on you in questions of food and drink. . . . These are a shadow of the things to come, but the substance belongs to Christ" (Col. 2:16–17). So the Old Testament dietary laws no longer apply in the age of the new covenant. Such laws are merely shadows, but Christ is the substance. Why would we want a shadow when we can have the substance? Jesus fulfills all such stipulations of the old covenant and makes them obsolete because he is the mediator of a "better covenant" (Heb. 7:22; 8:6). Therefore, we put our faith in him.

How then do we teach Leviticus 11? To determine that, we answer the question about the meaning of the command in its original context. The peoples who lived around Israel ate pork. In commanding his people *not* to eat pork God was creating a distinction between his people and other peoples. God's people were to observe that distinction; they were to be different, separate. If non-Jews got to know Jews well enough to share a meal with them, they would notice the difference, and if they pursued the issue they would learn that the Jews were different because of their God. "Why don't you eat pork?" "Because God told us not to eat pork." What is the similarity with today's context? People who live around us still do things God forbids, and God's people are still to be different. Now we have found a thematic connection to our contemporary context.

Fifth, honor the context of the legal text in salvation history. As noted above, all the laws of the Old Testament are located in the context of a historical narrative. That historical narrative is the story of God's work in calling and saving his people. Prior to God's gift of the law, historical highlights of the story are creation, the call of Abraham, and the miraculous deliverance from Egyptian bondage. The story includes three covenants: God's covenants with Noah and all creation, Abraham and his descendants, and Israel at Mt. Sinai. In a Christian sermon, a law's setting in salvation history is crucial. If we detach a legal text from that history, we also detach it from God's saving work and even from God himself. All that remains is legalism.

Christian preachers and teachers should also consider our post–resurrection perspective toward Old Testament law. From what position do we view the law? We are not standing with Israel at Mt. Sinai receiving the law and looking *forward* to the promised seed of Abraham. We are standing with the church looking *back* at the gift of the law. And we cannot look back without looking *through* the person and work of Jesus, the promised seed of Abraham who has come. In order to teach Old Testament law *as Christians*, we allow that perspective to affect our teaching. That means we will teach that God's gift of the law was good, but it was also temporary, preparatory, and pedagogical. It was temporary because God gave it with the foreknowledge that he would make it obsolete when he inaugurated the new covenant in Christ. It was preparatory because God used the law to demonstrate humanity's sinfulness and therefore our need for the Savior. It was pedagogical because God used the law to teach eternal principles such as the fact that sin leads to separation from God and death and God allows a substitutionary sacrifice to atone for sin. If indeed God was using the law to teach eternal principles and point to Christ, so can we. To do that, we will need to remember the context of the law in salvation history.

Sixth, identify principles that apply to both ancient and modern contexts. With respect to refraining from eating pork, we have already identified a principle that applies to both contexts. God doesn't want his people to be exactly like the people around them. That principle applies today, so we have identified a principle that applies to both ancient and modern contexts. Walter Kaiser refers to this process as "principlization."[12] Just as we ask how every legal text is fulfilled in Jesus, we also look for the underlying principle(s) in every legal text. The immediate and/or broader context always contains a principle about God, humanity, or God's way of relating to humanity. Once we identify a principle, we look for a statement of that principle elsewhere in the Old Testament and especially in the New Testament.

Seventh, consider what the New Testament teaches about each principle. It is crucial to find New Testament corroboration for the principle we identify in an Old Testament legal text, lest we teach a principle of our own making. Our principle derived from the dietary laws has to do with living differently from people who do not know God. Does the

---

12. Walter C. Kaiser Jr., *Toward an Exegetical Theology: Biblical Exegesis for Preaching and Teaching* (Grand Rapids: Baker, 1998), 150–63.

New Testament teach anything about the separation of God's people from those who do not know and love God? Yes, 2 Corinthians 6 tells Christians that such separation is perfectly normal, just like righteousness and unrighteousness are not partners, and just like light does not fellowship with darkness. "Therefore go out from their midst, and be separate from them" (6:17).

Jesus also spoke about his followers living differently from the people around them. He told his disciples that they were not of this world, and he prayed for them to be different from the world (John 15:19; 17:14–16). Jesus also fulfills that part of the old covenant law because he lived separate from the sin of the world, because he empowers his followers to be different, and because knowing him *is* the difference between his followers and those who do not know and love God.

Eighth, apply the principle to life. The principle is that God wants us to be different from those who do not know him. So we apply that principle in our own lives. We reject the sinful practices of the world and we love and obey Jesus. We also apply the principle to the lives of the people we teach. We testify to how the principle works in our lives, we explain how it will work in their lives, and we provide illustrations of how it has worked in the lives of people in the past.

Preaching and Teaching Prophetic Texts

As with the other sections of the Old Testament, preaching and teaching the prophets begins with understanding the prophetic genre, or the "rules" of interpretation that apply specifically to prophetic forms of communication. Determining how to apply prophetic messages to the lives of God's people today comes later. First we make sure we know what prophetic texts are saying, and not saying. Interpreting the prophets is not easy. All the prophets have their own unique challenges. The sheer volume of almost 250 chapters is daunting, often the material is not in chronological order, and the demarcation of separate units is not always clear. In his two-volume theology of the Old Testament, Gerhard von Rad devotes the entire second volume to the prophets. In that volume he quotes Martin Luther's words concerning the prophets: "They have a queer way of talking, like people who, instead of proceeding in an orderly manner, ramble off from one thing to the next, so that you cannot make head or tail of them or see what they are getting at."[13] No wonder, then, that so many Bible readers miss the point of prophetic texts, and so many Bible teachers avoid teaching them. The purpose of this section is to help preachers and teachers avoid interpretation errors and maximize the prophets' impact on contemporary people. Every time we read prophetic texts in preparation to teach or preach we should make the following six essentials part of our preparation routine.

1. Determine the subgenre of the prophetic text.

The contents of the books of the prophets consist of numerous subgenres.[14] Sometimes prophetic books contain narratives, like the stories of Isaiah's call (6:1–8), Amos' encounter with Amaziah the priest (7:10–17), and Jonah's famous mission trip to Nineveh (1:1–3; 3:1–5). Similar to narratives are vision reports. God showed prophets like Ezekiel, Daniel, Amos, and Zechariah multiple visions. The vision reports usually include dialogues between God (or an angel) and the prophets, descriptions of what the prophets saw, and statements about the meaning of the visions. Also, sometimes the prophets recorded their prayers, such as those found in Jeremiah 20, Jonah 2, and Habakkuk 1. Most of the remaining material in the prophetic books could be lumped together into the category "oracles"—the contents of the prophets' preaching, delivered originally either in oral or written form. The oracles are further subdivided according to their themes, so they are referred to as judgment oracles, salvation oracles, woe oracles, dirges, and lawsuit oracles, for example.

The subgenre of a prophetic passage will affect the way we teach it. We'll teach a prophetic narrative like, well, a narrative. We will not preach a sermon on a woe speech with lots of laughing, unless we conclude with the truth that in Christ all woes will be reversed one day. When we teach a lawsuit oracle, we will seek to identify the plaintiff, the defendants, and the judge. In teaching an oracle of judgment, we will identify the reasons God's judgment was coming, the parallels with

---

13. Gerhard von Rad, *Old Testament Theology*, trans. D. M. G. Stalker (New York: Harper & Row, 1965), 2:33n1.

14. A helpful resource that includes a consideration of various sub-genres is Leland Ryken, *Symbols and Reality: A Guided Study of Prophecy, Apocalypse, and Visionary Literature* (Bellingham, WA: Lexham Press, 2017).

the ways of God's judgment in the present and future ages, and the absence of condemnation for those who are in Christ (Rom. 8:1). With a little practice, determining the subgenre of a prophetic text should not be difficult, but it's an important place to start.

2. Enter the life of the prophet.

Jeremiah was different than Ezekiel. Jonah was different than Amos. Their historical setting was different, the circumstances of their lives were different, their experiences were different, and their personalities were different. I am not suggesting that we engage in paleo-psychology, which inevitably becomes speculative. I am urging us to read the entire work of each prophet and learn all the text says about him. When did the prophet live? What was going on in Israel, Judah, and the world during his lifetime? To whom did the prophet relate and speak? What did God call the prophet to do? All those questions will directly affect how we interpret and teach prophetic texts. Of course, some prophetic books contain almost no biographical information about the life and times of the prophet. All we know about Joel and Obadiah, for example, is what we may surmise from their sermons. Scholars debate even the dates of their ministries. But we should at least be familiar with such debates before we interpret individual texts in a prophetic book.

A helpful exercise for expositors is to ask a question like, what was it like to *be* Jeremiah? God called Jeremiah to remain single (16:2), so he lived alone out of obedience to God's command. God also told him not to attend funerals or feasts (16:5, 8). Thus, Jeremiah missed opportunities to comfort mourning loved ones and he missed occasions of celebration. As if that wasn't enough to isolate Jeremiah, God told him to preach the unpopular message that Judah was going to be destroyed by her enemies because of the sins of the people. As a result, the men of Anathoth, Jeremiah's hometown, plotted to kill him (11:21). Later they beat him and put him in prison (37:15). Evidently, his accommodations in prison were torturous, since he requested to be released, "Lest I die there" (37:20). King Zedekiah responded by ordering him to be placed in "the court of the guard" and gave him some bread every day. But when some men heard that he continued to preach that the Babylonians would conquer Judah, they threw him into a cistern where he sat in the mud until a man from Ethiopia pulled him out and incarcerated him again in the court of the guard (38:1–13). Jeremiah's suffering had an emotional impact on him. He accused God of deceiving him, he considered quitting preaching, and he even wished he had never been born (20:7–18). So what was it like to be Jeremiah? It wasn't much fun. Still, despite his emotional, physical, and spiritual struggles, Jeremiah was not intimidated into silence. Whether he was standing before the king, confronting powerful religious leaders, or suffering in prison, he spoke God's word faithfully.

The only way to learn about Jeremiah the man is to read the entire book and take notes about the biographical information in the book. We follow the same practice for any prophetic book we are teaching. Having such information in hand will make a tremendous difference in the way we teach a prophetic text. For example, unlike Jeremiah, Hosea was married, but his marriage to an unfaithful woman was a great hardship for him. The information we learn about Hosea's marital crisis alters the way we read much of his book. We feel the pathos of Hosea's description of God's relationship with unfaithful Israel: "My people are bent on turning away from me. . . . How can I give you up, O Ephraim? How can I hand you over, O Israel? . . . My heart recoils within me; my compassion grows warm and tender" (11:7–8).

The social locations of the prophets also varied. Isaiah counseled Ahaz and Hezekiah, kings of Judah (Isaiah 7; 37–39), but Amos was rejected by the people who had power in Israel (Amos 7:10–17). Micah preached that the sin of Israel and Judah was personified in their leaders (Micah 1:5; 3:1–7), while the preaching of Haggai and Zechariah seems to have supported the goals of civic leaders like Zerubbabel (Ezra 3:2–3; 4:2–3; 5:2; Haggai 1:1–14; 2:4; Zech. 4:6–9). Ideas about the prophets and their writings that do not take such circumstances into consideration will launch exposition in the wrong direction. The prophetic books are not collections of fortune cookie predictions about the end of the age or the second coming of Jesus. They were written by real men who preached God's word to real people in their lifetimes. Of course, under the inspiration of God's Spirit they sometimes predicted the future, but we will not know whether they were speaking to their times, to the near future, or to the distant future if we do not enter their lives and know their historical circumstances.

3. Identify the time period the prophet was addressing.

A common assumption about the prophetic writings is that they are all predictive and that the predictions relate to what is going to happen next on "God's prophetic calendar." For example, one popular writer wrote an article titled "What the Bible Says about a Palestinian State." In the article the author cites a passage from the third chapter of Joel and then writes, "It is clear from this prophecy that a distinct Palestinian State will become reality." Joel 3 refers to geopolitical entities like Tyre and Sidon, Philistia, Greece, and in later verses Egypt and Edom. No Palestinian State is mentioned, and the word "Palestine" did not exist during the lifetime of Joel. Furthermore, interpreting the precise time reference of Joel 3 is difficult and by no means certain. What seems clear is that it refers to a time after the fall and rebuilding of Jerusalem, like the period after the Babylonian exile in the sixth century BC, not the twenty-first century AD. The author of the article goes on to relate Ezekiel 35 to the second coming of Jesus, but that chapter is addressed to ancient Edom. And the author identifies Ezekiel's reference to an "ancient hatred" as modern Palestinian hatred for the State of Israel, but more likely it refers to the "ancient hatred" between Esau and Jacob, which became Edom and Israel.[15] Perhaps the author meant that Palestinian hatred is the latest iteration of the ancient hatred between Esau and Jacob, but he did not write that.

A question that we always ask of prophetic texts is, what time is it? The rather egregious interpretation errors of the author cited above seem to result from the assumption that prophetic texts must refer to our lifetime and predict something in the near future related to the second coming of Jesus and the modern State of Israel. Such an assumption results in the interpreter ignoring the original historical context of the prophet and losing the real message of the prophecy. Actually, the answer to the question, what time is it? varies. The prophets referred to the following time periods: the days that preceded them (events like the exodus, the giving of the law, etc.), their own lifetimes, their near

---

15. Joel Richardson, "What the Bible Says about a Palestinian State," at *World Net Daily*, 12-05-2012, http://www.wnd.com/2012/12/what-the-bible-says-about-a-palestinian-state/, accessed 9-27-2016.

future, the time of the coming of the Messiah, and the time of the second coming of the Messiah and the consummation of the age.

First, the prophets preached to their contemporaries about their own times. The prophets felt a great burden because of the sins of their times, a burden God's people should feel today. In preaching to their age, they brought to bear God's past revelation and gracious acts to Israel. Second, the extent of Israel's rebellion led the prophets to preach about God's judgment that would come in the near future. When the prophets who preached during the exile addressed the near future, they often gave a message of hope. Third, sometimes the prophets preached of events further in the future, predicting the coming of the Messiah.[16] Fourth, sometimes the prophets saw even further into the future to events that have not yet occurred, predicting the consummation of this age and the inauguration of the new age. In that age swords will be beaten into plowshares (Isa. 2:1–4; Micah 4:1–4), wolves will live with lambs (Isa. 11:1–10), and cosmic signs will signal its arrival (Joel 2:30–32).

To return to our main point, the question is, what time is it? To answer that question, the first requirement is to know the prophet's lifetime and all the major events in the history of Israel and their chronological sequence. How can we identify time references if we do not know what happened in each time period? To meet this requirement of knowledge, we should read the entire prophetic book, asking historical questions as we read. We should also be familiar with the contents of the books of Kings and Chronicles, and we should consult commentaries, books on the history of Israel, and Old Testament introductions. In addition, we should be familiar with the contents of the New Testament, since Old Testament prophecies sometimes are cited and interpreted in the New Testament. Of course, the shortcut to all this work is to read a few substantial commentaries on the passage under consideration. Unfortunately, the answer to the question, what time is it? is not always certain or unanimous. When that is the case, we hold our conclusions with humility.

---

16. See chapter 7 for some specific prophecies.

4. Demarcate the preaching/teaching passage.

It may seem to some people that this step should be first. However, the knowledge of the teacher should exceed the limits of the preaching/teaching passage. So the teacher starts with understanding the prophet, his times, and his writing, and then brings all that information to the study of the text he or she will teach. Selection of the limits of a passage is guided by three realities: time, audience, and theme. First, how much time do you have to prepare and to teach? If we had unlimited time, we could teach an entire prophetic book, or even the entire prophetic corpus. So the demarcation of the passage begins with a practical question, How much of the prophet's message can we teach well in the time that is allotted to us?

The answer to the question of time sometimes is determined, at least in part, by the nature of the audience. If the people we teach are ten-year-olds, the amount of time we can hold their attention is more limited. Thus, the passage will be shorter. If we are preaching to a congregation on a Sunday morning, it is likely that at some point the people will "check out" mentally, and the moment we go beyond that point we begin to see the operation of the law of diminishing returns. So we demarcate the text based on what we can teach effectively, since our goal is to maximize impact on the lives of hearers.

The third reality that guides the demarcation of a preaching/teaching passage perhaps is most obvious to Bible students. We determine the main theme—the big idea—of a passage, and when the subject of the text changes we draw the line of demarcation. Sometimes the main theme is developed further in verses that precede or follow the primary passage we are considering. How much of that development should we teach? Again, the answer to that question will likely be determined by time and audience.

5. Establish the original audience.

A common mistake in teaching the prophets is to proceed as if the only audiences of a given text are the contemporary church and the society in which we live. Since God's Word is eternal and he uses it to speak to every age, prophetic texts are relevant to our generation and at some point we will apply the meaning of the text to our modern context, but first we determine the original audience. The identity of the intended recipients of the message makes a significant difference in how we will interpret and apply prophetic texts.

In the summer of 2016, the water level in the Sea of Galilee was so low that an island appeared near the southern end of the sea. Some people saw the low water level as a sign that the second coming of Jesus is near. One reason given for this belief was the statement in Isaiah 19:5 that "the waters of the sea will be dried up, and the river will be dry and parched."[17] But those who use Isaiah 19:5 in that way neglect to note that the prophecy is directly addressed to Egypt. In fact, Isaiah 19 is located in the larger context of chapters 13–23, which are Isaiah's oracles against the nations. Furthermore, nothing in Isaiah 19 indicates that it relates to the first or second coming of the Messiah. Instead, the chapter uses literal and figurative language to describe the fall of Egypt.

Obviously, establishing the original audience of Isaiah 19 makes a difference in the way we will interpret the chapter. Since the issue of intended audience affects the interpretation of prophetic texts, preachers and teachers should make every effort to determine the audience as part of their exposition. Often the audience is Israel or Judah—God's covenant people who were being unfaithful to the covenant. Sometimes, as above, the audience is a foreign people group. At times prophets addressed only one person, and sometimes that person was the king or other leaders like false prophets or compromised priests. When the prophets prayed, the addressee was God. In every case, our interpretation of prophetic texts will be affected by the identity of the original audience.

6. Interpret symbolic language, actions, and visions.

Most prophetic writing is poetic writing. The prophets used language that is filled with irony, wordplay, sarcasm, and hyperbole, to name a few of their rhetorical techniques. Also, sometimes God commanded them to perform symbolic actions. Ezekiel alone recorded at least nine such symbolic actions, and other prophets like Jeremiah recorded them too. Finally, sometimes God showed the prophets visions that conveyed

---

17. Jay Baggett, "Island Emerges from Sea of Galilee—Called Messianic Sign," *World Net Daily*, September 15, 2016, http://www.wnd.com/2016/09/island-emerges-from-sea-of-galilee-called-messianic-sign/, accessed September 29, 2016.

symbolic meaning. For example, he showed Jeremiah a potter at his wheel (18:1–23), he showed Amos visions like a plumb line and a basket of summer fruit (7:7–9; 8:1–2), he showed Daniel visions of four beasts, a ram with two horns, and a man clothed in linen (7, 8, 10–12), and he showed Zechariah eight visions in the night (1:7–6:8).

Usually the text explains the meaning of symbolic actions and visions. But sometimes we can see the prophetic wordplay only when we read the text in Hebrew. Even when the poetic techniques can be seen in English, often we will discover them only after careful reading. For example, Micah composed a poetic lament over God's coming judgment because of Israel's sin. In Micah 1:10–15 he wrote thirteen place names with puns based on each place name. For example, verse 10 says, "Tell it not in Gath." That imperative echoes a passage in 2 Samuel (1:20), and the Hebrew word translated "tell" sounds like the word "Gath." Verse 10 also says, "In Beth-le-aphrah roll yourselves in the dust." Rolling in the dust was a sign of mourning, and the Hebrew word for "dust" sounds like "aphrah." Micah brooded over Israel's sin and lamented God's coming judgment. Like many poets, when he felt something deeply he wrote poetry that expressed his deep feeling. Recognizing and interpreting poetic techniques requires some skill. Preachers and teachers of the Old Testament will need to develop such skill to teach prophetic texts effectively. Books like hermeneutics texts and introductory books on the prophets can help, as can substantive commentaries on prophetic books.

Preaching and Teaching the Poetry of Psalms

The psalms powerfully express truths about God: his creative power, his sovereignty over all the created order, his providence in the lives of his people, his attentiveness to prayer, his salvation, his omniscience, his universal reign, his worthiness to be praised, and his opposition to sin are all affirmed in the psalms. Just as the psalms are about God, they are also about us. We are physical, spiritual, and emotional beings. The psalms address all those elements of our make-up. Every emotion we experience is expressed at some point in the psalms. If we want to teach people how our emotions relate to God, we can teach the psalms. And since so many of the psalms are addressed to God, they teach us to pray. In inspiring the book of Psalms, God gave us words to use when speaking to him. The praise psalms also teach us how to express praise to God, and voicing praise to God is an important part of a healthy spiritual life. Thus the psalter is part hymnal, part prayer book, part spiritual journal, and part anthology of theological poetry. When Christian Bible teachers teach or preach from the book of Psalms, they will never need to doubt the relevance of the message.

The psalms are poetry. To understand and teach the psalms properly, we have to appreciate their poetic form. We also have to know something about the way poetry works. Some people don't enjoy poetry and find it difficult to see its value. What's important, they think, is communicating information, not the unnecessarily flowery expressions of poetry. But God inspired the form of the psalms as well as their content. In his book on the psalms, literary expert Michael Travers asks an important rhetorical question: "If we do not find it difficult to accept the idea that the theology of the Psalms is inspired by God, why do we find it difficult to think of the form in which the theology is expressed as equally inspired by God?"[18] If we believe in verbal plenary inspiration, then we will affirm that when we see poetry in the Bible it is because God inspired the writers to write in just that way. It's important, then, that we come to grips with the value of the poetic form and become adept at interpreting its meaning.

The defining characteristic of Hebrew poetry is two-line parallelism.[19] Exactly what that means and how parallelism works in Hebrew literature is discussed broadly in Old Testament scholarship. James Kugel, for example, argues that parallelism is an inadequate way to think about Hebrew poetry. He points out that Hebrew has no word for poetry, parallelism can also be identified in much Hebrew prose, and Hebrew poetry exhibits a "disquieting refusal to present some clearly defined 'poetic structure'" like parallelism.[20]

---

18. Michael E. Travers, *Encountering God in the Psalms* (Grand Rapids: Kregel, 2003), 22.

19. Robert Lowth is often credited with articulating this idea first, in his *Lectures on the Sacred Poetry of the Hebrews*, first translated into English in 1787. It is more accurate to say that Lowth contributed to the popular acceptance of parallelism as the defining mark of Hebrew poetry. See James L. Kugel, *The Idea of Biblical Poetry: Parallelism and Its History* (New Haven, CT: Yale University Press, 1981).

20. Ibid., 23, 69, 76, 94–95, 185. Kugel recognizes the phenomenon of word pairs, or parallel lines, as obvious, but he thinks it is less accurate to refer to types of

The views of Kugel and others remind us that Old Testament scholarship is by no means unanimous about the precise nature of Hebrew
poetry, and Kugel's work in particular serves as a warning to read
Hebrew poetry on its own terms and refrain from superimposing the
forms of English poetry on literature that is not English. Still, however,
the psalms and other poetic passages in the Old Testament are clearly
dominated by lines that occur in pairs, or in parallel relationship to one
another.[21] In such parallelism, the second line serves to amplify the first
line in some way. A modern example of such parallelism is

> My son is thirteen;
> he is a teenager.[22]

The two lines are synonymously parallel in that "my son" is synonymous with "he," and "thirteen" is synonymous with "teenager." But
the second line amplifies the first line, carrying it further. The first line
gives chronological information, but any parent of a teenager knows
that the second line identifies the son with an entire complex of emotional, physical, and cultural indicators that go along with adolescence.
Old Testament poetry works in a similar way. Sometimes the second
line amplifies the first line by means of repeating the identical words
(Ps. 29:1–2). Sometimes the amplification occurs when the second line
carries the first line a step further (Ps. 46:7), or states the same truth
with synonymous words (Pss. 2:1; 19:1–2), or states the opposite to provide a clarifying contrast (Ps. 20:7–8).

---

parallelism and more accurate to refer to the second line as completing, or seconding,
the first line in some way, saying, "What's more . . ." He clarifies his position by
stating, "Paralleling is not a dependable, structural constant, but a fairly dependable,
variously manifested, feature of style," 39. The difference may seem slight, but Kugel's
point is that much of Western scholarship imports into the Bible poetic features and
structures that are alien to Hebrew literature and that such misconceptions have led to
widespread errors in interpretation (see 59–95).

21. For a description of Hebrew poetry that differs from Kugel's and that provides
an extensive system of classification of Hebrew poetry/parallelism, see Wilfred G. E.
Watson, *Classical Hebrew Poetry: A Guide to Its Techniques* (Sheffield: Sheffield Academic
Press, 1984).

22. I first saw this illustration in Thomas G. Long, *Preaching and the Literary Forms
of the Bible* (Philadelphia: Fortress, 1989), 49.

The relationship between the second line and the first line can be subtle, so readers are required to slow down and reflect on each word to arrive at the intended meaning. As Leland Ryken has expressed it, readers of poetry should not be afraid to stare at the poem.[23] Such meditation is in keeping with the nature of poetry, since the language of poetry is concentrated and heightened. Prose expresses ideas in sentences. Poetry, on the other hand, often uses individual words and their relationships with other words to communicate meaning. Poetry also uses figures of speech and wordplay to a higher degree than prose. To borrow metaphors from a literary critic, poetry has a "higher voltage" than other forms of communication, and it applies "greater pressure per word."[24] A great amount of truth is conveyed with a minimum number of words. Consequently, if we read poetry too quickly we'll miss much of the inspired meaning.

Poetry also uses numerous figures of speech, or symbolic language, like similes (Ps. 52:8), metaphors (Ps. 115:9), personification (Ps. 98:8–9), and word pictures (Ps. 97:2–6). Such techniques typically guide the reader to feel as well as to think. Poems go beyond the realm of the cerebral and draw readers into the experience of the poem. Thus the psalms remind us that a complete biblical theology is not limited to giving mental assent to correct propositions about God. Right theology also engages the senses and emotions as part of the experience of knowing God. The reader of the poetry in Psalms has experiences and emotions that go beyond dissemination of information. Poetry communicates ideas that, as the Irish have put it, are "better felt than tell't." We may even say that poetry is subjective in that it involves the subject, the reader, in the experience of the poem. Of course, lest we fall into a postmodern, relativistic mindset in interpreting the poetry of the psalms, we should remember that our experience and feelings are guided by the words of the poem.

As an example, read slowly the word pictures of Psalm 97:2–6.

---

23. Leland Ryken, *Words of Delight: A Literary Introduction to the Bible* (Grand Rapids: Baker, 1993), 215.
24. Laurence Perrine, *Sound and Sense: An Introduction to Poetry*, 2nd ed. (New York: Harcourt, Brace, & World, 1963), 10–11.

Clouds and thick darkness are all around him;
righteousness and justice are the foundation of his
throne.
Fire goes before him
and burns up his adversaries all around.
His lightnings light up the world;
the earth sees and trembles.
The mountains melt like wax before the LORD,
before the LORD of all the earth.
The heavens proclaim his righteousness,
and all the peoples see his glory.

If we read those lines and do not feel something powerful, then we read too quickly and did not enter the experience the psalm describes. As we move slowly through the pictures of those verses we see clouds and darkness veiling God. We see lightning flashing from him and mountains melting. We hear the heavens thunder his righteousness. This is God's glory and power in pictorial form. When we read Psalm 97 we move beyond acknowledging the idea of God's glory and power to *experiencing* his glory and power by means of being placed in the center of the drama of these explosive natural phenomena. Tremper Longman writes that this kind of imagery makes its own theological point. It declares that God is so great that his greatness cannot be expressed with mere words. Words only begin to approach a description of his majesty, and figures of speech like word pictures express that God's glory and mystery go beyond verbal expression. Longman writes, "Images, particularly metaphors, help to communicate the fact that God is so great and powerful and mighty that he can't be exhaustively described. . . . Metaphor preserves the mystery of God's nature and being, while communicating to us about him and his love for us."[25]

As we preach and teach the psalms, we should remember that God inspired poetry and providentially preserved it for our use. Furthermore, we have to learn something about the way poetry works in order to

---

25. Tremper Longman III, *"How to Read the Psalms* (Downers Grove, IL: InterVarsity Press, 1988), 121.

teach it well.[26] Robert Alter, a literature scholar, provides an excellent question to ask as we read the psalms: "What difference does it make to the content of the psalms that they are poems?"[27] Keeping such a question before us as we study the psalms will help us honor their God-given form and content. To help us preach and teach the poetry of the psalms, I offer five recommendations.

1. Help people see the illustrations in the poem.

As mentioned above, numerous psalms include word pictures that invite us to visualize or experience truth about God. Just as we slow down when we read such a psalm, we also slow down when we teach it to help people visualize the picture or illustration. Consider the way I once preached the illustration in Psalm 1 that contrasts the wicked with the righteous:

> Those who are on the Lord's side are like a perennially watered tree—always healthy and always fruitful. And to what shall the wicked be compared? Are they like a tree that is not perennially watered? No, they're not permanent enough to be compared with a tree. How about a small bush? No, still too big. Well, would it be accurate if we compared the wicked to a tiny, slender stalk of wheat? Now we're getting closer, but not the whole stalk. How about just the head of the stalk? No, still too large. Let's compare the wicked to the smallest part of the smallest part of that stalk of wheat—not the grain, but the worthless little sliver called the chaff. That's the right illustration for the wicked—the polar opposite from God's righteous and blessed people. Comparing the righteous with the wicked is like comparing a perennially watered tree that's permanent and prosperous to the chaff of wheat that is worthless and blown away by the lightest gust of wind. That's the illustration God has provided for us to represent the wicked.

---

26. For a helpful look at the genre of biblical poetry by a literary critic, see Leland Ryken, *Sweeter Than Honey, Richer Than Gold: A Guided Study of Biblical Poetry* (Bellingham, WA: Lexham Press, 2015).

27. Robert Alter, *The Art of Biblical Poetry* (New York: Basic Books, 1985), 113.

In Psalm 73 the psalmist wrote of a period in his life when he had doubted God's justice. He saw the prosperity of the wicked and the suffering of the righteous. His observations about life's apparent inequities caused him to question his faith in the holy God of Israel. Then he entered worship in the sanctuary and he "discerned their end" (v. 17). In the following verses the psalmist provided illustrations of his struggle and God's final justice. When I preached Psalm 73 I attempted to help people to "see" the illustrations by saying the following:

In verse 20, the illustration the psalmist used . . . was a dream—"like a dream when one awakes." What a great illustration. We dream some things that would *never* happen in real life. In our dreams, we can fly. In our dreams, we show up at school in our pajamas. . . . I preach a lot, and I dream a lot about preaching. And I worry about my preaching, so most of my dreams about preaching turn out to be nightmares. The other night I dreamed that I was talking with a church member about a worship service that was going to be really important in our church. But when the Sunday morning of that service arrived and it was time for me to get dressed, I couldn't find my clothes. In my dream I was turning the house upside down to find my clothes, but I couldn't find them. The time for the service came and passed, and I still couldn't find any clothes. The people at the church were wondering where I was, and somebody called me to ask why I wasn't there, and I said, "Because I can't find my clothes!"—like, "Why *else* wouldn't I be there?" That's the kind of weird thing that happens in our dreams. That dream was so real, but when I woke up I remembered that it's nowhere close to reality. Our dreams *seem* to make perfect sense while we're dreaming, but when we wake up we think, "That was weird."

That's the illustration the psalmist used in verse 20 to refer to this upside-down world in which wicked people are prospering and righteous people are suffering. It's as if we're in a dream state and weird things are happening. And God is *allowing* them to happen for a little while. But the psalmist also referred to the time when God rouses himself. That day will come, and when he rouses himself he's going to set things right. At the end, he'll give punishment to the wicked and reward to the righteous. When that happens, we'll say, "Remember when those people who mocked God and ridiculed Christians were on top of the world? And remember how that young lady who loved Jesus and served him was tragically killed in a car wreck? That was weird, wasn't it? It was like a dream, because now that young lady is having such a great time in heaven, and the people who scorned the very idea of God are suffering forever" (cf. vv. 18–19). When it appears that right is reversed and justice is perverted, remember what will happen at the end and for eternity. Remember that it won't be but a minute before God sets off the alarm and ends this dream. That's what the psalmist saw in worship. Sometimes God's people can go through a dark period when they think it pays to disobey God and serving him brings suffering. The psalmist went through such a period of doubt, but when he came out of it he said that he had been dreaming.

These explanations of the illustrations in Psalms 1 and 73 are not particularly eloquent or clever, but at least they help listeners to slow down and think about the meaning of the poetic illustrations. To help people see the illustration, expositors need to see it themselves. Time and meditation are necessary to allow expositors to arrive at an illustration's possible implications for meaning and application. Then expositors work for the right words that will open the imaginations of their hearers so they can see the illustration too. Of course, the end game is not to preach or teach an illustration but the truth to which the illustration points. But if we don't spend time with the illustration we are neglecting the poetic aspect of the psalm.

2. Help people feel the truth of the poem.

Some Christians seem afraid to show emotion. They should reconsider the psalms. The psalmists doubt, praise, lament, thank, complain, sing, fear, and trust. In one psalm they explode with ebullient hallelujahs, and in the next they wonder aloud why God doesn't answer their prayers. The psalms, in other words, reflect contrasting, sometimes conflicting, emotions. Bible teachers and preachers should make that plain to the people they teach. Such teaching will affirm their various feelings as common human experiences, even common experiences for God's people. Psalms 42 and 43, for example, address feelings of depression or despair. When preaching from Psalm 42, I included the following:

> In verses 5 and 11 of Psalm 42, and in verse 5 of Psalm 43, the psalmist wrote that he was in despair. At least that's the way the New American Standard Bible translates it. The Hebrew word here means "to be laid low," or "to be cast down." The King James and New International Versions translate the word in that more literal way. The psalmist was laid low emotionally; he was downcast. In verse 5 the psalmist also described his emotional state with the word "disturbed." That Hebrew word means to murmur, or growl, or to be in commotion. The psalmist was murmuring within himself. His soul was in commotion. . . .
>
> Have you ever felt that way? Laid low? Your heart in commotion? Charles Spurgeon wrote a book titled *Lectures to My Students*. One of his chapters was on pastoral depression; he titled the chapter "The Minister's Fainting Fits." He wrote of how common depression is and how he had suffered from it often himself. Like the writer of Psalm 42 and 43, Spurgeon wrote of the causes for these fainting fits. He wrote that sometimes we experience downcast hearts simply because we're human. God has made us with emotions. Ups and downs are part of the human experience—"hence these tears, hence these perplexities and castings down."
>
> Spurgeon also lectured that sometimes depression comes on us and we don't *know* the cause. "Then," he wrote, "it is all the more difficult to drive away." But he also wrote that it *can* be driven away. And the first thing he wrote about driving it away is also in Psalms 42 and 43. The first cure for a downcast spirit is to pray for God's help. Spurgeon wrote about our inability on our own to rise from emotional depths and the ineffectiveness of physicians and ministers in comparison with what God

can do. He wrote that the iron bolt that keeps us pinned down "needs a heavenly hand to push it back."[28]

Such words were an effort to help hearers linger over the psalmist's emotions. People who are in despair will resonate immediately with the psalmist's feelings. Other people will be prodded to think about what it's like to be in such an emotional state. The hope is that all the hearers who wrestle with dark emotions will learn something about how to handle them with God's help.

3. Use the corporate aspect of the psalms to connect hearers to the people of God.

Scholars debate the origin of individual psalms, the growth of collections of psalms, and the eventual development of the entire book of Psalms. While I have my own ideas about the growth of the psalter, what seems most certain is the beginning and the end of that process. At the beginning, individuals wrote psalms. That seems most likely, since typically committees do not write poems. Then, either immediately or eventually, many if not all the psalms gravitated to the setting of corporate worship. In some cases, the original words of a psalm may have been altered from singular to plural to facilitate their corporate use. A psalm's use in the context of corporate worship is indicated in the psalms in various ways. Many times the exhortations to worship are made with plural imperative verbs. For example, in Psalm 105:1, all three of the imperative verbs in the first line are plural, "Oh give thanks to the LORD; call upon his name; / make known his deeds among the peoples!" Other psalms indicate corporate use by means of first person plural pronouns, like Psalm 115:1, "Not to us, O LORD, not to us, but to your name give glory." Sometimes other worshipers are mentioned explicitly, as in Psalm 135:1, "Give praise, O servants of the LORD."

The corporate aspect of the psalms alters our perception of them and their application in our lives. As Thomas Long puts it, "It is one thing to read a poem with a religious theme. . . . It is another to encounter

---

28. Charles H. Spurgeon, *Lectures to My Students* (1889; reprint, Peabody, MA: Hendrickson, 2010), 159–60, 168.

a poem with a religious theme which has been used over and over in worship."[29] In the case of the psalms, they have been used in worship by God's people for thousands of years. When the people who hear us teach the psalms have problems and triumphs, sorrows and joys sometimes they feel that they are unique, alone. But God's people have faced problems and triumphs, sorrows and joys for millennia. They have felt the same emotions, faced the same struggles with sin and sinners, and turned to the same God for comfort and deliverance. Connecting the people of God today with all of God's people helps our hearers to see that their experiences are not utterly unique. What we face today is, after all, common and predictable. Thus we are not alone. We are part of a millennia-long gathering of God's people who have found the one true God ever a present help and always worthy of praise. Such a realization is one reason for the power of worship to transform us because in worship we are caught up in the consciousness that we stand with all of God's people around us in expressing praise, giving thanks, offering complaints, making petitions, crying out for deliverance, and confessing sin. Through the millennia God has given to his people in worship his listening ear, his deliverance, his comfort, his forgiveness, and his deliverance. He will give the same to us. Our preaching and teaching from the psalms offers more help to people when we call their attention to that reality.

4. Preach and teach the psalm, not the superscription.

Of the 150 psalms, 116 of them have superscriptions. The superscriptions are fascinating and evoke both questions and answers about the origin of individual psalms. The superscription of Psalm 78, for example, calls the psalm "a maskil of Asaph." The term maskil appears in the titles of thirteen psalms (32, 42, 44, 45, 52–55, 74, 78, 88, 89, and 142), and it is based on a verbal root meaning insight, understanding, or wisdom. Thus a maskil was likely a poem or song requiring contemplation and/or imparting insight or wisdom.

As for Asaph, he was a Levitical leader of music in worship in Israel. During most of the history of Israel, the Levites worked to support the service of worship, helping the priests in the tabernacle and temple.

---

29. Long, *Preaching and the Literary Forms of the Bible*, 46.

According to 1 Chronicles, King David appointed some of the Levites to lead in music in worship, "to invoke, to thank, and to praise the Lord" (1 Chron. 16:4). Asaph is referred to as "the chief" of that group of praise leaders (v. 5). Later, David divided the Levites into four divisions (23:2–5). The fourth division was responsible for the music of worship. Levites in the fourth division "prophesied with lyres, with harps, and with cymbals . . . in thanksgiving and praise to the Lord" (25:1, 3). David placed all those worship musicians under three leaders, and one of the leaders was Asaph. Asaph seems especially prominent among music leaders, because wherever they are listed Asaph is mentioned first (25:1–9). Second Chronicles 29:30 also refers to Asaph as a seer, or prophet.

The work of Asaph endured. Over 250 years after his lifetime, King Hezekiah "told the Levites to sing praise to the LORD in the words of David and of Asaph the seer" (2 Chron. 29:30). Even as late as the post-exilic period, Asaph was remembered as a praise leader (Neh. 12:46), and Ezra 3:10 mentions that his descendants were still leading music in worship. The superscription of Psalm 78 ascribes authorship of the psalm to Asaph, and the strong record of Asaph's leadership in worship serves to confirm the authenticity of the ascription. It makes sense that someone who led music in worship would write worship poetry and music. Since Asaph's descendants were also worship leaders, they may have also written psalms.

Such historical information is interesting and important to anyone studying the history of Israel and her worship. But we must ask whether it helps us to understand the contents of Psalm 78, or any other psalm headed with Asaph's name. Furthermore, what if the superscriptions were added centuries after the psalms were written? What if the superscriptions should not even be regarded as canonical and the accuracy of their information is dubious? All these are relevant questions and answered variously by scholars. Therefore, Tremper Longman's advice seems prudent here:

> When all the evidence has been surveyed, it is best to treat the titles as noncanonical, but reliable early tradition. Practically speaking, the implications for reading a psalm are twofold. We should let the psalm title initially inform the reading of a psalm.

However, we shouldn't bend the interpretation of a psalm un-naturally to make it conform to the title.[30]

If we adopt such a posture toward the superscriptions, the conse-quence for preaching and teaching the psalms will be that we will mar-ginalize the superscriptions to a position of relative unimportance. In most cases we will not mention the superscriptions at all. Even when a superscription contains historical references, like Psalms 51 and 142, I recommend that we follow Steven Smith's advice and "preach the psalm, not the story."[31]

The relative unimportance of the superscriptions for preaching and teaching also applies to the position of each psalm in the psalter. A growing number of scholars are making much of the order of the psalms, and their interpretations of individual psalms are influenced by considerations of order and relationships to nearby psalms. In fact, some scholars seem surprisingly dogmatic about the importance of a psalm's position in the psalter. We should emphasize, however, that we know nothing about why the psalms were placed in their present order. The psalms were also divided into five "books" in antiquity, and we don't know why or according to what principles the divisions were made. Therefore, the best way to teach and preach the psalms is to focus on the content of the psalms, not their position. The only evidence that may indicate a reason for a psalm's position are verbal parallels with nearby psalms. Such parallels are also evidence for shared ideas, or theology, between the psalms, and it is more important to teach that theology than to make a point about a psalm's position.

5. Make the connection to the New Testament.

The book of Psalms is quoted more in the New Testament than any other Old Testament book. For example, in a clash with the Pharisees Jesus quoted Psalm 110:1 (Matt. 22:41–46), and while he was dying on the cross he quoted Psalm 22:1 (Matt. 27:46). In his historic sermon on the day of Pentecost, the apostle Peter quoted from Psalms 16 and

---

30. Longman, *How to Read the Psalms*, 41.

31. Steven W. Smith, *Recapturing the Voice of God: Shaping Sermons like Scripture* (Nashville: B&H, 2015), 135.

110 (Acts 2:25–28, 34–35), and in the apostle Paul's sermon in Pisidian Antioch he quoted from Psalms 2:7 and 16:10 (Acts 13:33, 35).

The frequent use of the psalms in the ministry of Jesus, the sermons of the early church, and the Pauline and General Epistles demonstrate three facts. First, the book of Psalms is theological, not merely devotional. It teaches about God's nature and plan. Second, the book of Psalms is messianic. Jesus referred to "everything written about me in the Law of Moses and the Prophets and the Psalms" (Luke 24:44). Evidently, Jesus taught his apostles how the psalms pointed to him, since they cited them so often in their preaching and writing. Third, the book of Psalms is practical. Just as the early church used the book of Psalms frequently to teach about Jesus and how to follow him, so can we.

Consider one example of moving from a psalm to the New Testament. The latter part of Psalm 24 poetically portrays God's entrance into Jerusalem. The city gates are exhorted, "Lift up your heads, O gates! . . . that the King of glory may come in" (v. 7). The gatekeepers ask in reply, "Who is this King of glory?" and the answer comes back, "The LORD, strong and mighty." When I preached from Psalm 24, I stated the following:

> We don't know for sure that this psalm was written on the occasion of the entry of the ark into Jerusalem, but we do know that the Lord entered Jerusalem. About 1,000 years after this psalm was written, the Lord Jesus entered Jerusalem accompanied by shouts of "Hosanna." The Gospel of Luke records that they said, "Blessed is the King who comes" into Jerusalem (Luke 19:38), and the Gospel of Matthew says that everybody was asking, "Who is this?" (Matt. 21:10), just as they were asking in Psalm 24. Who is this? He is the Lord and Savior who entered Jerusalem to die as the final sacrifice for the sins of all humanity. And three days after he died, he rose from the dead and lives today. And the books of Zechariah and Revelation say that one day he will enter Jerusalem again. He will enter in victory as a king to set up his reign that will be universal and eternal, and his people will live in his presence forever.

Arriving at such a connection is simple. We identify the theme: God's entry into Jerusalem. We ask, What does God's entry into Jerusalem have to do with Jesus? The answer: Jesus entered and will again enter Jerusalem.

The procedure of making a connection between Old Testament texts and Jesus may sometimes seem simple, but it is absolutely necessary. We and our hearers cannot be rightly related to God without the gospel of Jesus, and we cannot live the life of the righteous without Jesus' help. Also, we cannot use the psalms to offer right praise to God without Jesus, since the writer of Hebrews referred to Jesus when he wrote, "through him then let us continually offer up a sacrifice of praise to God" (13:15). In chapter 7 we will see the priority of presenting Jesus in every sermon or lesson, not only from the psalms but from every genre in the Old Testament.

Chapter 4

WHAT IS THE TEXT'S CONTEXT?

8-STEP METHOD

STEP 1	Translating the text
STEP 2	Considering text criticism
STEP 3	Interpreting the genre
STEP 4	**Exploring the context**
STEP 5	Defining important words
STEP 6	Identifying the big idea
STEP 7	Connecting to Jesus
STEP 8	Applying the text to contemporary people

Step 4 of our 8-step process of exposition is context exploration. Every text has a context, and the meaning of every text depends on its context. Suppose I said, "The youth pastor was told to stop fighting at youth lock-ins." The context of that statement would make a significant difference in its meaning. On the one hand, it could mean that some teenagers had been playing too roughly at youth functions, and the youth pastor was directed to put a stop to it. On the other hand, it could mean that the youth pastor himself had been fighting at youth events, and he was told to change his behavior. The youth pastor would no doubt agree with Dean Deppe, who wrote, "Context is everything!"[1]

In this chapter we will consider the fact that every text has multiple contexts. First, every text has a literary context, since it is situated in a larger textual unit, within a biblical book and in the entire canon. Second, every text is set in a particular time period and in a particular cultural setting. Hence, every text has a historical/cultural context. Third, every text has a geographical context. Sometimes if we do not consider the geographical setting we may miss the full meaning of the text. Fourth, every text is located at some point in salvation history. When we explore a text's redemptive-historical context, we ask how it fits in God's salvation plan that culminates in Christ. Every biblical text has something to do with God, and asking about redemption history helps us to relate texts to God, his work in history, and his work in our lives. Good exposition requires a consideration of all these contexts. However, before we launch into such study we will not forget to pray.

Pray

Just as every text has a context, all prayer is contextual. We pray in a particular place and in a particular time. Our prayers today are different than the prayers we prayed five years ago. Our needs today are different, and perhaps we live in a different place geographically. We are also different people. Maybe today we are five years more mature or more jaded, more devoted or more cynical, more joyful or more disappointed. Regardless of how we may have changed, we *have* changed and our circumstances have changed. Our prayers will change too. Prayer will mirror our mindset or it is not prayer. Prayer is intimate conversation between us and the God who knows our thoughts. Therefore, prayer is too personal to be routine, too real to be rote. People who do not want to be intimate with God do not pray. They may recite words, but they do not pray.

Hannah was childless, barren. She was brokenhearted over it, so she did not pray a happy prayer. She told Eli that she had been praying "out of my great anxiety and vexation" (1 Sam. 1:16). She prayed her

---

1. Dean Deppe, *All Roads Lead to the Text: Eight Methods of Inquiry into the Bible* (Grand Rapids: Eerdmans, 2011), 131, 136.

feelings, her life. If it had been otherwise, her prayer would have been phony. She also referred to her praying by saying, "I have been pouring out my soul before the Lord" (v. 15). That's prayer—pouring out the contents of our souls before God. To interpret Scripture correctly we do not ignore the context. To pray correctly we do not ignore our context. We pour it out to God.

Sometimes our context overwhelms us and makes us feel incompetent to interpret the Bible adequately. We're too distraught, too distracted, too weak to think ourselves adequate to teach God's Word. Think again. Moses did not feel adequate. Neither did Gideon or Jeremiah. If you find yourself feeling like they felt, do what they did. Tell God your thoughts in prayer. Pour out your soul to God. Ask him to help you. He will. You didn't see these circumstances coming, but he did.

Literary Context

In his book on biblical interpretation and application, Daniel Doriani writes, "The study of literary context is the first and perhaps the most important method of all."[2] The Old Testament is, after all, a literary work. The meaning of any text in literature is not derived merely from determining the meanings of individual words and phrases. Meaning is determined by the way words and phrases function in the larger units of clauses, sentences, paragraphs, and an entire document. As McCartney and Clayton express it, "Meaning is not just a function of words, but of the complex of words and context."[3] Consequently, studying the literary context to grasp its message is a necessary step in understanding the meaning of any passage of Scripture. Teachers of the Old Testament, then, will prioritize careful consideration of the context as part of their study routine. To do so, I suggest seven habits of studying the literary context.

1. Read the entire book three times.

When we receive a lengthy email from a co-worker or friend, we don't select one passage to ponder, then return to the email a few days later

---

2. Daniel Doriani, *Getting the Message: A Plan for Interpreting and Applying the Bible* (Phillipsburg, NJ: P&R, 1996), 44.

3. Dan McCartney and Charles Clayton, *Let the Reader Understand: A Guide to Interpreting and Applying the Bible* (Phillipsburg, NJ: P&R, 2002), 149.

to study another passage until eventually we have finished carefully studying the entire email. We read through the entire email right away, and the result is that we understand each part of the email in the light of the whole message. Biblical books are significantly more substantive than the average email message, and longer. Why would we attempt to interpret one part of a book before reading the entire book?

Most of the preaching I have done has been expositional preaching through books of the Bible, verse by verse or chapter by chapter. My Bible teaching in contexts other than worship has followed the same format. Elsewhere I have recommended that pastors follow such a method.[4] Teaching through an entire book follows the pattern of revelation God has given in the Bible. It also trains the people we are teaching to read the Bible as it was written—not as a collection of spiritual principles for living, but as a collection of books that were written in various ways at various times for various purposes. Teaching or preaching through a book in the Old Testament requires understanding the entire book from the beginning. What is the book's purpose, major themes, origin, and audience? The answers to such questions will affect the way we teach through a book from the first sermon or lesson. Even if we teach from only one passage in a book, the meaning of that passage is affected by its larger context, sometimes in subtle ways and sometimes in definitive ways. Therefore, awareness of the contents of the entire book is foundational.

Consider an example of the importance of studying the contents of an entire biblical book before teaching an individual passage in that book. During the Protestant Reformation of the sixteenth century, reformers found multiple reasons to separate from the Church of Rome. One of them, perhaps surprisingly, had to do with the book of Ecclesiastes. In the first two chapters of Ecclesiastes the author wrote that pursuing a happy and meaningful life in things like knowledge, wealth, work, and pleasure is pointless. We cannot find a happy and meaningful life in the things of this world apart from God. Jerome was one of the fathers of the Roman Church who lived approximately AD 347–420. Jerome read that passage in Ecclesiastes and concluded that since happiness is not

---

4. Allan Moseley, "Preaching Expository Sermons," in *Entrusted to the Faithful: An Introduction to Pastoral Leadership* (Spring Hill, TN: Rainer, 2017), 58–59.

found in the things of this world, then a life of true godliness consists of separating ourselves entirely from the things of the world and living a monastic life. That idea took hold, and the canons of monasticism began to spread. Living the ideal Christian life, according to the monastic model, involves forsaking commerce, the household, and the political order, and going to the desert to isolate oneself from human society.

During the Reformation, Martin Luther said that monasticism was one of the ideas the Roman Church had wrong. Luther wrote that Jerome had misread and misapplied the book of Ecclesiastes. So in 1526, from July to November, Luther delivered some twenty-seven lectures on the book of Ecclesiastes. Luther taught that it's not necessary to flee from the world to serve God; we ought to serve God *in the midst of* the world. To make his point, Luther moved beyond the first two chapters of Ecclesiastes and found that enjoyment of this world is a repeated theme in the book (2:24–26; 3:12–13; 5:18–19; 8:15; 9:7–9). It appears first at the end of Ecclesiastes 2. This is what Martin Luther wrote about Ecclesiastes 2:24: "This is the principal conclusion . . . of the whole book, which he will often repeat. This is a remarkable passage, one that explains everything preceding and following it."[5] Luther emphasized that the theme of Ecclesiastes has to do with living in a relationship with God and enjoying life in this world as a gift from him. I think Luther was correct, and he arrived at his conclusion about the main theme of Ecclesiastes by reading the entire book and interpreting the parts in the light of the whole. The theology of monasticism, on the other hand, resulted in part from reading a portion of Ecclesiastes in isolation from the whole.

Why read an entire book three times? If our reading comprehension was 100 percent, maybe one or two readings would be sufficient. However, since our memory and understanding are not perfect, each time we read a text we learn something we missed in earlier readings. The purpose of the first reading is to get a general idea about the contents of the book, the flow of the narrative, themes, and argumentation. In the second reading we notice things we missed in the first reading, like repeated words or phrases. In the third reading we begin to make

---

5. Martin Luther, "Notes on Ecclesiastes," in *Luther's Works*, vol. 15, ed. Jaroslav Pelikan (St. Louis: Concordia, 1972), 46.

notes about the contents of the book and perhaps even write a rough-draft outline. Grant Osborne recommends creating a chart of the contents of the book to aid in visualizing the book's themes or action and the movement from one section or scene to the next.[6] Regardless of the form our notes take, it will be helpful to write down as many observations as possible, because when we leave the book and resume our study a day or two later, we will have forgotten some of what we learned unless we write down the ideas.

2. Note repeated words or phrases.

As we read an entire biblical book, we keep in mind the words of the passage we will be teaching. Are some words or phrases in the teaching passage repeated elsewhere in the book? Make a note of them. The meaning of the word or phrase in your passage may be affected by the way that word or phrase is used elsewhere in the same book.

Suppose we are studying the temptation/fall narrative in Genesis 3. We notice the serpent's statement about the consequence of eating from the tree of the knowledge of good and evil: "You will not surely die" (v. 4). In the immediate context, his words contradict the woman's citation of God's prohibition, but if we also read the larger context we will observe God's statement about the consequence of eating from that tree: "You shall surely die" (2:17). Here we encounter an important parallel. The serpent's statement is a direct contradiction of God's statement. If we read the two statements in Hebrew, the serpent's contradiction is even more obvious. In Hebrew, the grammatical form of God's statement is emphatic. The serpent repeats the same grammatical form. He also repeats the words God used, with one exception: "not." The serpent's refutation of God could not be more unmistakable, but we see how the statements match only when we read both chapters.

If we want to teach what the Bible says about the importance of relationships, it is likely that we will include Genesis 2:18, where God says, "It is not good that the man should be alone." God made humanity in such a way that relating to others is an inherent good. But reading that

---

6. Grant Osborne, *The Hermeneutical Spiral: A Comprehensive Introduction to Biblical Interpretation* (Downers Grove, IL: InterVarsity Press, 1991), 22–27.

verse in the context of the book of Genesis as a whole complicates the subject considerably. First, one cannot read Genesis 1 without noticing the repetition of the word "good" (vv. 4, 10, 12, 18, 21, 25, 31). "God saw that it was good" is the refrain expressing the eminent worth of God's creative work. What a stark contrast, then, to read in chapter 2 that God said, "It is not good" for the man to be alone. God's design for humanity was not complete until he had the opportunity for relationships. However, reading the following chapters in the book of Genesis demonstrates powerfully that relationships can also cause anguish and provide opportunities to rebel against God's will. Therefore, when teaching what the Bible says about relationships, using Genesis 2:18 as a "proof text" for the goodness of relationships would diminish the full biblical witness unless the verse is qualified by its larger literary context.

3. Identify the purpose of the book.

Every book in the Bible has a purpose. Some books may have multiple purposes, or one primary purpose plus a few subordinate purposes. Even in the case of historical books like Samuel and Kings, the authors did not write their books merely because they thought writing was a fun hobby or because they wanted to record some interesting facts about the past. Therefore, I recommend a teleological reading of every Old Testament passage—that is, reading a text in light of where it is heading and how it contributes to the end purpose of the book. We can discover such a purpose only when we read the entire book in which our passage is found.

A helpful exegetical question is, what was the author trying to accomplish in this passage and in this book? We cannot read the minds of biblical authors, but we can look at what they wrote and assess the primary achievements of their work based on textual evidence. Asking about a book's purpose can easily become speculative: what was most important to the author(s)? and why did he or she write this book? Ultimately, we cannot know the answers to such questions with much degree of certainty. The expositional goal of teachers and preachers of the Old Testament is more empirical and practical. We want to find the main emphases of the book and how our teaching passage fits into the overall scheme or purpose of the book.

Think about the purpose of the book of Ruth and how that purpose may impact the exposition of any passage in the book. The question can become academic. For example, Robert Pfeiffer writes the following about Ruth's author: "He simply set out to tell an interesting tale of long ago, and he carried out his purpose with notable success."[7] But how can we know whether the author's purpose was so limited? We cannot. Pfeiffer offers a guess, and those who teach the Old Testament in the church need more than guesswork to guide their teaching.

What are the textual clues that may indicate an overall purpose of the book? First, at several points the story mentions God's sovereignty over events. When Naomi referred to the difficult circumstances of her past, she did not say, "I have had a hard life." Instead, she said, "The hand of the LORD has gone out against me" and "The Almighty has dealt very bitterly with me" (1:13, 20; cf. 1:6, 9, 20, 21; 2:12; 4:12, 13, 14). Such statements may indicate that the purpose of the book is to stress God's sovereignty over the events of history and over our lives. Whether that is the main purpose or not, it is at least an emphasis or achievement of the book.

Second, the ending of the book may signal its main purpose. The final verses are devoted to a genealogy that ends with the name of King David. In fact, David is mentioned twice (4:17, 22), and his name is the final word in the book. Why end at that point? Why not carry the genealogy further? Perhaps at the mention of David's name the author had achieved his purpose. He wanted to show that the difficult, often ugly events of the period of the judges ultimately led to God's desired outcome: the reign of David that would lead eventually to the reign of the Davidic Messiah. Thus, beyond showing that God is sovereign over the events of our lives, the author wanted to show that God sovereignly guides the events of our lives to his redemptive purpose in the end. So the theological message of the book extends beyond the truth of God's control; it includes his redemptive purpose for all people. Such a telos, or final purpose, for the book as a whole impacts the way we teach every individual passage in the book of Ruth. We can access that purpose only if we read and consider the entire book.

---

7. Robert Pfeiffer, *Introduction to the Old Testament*, 2nd ed. (New York: Harper & Brothers, 1941), 719.

4. Read an outline of the book in a commentary.

Typically the writers of commentaries on biblical books have spent many hours, sometimes years, studying their subject. Often at the beginning of a commentary the author will include an outline of the entire biblical book. Before producing such an outline, he or she will have exegeted the book, revising the outline as necessary to reflect their conclusions about the flow of the book and how it should be divided. The outline provides an overview of the entire book at a glance. Since one initial goal of the exposition of any passage is to understand the context of the book as a whole, it is wise to take advantage of such an outline. If the expositor produced an outline during the third reading of the book, as suggested above, the outlines in commentaries can be compared with the expositor's outline. Also, in reading an entire biblical book sometimes expositors can "lose the forest for the trees." In other words, we focus on the details of the text, or become preoccupied with some of the details, and we miss the overall flow the book. An outline in a commentary can help to mitigate that problem.

5. Determine the original audience and the author's relationship to the audience.

King Ahab of Israel and King Jehoshaphat of Judah were seeking counsel from the prophets about whether to attack Syria. Micaiah the prophet said, "Go up and triumph; the LORD will give it into the hand of the king" (1 Kings 22:15). If the reader of that story does not pay attention to the literary context, and specifically the relationship between Micaiah and Ahab, Micaiah's meaning will be missed. Ahab had told Jehoshaphat that Micaiah "never prophesies good concerning me, only evil" (v. 8). Ahab's statement foreshadows Micaiah's sarcastic proclamation of victory: his "good" prophesy is actually "evil." The reader, though, has to understand the relationship between the two men to interpret Micaiah's words correctly. Micaiah was being sarcastic, and that interpretation is confirmed by the additional words Micaiah spoke after he was pressured by Ahab. Micaiah went on to make explicit his prediction that Syria would prevail if Israel and Judah attacked (v. 17).

In 2 Kings 22 the story itself supplies enough information about the relationship between Ahab and Micaiah to interpret Micaiah's words correctly. However, expositors often must read between the lines to reach conclusions about the relationship between the writer of a biblical book and the original readers or hearers. Sometimes we have to admit that such a relationship is unknowable, so any conclusions we reach will be speculative. In other cases, the relationship between the writer and readers appears clear and immediately relevant. For example, if Amaziah's reaction to Amos is indicative, Amos was not well received. Amaziah told him to leave Israel and go back to Judah (Amos 7:10–17).

Similarly, Malachi affirmed numerous truths about God and about the spiritual condition of the people to whom he preached, but his affirmations were met with denials. Malachi quoted his audience as arguing with virtually every point he made, and he responded by defending his point. In fact, the book of Malachi is usually outlined according to the pattern of affirmation, denial, and defense. The pattern is repeated six times. Scholars debate whether Malachi's audience was actual or rhetorical, but in either case Malachi portrayed the relationship as contentious.

On the other hand, when Haggai preached the people who heard him responded positively. He told them they should be working to rebuild the temple. They obeyed his words, feared the Lord, and went to work on the temple (Hag. 1:12, 14). Likewise, it appears that the people of Jerusalem responded positively to Nehemiah. He called them to work on the wall and to reform their lifestyles, and they did both (Neh. 1:18; 5:11–13; 6:15).

How much do we know about the audience of the Pentateuch and how its message was received? Most answers to that question involve speculation, but sometimes it is both possible and fruitful for expositors to reach some conclusions about the identity of the audience. For example, if we affirm Mosaic authorship of the Pentateuch, the primeval history in Genesis 1–11 was written before the Israelites' entry into the Promised Land, that is, about 1400 BC (assuming the early date for the exodus). The original audience for the Pentateuch was the congregation of Hebrews in the Sinai wilderness. They had just fled Egypt, and Egypt had several stories about the origin of the universe that included references to numerous gods. Also, the Hebrews were descendants of Abraham, who had lived on the other end of the Fertile Crescent from Egypt and had worshiped an entirely different pantheon of deities (Josh. 24:2). The primeval history in Genesis presents a different explanation for the origin of the universe from the myths of other ancient Near Eastern cultures. The process of creation is different and the God of creation is different. Possibly the Hebrews in the wilderness would have been more or less familiar with the origin stories of Egypt and Mesopotamia. Therefore, when Moses presented the contents of the primeval history in Genesis, the people had to make a choice. Would they receive Moses' creation story as a perfect revelation from the one true God, or would they join their neighbors in affirming the origin stories of the most powerful cultures in the world? When expositors think about such a relationship between author and audience, the result can shed further light on the meaning and significance of a text.

6. Establish whether the context is prescriptive or descriptive.

The distinction between prescription and description is used in numerous fields. Grammarians and ethicists, for example, have seen the heuristic value of such a binary opposition. When grammarians are prescriptive, they encourage us to use language properly. They tell us how language *ought* to be used. They prescribe. When they are descriptive, they teach how language is used in actual practice and perhaps explore the mental processes that led to a particular use of language. Put another way, prescriptive grammarians are concerned that we use language in the correct way, whereas descriptive grammarians are concerned with a correct description of the way we actually use grammar.

What does this have to do with considering the literary context of a passage in the Bible? Genesis 16 says that Abram's wife Sarai gave Hagar to Abram so Abram could father a child by Hagar. In that passage the author described what Sarai and Abram did; he did not prescribe that men should take mistresses to bear children for them. In the literary context of Genesis, God had already prescribed his design for marriage: one man and one woman (2:24). The actions of Sarai and Abram constitute deviations from that established norm, and the writer of Genesis 16 simply described their actions accurately. The same is true for the description of Solomon's seven hundred wives and three hundred concubines (1 Kings 11:3). Such a description does not constitute an endorsement of polygamy or adultery. That fact should be evident from texts that are clearly prescriptive, like God's original design in Genesis and the commands against adultery in the legal corpus (e.g.,

Exod. 20:14, 17). Also, the context of the description of Solomon's polygamy mentions the disastrous spiritual and national consequences of
Solomon's actions, which serve as confirmation of God's displeasure
with Solomon's chosen way of life (1 Kings 11:3–11).

Scriptural descriptions of the activity of God can also be descriptive
or prescriptive. The fact that God acted in a specific way in someone's
life in the past does not necessarily mean that he will always act in the
same way in our lives. "Although God's character is immutable, his
actions are not."[8] Therefore, when we read that God acted in a certain
way toward Abraham or Israel or Babylon, we cannot necessarily teach
that contemporary people can expect him to act in just the same way
in their lives. To draw such a universal conclusion, we need corroboration about God's ways from other passages of Scripture. Throughout
history God has responded in various ways to various people in various
circumstances. Therefore, we should be careful to classify passages as
descriptive or prescriptive before we draw universal conclusions about
God's actions.

Classifying a passage as descriptive or prescriptive serves a practical
function in teaching the Old Testament. In passages that describe sinful actions, Old Testament writers customarily did not interrupt the
progress of their narratives to write, "And remember, God's law says
this is wrong." They assume their readers possess a basic knowledge
of morality that arises from creation and covenant law, and they trust
their readers to apply that law to their stories and assess the rightness or
wrongness of the characters' actions. However, if a teacher of the Old
Testament is speaking to people who are not familiar with the contents
of the Old Testament, it may be wise to state clearly that a descriptive
passage is not prescriptive, lest hearers wrongly assume that the passage
offers tacit approval of behavior that the Bible elsewhere condemns as
sinful.

7. Consider the canonical context.

To interpret each Old Testament passage in light of its literary context
we have recommended reading the entire biblical book in which the

---

8. Henry A. Virkler and Karelynne Gerber Ayayo, *Hermeneutics: Principles and Processes of Biblical Interpretation*, 2nd ed. (Grand Rapids: Baker, 2007), 88.

passage is located. Before we conclude our consideration of literary context we should look beyond the book to think about the implications of the fact that the passage is also located in a canon of Scripture. If we do not think about how a particular passage relates to revelation in other books of the Bible we may miss crucial truths.

This is a confessional perspective. The believing church has always affirmed that God inspired the entire canon. That plenary inspiration makes the Bible a theological unity, despite the obvious diversity of its various books. Such theological unity means that all the books of the Bible will relate to one another in some meaningful way. For teachers of the Old Testament, it means that arriving at "Isaiah's theology" or "the Chronicler's theology" will be a penultimate achievement. The ultimate goal will be to integrate our passage into a theology that can be called "biblical." This will require considering the light the entire canon may shed on the passage we are teaching or preaching.

At several places in this book we are contending that Old Testament exposition should lead to the New Testament gospel at some point. Here it should be mentioned that if we bring to bear the entire canon on our exposition, then we will look for the ways the New Testament may shed light on the Old Testament passage we are studying. That is why Jeannine Brown writes, "It is at the canonical level that a particularly Christian interpretation emerges."[9] We will have more to say about the relevance of the New Testament in the section below on redemptive-historical context.

An example can demonstrate the helpfulness of considering the canonical context. The book of Nahum announces God's judgment on Nineveh. After the superscription, the book opens with a threefold emphasis on God's wrath: God is "jealous," "avenging," and "wrathful." Also, the word translated "avenging" appears three times in one verse (1:2). And God's wrath on Nineveh does not relent at any point in the book. In Nahum, even the possibility of God's mercy toward the Ninevites is absent.

However, when we consider where Nineveh is mentioned elsewhere in Scripture, we remember that the book of Jonah describes how God's

---

9. Jeannine K. Brown, *Scripture as Communication: Introducing Biblical Hermeneutics* (Grand Rapids: Baker, 2007), 225.

mercy had been shown to the Ninevites some 150 years before Nahum. God had sent at least one prophet, Jonah, to warn Nineveh to turn from sin. In response to Jonah's preaching they turned from sin. However, at some point they returned to their barbarous ways. Even then, God waited a century and a half before inspiring Nahum to announce God's final judgment.

Thus looking beyond the book of Nahum and considering its canonical context leads us to a theological picture that is more complete than the conclusions we may reach when we limit our study to the three chapters of Nahum. We may even say that if we consider the book of Nahum in isolation that we are taking its message "out of context," since we are not including in our study the full context of all God's dealings with Nineveh.

Historical and Cultural Context

Studying the historical and/or cultural context of a passage of Scripture is often referred to as background study. Such background study is a necessary part of the exposition of every Old Testament text. The emphasis on the importance of considering a passage's historical/cultural context as a part of the interpretation process arises from three foundational presuppositions. First, the meaning of a text is the author's intended meaning. As E. D. Hirsch put it, "Verbal meaning is whatever someone has willed to convey by a particular sequence of linguistic signs."[10] We cannot know the minds of the biblical authors, but we can know what they willed to convey when we read what they wrote. If we abandon the principle that a text's meaning is determined by the author of the text, we will have no objective criterion by which to establish the meaning of any text. All that is left is a postmodern, relativistic reading by which meaning is determined by the preferences that readers impose on a text. In such a situation, ultimately no absolute Truth exists, only "truths" that are relative to each situation and person.[11]

---

10. E.D. Hirsch, *Validity in Interpretation* (New Haven, CT: Yale University Press, 1967), 31.

11. See the description of postmodernism and its impact on the way people think about truth in Allan Moseley, *Thinking Against the Grain: Developing a Biblical Worldview in a Culture of Myths* (Grand Rapids: Kregel, 2003), 56–73.

Such an approach to reading has never been the church's approach to reading the Bible. Instead, the church has affirmed what Scripture says about itself, that God inspired persons to write his Word (Mark 12:36; 2 Tim. 3:16; 2 Peter 1:20–21). Therefore, the meaning of every text is determined by the human author and the divine Author. Since, then, the meaning of Old Testament texts was determined long ago, we are helped by knowing as much as possible about the authors, their times, and the original referents for phenomena like "horns" on an altar, the "King's Highway," and the "Millo."

The second foundational presupposition that makes historical/cultural study necessary is the belief that the contexts of Scripture were not accidents. God chose to reveal himself to the patriarchs and to their descendants the Jews. God chose to lead Abram and his progeny from Mesopotamia to Canaan, then to Egypt and back to Canaan. God also chose specific moments in history to lead his people out of Egypt, to raise up leaders, to inspire writers, and to send prophets to speak his words. Hence, God chose specific people, periods, and places to do his work and write his word. When we study that context (the matrix of biography, culture, history, and geography), we are essentially walking on holy ground, since we are entering the spaces and times in which God revealed himself and his word.

The third presupposition that is foundational for background studies is the most obvious—we do not live in the same times, cultures, and places as the authors of Old Testament texts. The authors of Scripture lived thousands of years ago, wrote in a different language, and lived in cultures that were vastly different from ours. If we wish to understand what an author meant by what he wrote, we will often be required to learn something about his times and culture. We will be helped by "entering the world" of the writer. Once we see how his words worked in his world, we will know how their meaning and significance can be transferred to our world. John Walton explains the necessity of studying Scripture's historical/cultural context:

> Without the guidance of background studies, we are bound to misinterpret the text at some point. . . . We can . . . speak of the potential meanings that words point to as gaps that need to be filled with . . . meaning by the audience. The writer . . . assumes

that those gaps will be filled in particular ways based on the common language and worldview he shares with his audience. Interpreters of the Bible have the task of filling in those gaps, not with their own ideas . . . but with the ideas of the writer. . . . Often the words . . . and the ideas . . . are rooted in the culture and therefore need the assistance of background studies.[12]

Preachers and teachers of the Old Testament who aim at excellence in their exposition will become students of ancient Near Eastern history and culture. As we grow in our knowledge of such subjects, we will grow in our ability to apply our knowledge to our exposition of specific texts. Growth in knowledge will require adequate resources. Depending on commentaries will not suffice since even extensive commentaries sometimes refer in passing to documents like "Mesopotamian origin stories" or "Egyptian wisdom texts." Expositors will ask, What origin stories? What Egyptian wisdom texts? and How do they relate to the Old Testament? I recommend collecting and using resources in the following categories:

1. *Volumes on the history of Israel.* Every serious Bible student should read at least one history of Israel. As a part of preparation to teach a particular passage, expositors should also consult a few books that examine the historical information behind the passage. Such books consider the biblical text, plus the data available by means of archaeology. Reading such volumes helps expositors exegete the passage they are studying, and it provides a historical context that will aid them in their future study of other passages.[13]

---

12. John H. Walton, *Ancient Near Eastern Thought and the Old Testament: Introducing the Conceptual World of the Hebrew Bible* (Grand Rapids: Baker, 2006), 25.

13. Ancient Israelite historiography is a highly contested field, with differing views concerning such things as Israel's conception of history, the accuracy of historical information in the Bible, and the proper interpretation of archaeological data. For that reason expositors should be aware of the presuppositions of the authors of various histories of Israel. I recommend a history text written by an author who places confidence in the history of Israel as presented in the Old Testament, such as Walter C. Kaiser Jr., *A History of Israel: From the Bronze Age Through the Jewish Wars* (Nashville: Broadman & Holman, 1998); and Eugene H. Merrill, *Kingdom of Priests: A History of Old Testament Israel,* 2nd ed. (Grand Rapids: Baker, 2008).

2 *Books that are collections of ancient Near Eastern texts.* Commentaries often refer to texts from ancient cultures in Mesopotamia and Egypt. Shouldn't expositors read those texts for themselves? Only then can they reach their own conclusions about similarities and dissimilarities with Old Testament texts. Such texts were written in languages like Akkadian, Egyptian, and Ugaritic, but English translations are available.[14] My favorite, though expensive and with older translations, is Pritchard's *Ancient Near Eastern Texts Relating to the Old Testament.*

3. *Books that have collections of ancient Near Eastern texts with commentary.* Some resources include texts from the ancient Near East, or excerpts, plus the author(s) perspectives on how those texts compare and contrast with similar texts in the Bible. Of course, each author's perspective is different, and Old Testament expositors may or may not be satisfied with the author's conclusions. However, it is helpful to be aware of the ideas of the experts in the field, and typically they have spent decades reflecting on how Old Testament texts may relate to other ancient Near Eastern texts.[15]

4. *Commentaries that specialize in providing background information.* Some commentaries on specific books or sections of the Old Testament focus especially on providing as much background information as possible. Such books are convenient because expositors may turn to the pages relevant to the passage they are studying to access specific information. Hence, the advantage of such resources is time conservation.

---

14. For example, Bill T. Arnold and Bryan E. Beyer, *Readings from the Ancient Near East: Primary Sources for Old Testament Study* (Grand Rapids: Baker, 2002); Walter Beyerlin, *Near Eastern Religious Texts Relating to the Old Testament* (Philadelphia: Westminster, 1978); Michael David Coogan, *Stories from Ancient Canaan* (Philadelphia: Westminster, 1978); Victor H. Matthews and Don C. Benjamin, *Old Testament Parallels: Laws and Stories from the Ancient Near East*, 3rd ed. (Mahwah, NJ: Paulist Press, 2006); and James B. Pritchard, *Ancient Near Eastern Texts Relating to the Old Testament*, 3rd ed. (Princeton, NJ: Princeton University Press, 1969).

15. Examples include Christopher B. Hayes, *Hidden Riches: A Sourcebook for the Comparative Study of the Hebrew Bible and Ancient Near East* (Louisville: Westminster John Knox, 2014); Kenton L. Sparks, *Ancient Texts for the Study of the Hebrew Bible: A Guide to the Background Literature* (Peabody, MA: Hendrickson, 2005); and John H. Walton, *Ancient Near Eastern Thought and the Old Testament: Introducing the Conceptual World of the Hebrew Bible* (Grand Rapids: Baker, 2006).

The disadvantage is that if expositors limit their reading to information about one passage, it is possible to misinterpret the data without knowledge of the larger historical and archaeological context. Hence, expositors should use these specialty commentaries after they have become familiar with the history of Israel and the general cultural information that pertains to each period of that history.[16]

5. *Books that describe the people groups of the ancient Near East.* Old Testament expositors regularly encounter references to the peoples who lived around Israel. For example, what do we know about Egypt during the Egyptian sojourn of Abraham's descendants? What has archaeology revealed about the Philistines during the periods of the judges and united monarchy? Actually, quite a lot, and the same is true for the Canaanites, Syrians, Assyrians, Babylonians, Persians, etc. Thorough Old Testament commentaries provide some relevant information about such peoples when such information relates to specific texts, but for more extensive background information expositors will consult more comprehensive sources.[17] In addition, some resources address one particular nation or people group in more detail.[18]

At this point some recommendations regarding background studies may be helpful. How should expositors use such studies in their

---

16. Examples of this type of commentary are John J. Davis, *Moses and the Gods of Egypt: Studies in Exodus*, 2nd ed. (Winona Lake, IN: BMH Books, 1986); John J. Davis and John C. Whitcomb, *Israel from Conquest to Exile: A Commentary on Joshua-2 Kings* (Winona Lake, IN: BMH Books, 1989); Alfred J. Hoerth, *Archaeology and the Old Testament* (Grand Rapids: Baker, 1998); Philip J. King, *Amos, Hosea, Micah: An Archaeological Commentary* (Philadelphia: Westminster, 1988); John H. Walton, Victor H. Mathews, and Mark W. Chavalas, *The IVP Bible Background Commentary: Old Testament* (Downers Grove: IL, InterVarsity Press, 2000).

17. For example, Bill T. Arnold and Brent A. Strawn, eds., *The World Around the Old Testament: The People and Places of the Ancient Near East* (Grand Rapids: Baker, 2016); Alfred J. Hoerth, Gerald L. Mattingly, Edwin M. Yamauchi, eds., *Peoples of the Old Testament World* (Grand Rapids: Baker, 1994); Sabatino Moscati, *The Face of the Ancient Orient: Near Eastern Civilization in Pre-Classical Times* (New York: Dover, 2001); and Jack Sasson, ed., *Civilizations of the Ancient Near East* (Peabody, MA: Hendrickson, 2000).

18. For example, John D. Currid, *Ancient Egypt and the Old Testament* (Grand Rapids: Baker, 1997); Edward E. Hindson, *The Philistines and the Old Testament* (Grand Rapids: Baker, 1971); and Edwin M. Yamauchi, *Persia and the Bible* (Grand Rapids: Baker, 1990).

preaching and teaching? How much should they talk about historical/ cultural backgrounds in their preaching and teaching?

First, we keep in mind that the scriptural text, not the background information, is most important. We master cultural/historical information not as an end in itself, but as a necessary means to understand and explain God's Word. A mistake some expositors make is getting so involved in the historical context that they devote more time in their exposition to an attempt to reconstruct what actually happened than they devote to teaching what the text says. A fundamental principle to remember is that the locus of revelation is the text, not our reconstruction of the event. The event is over and we have no access to it except through the text. Furthermore, the text is what God inspired as his communication to humanity.[19] The theological message for today is in the text. Background material is supplementary and explanatory; the text of the Bible is primary and revelatory. Therefore, we begin and end the process of exposition by reading the text.

Second, we make sure we use credible sources. In a perfect world, we could trust all the information we hear in a Bible study or sermon and we could repeat the information in our own exposition without fear of being inaccurate. However, in the real world it is necessary to be more careful. Mistakes about background material are common. If our goal is excellent exposition, we will not repeat them. As for media reports about archaeological discoveries that "prove" or "disprove" the Bible, we should trust them even less. Media reports commonly sensationalize such discoveries and quote advocates for an ideological agenda. The result is mischaracterization of facts. Therefore, expositors who aim at accuracy will use the kinds of sources footnoted earlier in this chapter and written by authors whose expertise and theological commitments are clear.

---

19. See John Sailhamer's helpful discussion in *Introduction to Old Testament Theology: A Canonical Approach* (Grand Rapids: Zondervan, 1995), 36–85. Sailhamer affirms the historicity of God's acts in history as recorded in Scripture, but at the same time argues that Scripture, not historical events, is the locus of revelation. Similarly, J. I. Packer writes, "No historical event, as such, can make God known to anyone unless God Himself discloses its meaning and place in His plan." J. I. Packer, *God Speaks to Man: Revelation and the Bible* (Philadelphia: Westminster, 1965), 51.

Third, we guard against generalizations about ancient cultures. No culture is monolithic. Every culture has some variations in morality, economy, politics, and theology. For example, the Old Testament depicts Canaanite culture during the time of Moses and Joshua as wicked (Lev. 18:6–27). However, the book of Joshua records that at least one Canaanite during that period put her faith in the one true God and gave her allegiance to the invading Israelites (Josh. 2:1–21). If we say, "Nineveh, the capital city of Assyria, was pagan and barbaric," we would be generally accurate. But during at least one period in the history of that city the populace repented and believed God (Jonah 3:4–10). In light of such exceptions, the wise approach is to make specific statements about specific people and situations instead of generalizations about entire cultures.

Also, we should guard against generalizations concerning the conclusions of archaeologists and historians. The fields of Near Eastern archaeology and history are notoriously contested.[20] Virtually every artifact that is discovered sparks new debates. Therefore, we avoid generalizations about ancient civilizations and modern scholarship. Our goal is absolute accuracy in the information we share in our exposition.

Fourth, we don't speculate about contextual issues. Speculation is going beyond the evidence to suggest something that *might* have happened. The job of an Old Testament preacher or teacher is to affirm, explain, and apply what the Bible says. That job precludes guessing. When we guess we are engaging in something other than biblical exposition. If the Bible states it, we should state it. But if the Bible leaves some questions unanswered, we let those questions remain unanswered and we leave speculation in the coffee shop where it belongs.

Fifth, we check the Old Testament itself for historical and cultural information. The Old Testament contains a lot of background data, so we make the scriptural text our first source in studying the background of a text. Since we believe that God inspired the text of the Old

---

20. Even the title for the archaeology of the land of Israel can be controversial. Some prefer the older "Biblical Archaeology," while others use "Syro-Palestinian Archaeology" or "Levantine Archaeology." Such titles can be ideologically and even politically loaded.

Testament, we can trust the accuracy of its assertions about history and culture.[21] For example, the book of Ruth opens with the circumstantial clause, "In the days when the judges ruled" (1:1). To learn something about what those days were like, we read the book of Judges. Reading that historical information gives us numerous snapshots of the prominent people and events in the times in which Ruth lived.[22] The same is true for the prophetic books. To gain information about the historical, cultural, and spiritual setting of Haggai and Zechariah, for example, we can read the book of Ezra.[23]

The history and archaeology of the ancient Near East is an enormous, daunting subject. Many scholars labor for a lifetime and master only one aspect of the subject. And before long their mastery is out of date as new discoveries are made. Therefore, a final recommendation to Old Testament expositors is to exercise persistence and patience. We start where we are and we commit to grow in our knowledge month by month, year by year. The greater the breadth and depth of our knowledge of historical and cultural backgrounds, the better we will be able to interpret Old Testament texts.

---

21. In the confessing church, by far the dominant position has been complete trust in the Old Testament's historical data, even when historical accounts include the suspension of the laws of nature, or the supernatural. On the other hand, in academia "minimalists" and "maximalists" continue to wrangle over whether or to what degree to trust the accuracy of the historical information in the Old Testament. For reviews of the debate, see V. Philips Long, David W. Baker, and Gordon J. Wenham, eds., *Windows into Old Testament History: Evidence, Argument, and the Crisis of "Biblical Israel"* (Grand Rapids: Eerdmans, 2002); and Iain Provan, V. Philips Long, and Tremper Longman III, *A Biblical History of Israel* (Louisville: Westminster John Knox, 2003), 1–104. For sources that provide evidence for the trustworthiness of the historical data in the Old Testament, see Daniel I. Block, ed., *Israel: Ancient Kingdom or Late Invention?* (Nashville: B&H, 2008); K. A. Kitchen, *On the Reliability of the Old Testament* (Grand Rapids: Eerdmans, 2003); and Randall Price, *The Stones Cry Out: What Archaeology Reveals about the Truth of the Bible* (Eugene, OR: Harvest House, 1997).

22. The picture of military and political unrest portrayed in the book of Judges is corroborated by a group of over three hundred letters discovered in the late nineteenth and early twentieth centuries. They are called the Tell el-Amarna letters, and they date to the fourteenth century BC. They are correspondence between the Pharaohs Amenhotep III and Akhenaten and numerous leaders in Canaan and elsewhere.

23. Also, in recent decades scholars have produced an impressive body of literature analyzing this Second Temple Period sociologically, economically, politically, literarily, and religiously. A good example is T&T Clark's Library of Second Temple Studies, with almost ninety volumes exploring the literature of that period.

Geographical Context

As Old Testament expositors study any text, a good question to ask is, where are we right now? Sometimes the location of the action or dialogue makes a difference in how we interpret a text, or whether we even understand it. As John Monson puts it, "Texts, material culture, and geography form an inseparable triad, which together help us define the context of Scripture."[24] For example, Amos 4:1 refers to "cows of Bashan, who are on the mountain of Samaria." Amos wrote of two geographical locations: Bashan and Samaria. Samaria was the capital of the northern kingdom of Israel during Amos' lifetime, and it was located on a hill, or mountain. The cows seem to be located in Samaria, so why the reference to Bashan? Bashan was not a city; it was a geographical region east and north of the Jordan, stretching from Gilead in the south to the Mt. Hermon region in the north. In antiquity it was known for the fertility of its soil and hence its green pastures. So cows that lived in Bashan were well-fed, plump. Amos' statements that follow accuse these cows of oppressing the poor and ordering their husbands to bring them drinks. Clearly these were not cows but women. Now it is clear that Amos was addressing wealthy women who lived in the capital and referring to them as fat cows.

Geographical information also helps to illuminate a story in 1 Samuel 24. King Saul was pursuing David to capture and kill him, and he heard David was "in the wilderness of Engedi" (v. 1). Without some knowledge of Engedi, expositors could reach incorrect conclusions about where David was hiding. Engedi is indeed located in the wilderness, but Engedi itself is no wilderness. It is a beautiful oasis located on the eastern edge of the Judean wilderness and overlooking the Dead Sea. At Engedi David and his men would have had plenty of water and the opportunity to hide in the caves near the spring. To reach David at Engedi Saul and his men would have to trudge through miles and miles of wilderness. Plus, rising over the spring of Engedi is a mountain, and from the top David's scouts could have watched scores of miles in every direction. It was the perfect location for David and his men.

---

24. John M. Monson, "Contextual Criticism as a Framework for Biblical Interpretation," in *Israel: Ancient Kingdom or Late Invention?*, ed. Daniel I. Block (Nashville: B&H, 2008).

Since geographical location is often crucial for understanding a text, accessing geographical information should be a part of every exposition. Maps in the back of Bibles are helpful, but typically not adequate. Therefore, Old Testament expositors should have at least one historical Bible atlas. Such atlases correlate geographical information with the history of Israel and specific texts in the Old Testament. Therefore, expositors can use such a resource to trace the action of Old Testament stories on a map. The better atlases also provide verbal descriptions of many sites mentioned in the Old Testament. Most major Christian publishers have produced such atlases. For the greatest help in preaching and teaching the Old Testament, expositors should have an atlas with maps that consistently relate to the biblical text. Personally, I have used the atlas edited by Thomas Brisco with profit.[25] Expositors also profit significantly from traveling to Israel and studying the land for themselves.

Redemptive-Historical Context

In every age, people have adopted differing philosophies about the way history develops. Some people have conceived of history as cyclical. Events repeat themselves in a recurring pattern. They live with the feeling that what is happening now has happened before and it will happen again. Others embrace an evolutionary view of history. Humanity and the world are changing (either improving or devolving) because of the interaction of natural forces on one another. Still others advocate determinism. To determinists, free will is an illusion. Events in the past, present, and future are determined by God, natural laws, or some other force. The best response to the fixed nature of reality, according to this view, is to submit to the inevitable.

In contrast with such philosophies of history, the view of history reflected in the Bible is linear and teleological. History is linear because it moves forward on a time line. Time moves forward inexorably, never circling back. History is teleological because it always has been and still is headed toward an intended end. Events in history have a purpose, a goal, and God is the One directing history toward his desired outcome.

---

25. Thomas V. Brisco, *Holman Bible Atlas: A Complete Guide to the Expansive Geography of Biblical History* (Nashville: Broadman & Holman, 1998).

What is the end to which God is guiding history? Repeatedly the Bible asserts that history ends in redemption for God's people. From the beginning of biblical history, God's work, God's words, and human faith look forward to the end God has in mind. In the garden of Eden, God's promise to defeat his adversary signals that God is leading history toward an outcome, and that outcome is good news for people who put their faith in him and bad news for those who oppose him (Gen. 3:15). The scriptural record of Enoch, who "walked with God, and he was not, for God took him" also foreshadows a better outcome for God's people (Gen. 5:24). In the patriarchal period, as the writer of Hebrews summarized, once Abraham exercised faith, he "was looking forward to the city that has foundations, whose designer and builder is God" (Heb. 11:10). After Abraham, his descendants who "died in faith" desired "a better country, that is, a heavenly one," and God "has prepared for them a city" (Heb. 11:13, 16).

Several psalmists also saw God's salvation reaching into the glorious future he has in store for the faithful. For example, one psalmist prayed, "At your right hand are pleasures forevermore" (Ps. 16:11). Being in the presence of God forever is also expressed in Psalm 73, where the psalmist testified to God, "You guide me with your counsel, and afterward you will receive me to glory. . . . God is the strength of my heart and my portion forever" (vv. 24, 26). The author of Psalm 23 affirmed, "I shall dwell in the house of the LORD forever" (v. 6).

The prophets also saw history progressing toward a goal that God had in mind. Isaiah and Micah wrote of a peaceful future in which all nations would desire to know and obey God (Isa. 2:2–4; Micah 4:1–3). Isaiah also wrote of future reversals of the curse throughout the natural order (11:6–10), and in chapters 24–27 he envisioned an eschatological age of cataclysmic destruction on the earth and the salvation of God's people. Examples could be multiplied of old covenant saints looking forward to what the writer of Hebrews called "a better country, that is, a heavenly one" and "a better life" (Heb. 11:16, 35).

In light of history's purposeful movement from beginning to end, every part of the Old Testament can be placed on a timeline that stretches from creation through each of the Old Testament covenants to the new covenant in Christ and finally to the consummation of the age and the presence of God's people with God forever. Part of good exposition is placing the text being studied on that timeline and considering how its location may affect its meaning. As Jeannine Brown puts it, "How does the text I am studying draw upon and contribute to the overarching story of God's redemptive activity in and through his covenant people on behalf of creation and all humanity?"[26] Such a question is especially important to ask of texts in the Old Testament. Our exposition of the Old Testament is not *Christian* unless we make a connection between the text and Christ. Such a connection is not always apparent, so expositors intentionally ask questions that will place the Old Testament text in the context of God's redemptive work.

To illustrate, Exodus 22:20 calls for the death penalty for any Israelite committing idolatry. During that period in redemptive history and within the nation of Israel, God invested Israel's leadership with the authority to use the death penalty. However, after the coming of Christ and the establishment of the church, God has not given the church the authority to impose his law on civil entities such as nations. When teaching Exodus 22 in the church, therefore, an exposition would be incomplete without reference to passages like Romans 13 in order to point out this difference concerning the way God's people relate to civil authority today. Furthermore, it would be helpful to complete the picture of redemptive history by referring to the fact that one day God will judge all sinful human governments when he establishes his universal rule and "the kingdom of the world has become the kingdom of our Lord and of his Christ, and he shall reign forever and ever" (Rev. 11:14; cf. Rev. 13–14). In teaching Exodus 22, then, it is essential to point out that God gave his Sinai commands in a redemptive-historical context that no longer exists.

To cite another example, Micah 6:8 states, "He has told you, O man, what is good; and what does the LORD require of you but to do justice, and to love kindness, and to walk humbly with your God?" Some Old Testament scholars have considered that verse a summary statement of the ethical message of the prophets who preached in the eighth century BC.[27] Indeed, the verse calls people to a high ethical standard:

---

26. Brown, *Scripture as Communication*, 230.

27. See James O. Newell, "The Means of Maintaining a Right Relationship with Yahweh: An Investigation of Selected Passages from the Hebrew Prophets of the Eighth Century BC" (PhD diss., New Orleans Baptist Theological Seminary, 1988).

the combination of justice, kindness, and walking with God. Similarly, Amos preached, "Let justice roll down like waters, and righteousness like an ever-flowing stream" (5:24).

As powerful as such verses are in calling people to ethical behavior, Christian expositors have not finished their work until they place the verses in their redemptive-historical context. Using such passages to challenge people to live righteously is commendable, but insufficient because it falls short of the gospel. If we do not refer to New Testament truth, we may give people the impression that living according to ethical standards and believing in the existence of God is the totality of right religion. It is not. Therefore, we remind people of the redemptive-historical context. Even in the context of the old covenant, faith was required to be justified before God. Good works were not sufficient (Gen. 15:6; Rom. 4:1–12). In the age of the new covenant in which we live, we are "not justified by works of the law but through faith in Christ Jesus" (Gal. 2:16). Therefore, when we join Micah and Amos in calling people to live according to high moral standards, we remember our responsibility to complete the redemptive-historical picture. Our "moral living" will always fall short (Isa.64:6; Rom. 3:23). For such sin we need a Savior. God has provided that Savior: "the Father has sent his Son to be the Savior of the world" (1 John 4:14). God requires us to exercise saving faith in the Savior, then we live ethically as he transforms us into new people and as saving faith produces good works (2 Cor. 5:17; Gal. 3:10–14; James 2:20–24).

Remembering the redemptive-historical context of every Old Testament passage protects us from hermeneutical tunnel vision. In studying a particular passage it is possible to spend all our time learning about the verses in front of us and their immediate context. There is so much to learn, and so much to teach! However, we cannot forget that the passage before us is located in a canon of Scripture that culminates in Christ. The Christocentric canon reflects the fact that God has guided all redemptive history to culminate in Christ. Therefore, the passage we are teaching, wherever it is located in the canon, also culminates in Christ. A text's context is highly important, but ultimately we look beyond immediate contextual issues and lead people to Christ.

Chapter 5

WHAT IS THE MEANING OF KEY WORDS?

8-STEP METHOD

STEP 1	Translating the text
STEP 2	Considering text criticism
STEP 3	Interpreting the genre
STEP 4	Exploring the context
STEP 5	**Defining important words**
STEP 6	Identifying the big idea
STEP 7	Connecting to Jesus
STEP 8	Applying the text to contemporary people

Our goal as expositors of the Old Testament is complete compre-hension and accurate, cogent communication. That is, we want to understand what the text says—both its original contextual issues and its abiding message—and we want to communicate what it says in a way that people understand it and feel compelled to submit to its truth. To that end, we make sure we know what the text says, which requires the first two steps of translation and text criticism. Third, we note the genre and interpret its relevance for understanding the passage we are studying. Fourth, we explore the context of the passage and discover how the context impacts the text's meaning. The fifth step is the subject of this chapter. We identify words in the text that require further study and we make sure we understand them.

A commitment to study and teach the Bible well involves a corresponding commitment to words. The Bible consists of words. Devotion to the Bible is devotion to its words. In preaching and teaching the Bible, our tools are words. Whether we use the right tools and use them effectively will depend largely on the amount of effort we expend to develop our verbal skill. Expositors are gifted in the use of words in different degrees. But no matter what may be the extent of one's inborn ability, if expositors work hard they can become masters of understanding and using words.

The title of this chapter is not meant to suggest that some words in the Bible are not key or important. When we believe in verbal, plenary inspiration, all the words of the Bible are important to us because they are all inspired by God (2 Tim. 3:16). However, in our efforts to teach the contents of a verse accurately and effectively, some words will require more explanation than others. For example, Genesis 15:6 says that Abraham "believed the LORD, and he counted it to him as righteousness." Every word in that verse is important, but the New Testament citations of this verse indicate that a few of the words carry more theological weight. To teach that verse adequately, expositors will need to give special attention to "believed," "righteousness," and perhaps "counted." Is the righteousness in that sentence imputed righteousness or practical righteousness? When Abraham believed, what exactly did he do? In this case, the New Testament provides help with answering such questions, since Paul regarded this verse as decisive in building the case for salvation by grace through faith apart from works of the law (Rom. 4:9–25; Gal. 3:5–10).

Ideally, expositors could spend an equal amount of time on every word in every verse. However, since we always work within time constraints, prioritizing certain words is necessary. Before we prioritize certain words, though, we should prioritize prayer.

Pray

In the Pastoral Epistles, the apostle Paul warned Timothy twice about inappropriately wrangling over words. First, in 1 Timothy Paul referred negatively to people who have "an unhealthy craving for controversy and for quarrels about words, which produce envy, dissension, slander, evil suspicions, and constant friction among people who are depraved in mind and deprived of the truth" (6:4–5). Second, in 2 Timothy Paul exhorted Pastor Timothy to be faithful in a whole list of responsibilities to the flock. One of those responsibilities was "charge them before God not to quarrel about words, which does no good, but only ruins the hearers" (2:14).

It should sober all Bible expositors that we can "produce envy, dissension, slander, evil suspicions, and constant friction" by handling words the wrong way. How does such a disaster happen? It's easy, and it happens all the time. We push a little too hard for our definition of a theological word, we fail to demonstrate love to someone who uses a different definition, or we show people that we derive more pleasure from debating them than serving them. The scariest part is that we can do all that without really thinking about it. We become convinced of the rightness of our position, we begin to push for our agenda to prevail, we don't pay careful attention to the feelings of our brothers and sisters, and sooner than we would have thought possible we see "envy, dissension, slander, evil suspicions, and constant friction" (1 Tim. 6:5). According to 2 Timothy 2:14, such behavior "ruins the hearers." The word translated "ruins" occurs in 2 Peter 2:6, where it refers to the destruction of Sodom and Gomorrah. Clearly Paul was warning Timothy that quarreling about words causes significant damage in the flock.

The possibility that we could become experts in handling words while simultaneously creating division in the church and harming the people we teach should drive us to our knees. Rather than attempting to describe how to pray about the way we handle words, I offer an example of a request for God's help. I hope it's the kind of prayer we will want to pray every time we begin the work of word study.

God, as I begin studying these words, please help me to remember that they are your words—holy words from the holy God. Since they are holy, help me to treat them as holy, with reverence and great care. I know I did nothing to deserve the gift of these words; you gave them because of your grace and love. As I receive them as a gift of love from you, please help me to study them with love for you and for the people I teach.

Please prevent me from harming those who hear me. Instead, enable me to help them. Use my words to explain and apply your words so that the people who hear me will love you more and will be more equipped to live for you. As a result of being together before your Word, may we love one another more and be more effective in our witness to this world that is full of people who need you desperately. I pray all this with a desire for you alone to be glorified in my study and teaching. And when I teach, please help me to "make it clear, which is how I ought to speak" (Col. 4:4), and "let the words of my mouth and the meditation of my heart be acceptable in your sight, O LORD, my rock and my redeemer" (Ps. 19:14), in Jesus' name, Amen.

The Way Words Work

It is likely that expositors commit more interpretation and application errors when doing word studies than when doing any other task. Even experienced teachers say things that are not true because they don't seem to understand the way words work to convey meaning. Most words have a semantic range, sometimes referred to as a semantic domain, semantic field, or lexical field. Grant Osborne provides a simple definition of semantic range: "A list of the ways the word was used in the era when the work was written."[1] A good example in English is the word "run." If asked to define the word, many people would say something like "to move on foot quickly." But I have often asked students in hermeneutics classes if they can think of other meanings of run, and they quickly provide uses like the following:

"He's going to run for office."
"I'm going to run some errands."
"Can your run that by me again?"
"The boss will run things in the office."
"It's unusual for him to run his mouth so much."
"I run that machine so much that it's going to wear out."

---

1. Grant R. Osborne, *The Hermeneutical Spiral: A Comprehensive Introduction to Biblical Interpretation* (Downers Grove, IL: InterVarsity Press, 1991), 81.

"She has a run in her stocking."
"In the sixth inning he scored a run."[2]

Clearly, "run" has a significant range of meanings, and some of the meanings contrast rather dramatically with one another. Normally such contrasts within a word's semantic range do not create problems in communication, since the context in which the word appears indicates which meaning a writer or speaker intends. However, when we forget the reality of semantic range and the importance of considering a word's context, we begin to make exegetical errors.

To impress on us the importance of this issue and the ease of going awry in exegesis, perhaps an illustration will help. I try to refrain from critical comments about fellow preachers. However, I believe correcting word study errors for the purpose of promoting biblically faithful preaching justifies this illustration, though it does not reflect well on the preacher. I heard the following statement in a sermon preached by a pastor whom I regard as an otherwise excellent Bible preacher. He was explaining the meaning of the Greek word *agape*, which is typically translated "love."

> [Agape is] self-giving love, not emotionally driven, but it is empowered by the Holy Spirit. . . . Agape love is a love of worth, or esteem, that which ascribes value to another person, that which prizes another person. It's used over three hundred times in the New Testament. . . . Agape love is not to be known only in a cognitive sense, but it is to be expressed.

This preacher described *agape* as if it has certain inherent qualities that are part of the word and will be present whenever that word is used. That's not the way words work, so his description does not hold up under examination. In the Septuagint translation of 2 Samuel 13:15, *agape*

---

2. I am not alone in using the word "run" to illustrate the concept of semantic range. I have seen it also used in Peter Cotterell and Max Turner, *Linguistics and Biblical Interpretation* (Downers Grove, IL: InterVarsity Press, 1989), 138; William D. Mounce, ed., *Mounce's Complete Expository Dictionary of Old and New Testament Words* (Grand Rapids: Zondervan, 2006), xiii; and Moisés Silva, *God, Language, and Scripture: Reading the Bible in the Light of General Linguistics* (Grand Rapids: Zondervan, 1990), 94.

occurs twice to refer to Amnon's illicit love for his half-sister Tamar that drove him to rape her. Such love was hardly "empowered by the Holy Spirit," or "that which prizes another person." In the Septuagint translation of Song of Songs, *agape* occurs in contexts in which it clearly refers to emotional, even sensual sentiment (Song 2:5; 2:7; 3:5; 5:8; 8:4), contradicting the pastor's claim that *agape* is "not emotionally driven." Moving to the New Testament, *agape* appears in 2 Timothy 4:10 to describe a man named Demas, about whom Paul wrote, "Demas, in love with this present world, has deserted me." Again, this use of *agape* does not connote "self-giving love" or prizing "another person." To the contrary, Demas' *agape* was for the sinful world and led him to abandon his Christian brother who needed him. This preacher made the mistake of selecting one connotation of a word (possibly the dominant connotation) and describing the word as if that one connotation is inherent in the word itself. If that is true, we should have that connotation in mind every time we see the word. But as we have seen, many words carry more than one connotation, so we have to consider the context in which a word appears before we draw a conclusion about the meaning of a word in a given context.

In doing exegesis, it may be helpful to think of word meanings this way: words don't have meanings, they have usages. Therefore, we always ask, What meaning did this author intend when he used this word in this sentence? We determine the meaning of a word by paying attention to the way a speaker or writer uses that word in a sentence and paragraph. In Lewis Carroll's *Through the Looking Glass*, Humpty Dumpty is discussing word meanings with Alice. Carroll wrote, "'When *I* use a word,' Humpty Dumpty said, in rather a scornful tone, 'it means just what I choose it to mean—neither more nor less.' 'The question is,' said Alice, 'whether you *can* make words mean so many different things.' 'The question is,' said Humpty Dumpty, 'which is to be master—that's all.'"[3] Humpty's approach to semantics is right on target. A word means just what the person using the word chooses it to mean. The word is not the master; the person who uses the word is the master of its meaning. When a word has a range of meaning, the exact meaning of the word

---

3. Lewis Carroll, *Alice's Adventures in Wonderland and Through the Looking Glass* (New York: Oxford University Press, 2009), 190.

in a given context is determined by the person who uses that word. And typically the speaker or writer signals the intended meaning by the way he or she uses the word in the sentence and paragraph.

Of course, there are limits to a word's semantic range and therefore limits to the ways we may use a word and still be understood. While *agape* may refer to things like selfless altruism, emotional sentiment, or carnal desire, it cannot refer to an olive tree, for example. Words function in a language as signs.[4] They serve to point to realities. When we hear someone say "apple," the idea or image of a round, red fruit comes to mind because the word "apple" is a sign for that reality. Words can function as signs for different things (an Apple computer), but not for *everything*. That would result in a language with no rules at all, and therefore no intelligible communication.

How does this work when interpreting a text in the Old Testament? Consider the Hebrew word *ra'ah* as it occurs in the book of Jonah. A standard Hebrew lexicon lists the English equivalents for *ra'ah*, as "evil, misery, distress."[5] "Evil" or "distress"? Quite a semantic distance separates those two meanings. When we encounter *ra'ah* in the Old Testament, obviously we will have to pay careful attention to the context to determine which meaning the writer intended. In the four chapters of Jonah, *ra'ah* appears eight times. In two occurrences the intended reference is clearly moral evil, since the Ninevites were repenting, or turning from their *ra'ah* (3:8, 10). Four times the word clearly refers to distress: the distress of the storm (1:7, 8), and the destruction God was prepared to bring on Nineveh (3:10; 4:2). Two occurrences of the word are ambiguous, perhaps intentionally so. First, God commanded Jonah to go to Nineveh and "call out against it, for their *ra'ah* has come up before me" (1:2).[6] Was God telling Jonah to preach against the Ninevites because of their evil? In light of what the book reveals later

---

4. Because of this, linguistics is considered a branch of semiotics. Semiotics is the study of a culture's signs, and the word "semiotics" is from the Greek word for "sign."

5. Francis Brown, S. R. Driver, and Charles A. Briggs, eds., *The Brown-Driver-Briggs Hebrew and English Lexicon* (1906; reprint, Peabody, MA: Hendrickson, 2006), 949.

6. The preposition translated "against" is another example of a word's possible semantic range. Typically, dictionaries provide English equivalents like "upon" or "over" to translate this preposition. But its semantic range includes ideas like "on account of" and, as is likely in Jonah 1:2, "against."

about Jonah, he might have been eager to obey a command to excoriate the Ninevites for their wickedness. On the other hand, Jonah might have been loath to preach to them about turning to the one true God so he could help them in their distress. The exact meaning is ambiguous, so perhaps we're meant to be left to contemplate the possible relationship between the Ninevites' wickedness and their distress, and how Jonah might have responded to each.

The use of *ra'ah* in Jonah 4:6 also seems ambiguous. In that verse, Jonah was in distress because of exposure to the heat of the sun, and he was in sin because of his hatred of the Ninevites, which he had just expressed. God caused a plant to grow "to save him from his *ra'ah*." Was God acting to rescue Jonah from his distress, or to rescue him from his sin? Since Jonah was in distress and in sin, it is difficult to determine which meaning of *ra'ah* is intended. Again, the reader is left to consider Jonah's situation of being in both distress and sin, and how the two might be related. What is clear, however, is that in considering the uses of *ra'ah* in Jonah, the context of each occurrence of the word is determinative for its meaning. That is true because words don't have meanings; they have usages.

More about the Controlling Influence of a Word's Context

The reality of semantic range can be frustrating to people who are learning a new language. Typically, language students learn an English word or two that serve as equivalents of the word in the new language. After learning such equivalents, students naturally assume them in their translation whenever they encounter the word in the source language. They are then vexed to learn that in some contexts the word means something entirely different.

Once when in Japan, an English teacher asked me a question related to this phenomenon. She was from New Zealand and she was teaching English to Japanese students. Her students wanted to speak English in the United States, but she was using a textbook written in the United Kingdom. She asked me, "What is a biscuit?" She knew what "biscuit" means in New Zealand, the textbook taught her students what a biscuit is in the United Kingdom, but biscuits usually are different in the United States. The same word has three different meanings. To determine the meaning of biscuit, one would have to ask, "Am I in New Zealand, the United States, or the United Kingdom?" Context even makes a difference in understanding what we are having for breakfast or for afternoon tea.

To repeat, words don't have meanings, they have usages. For example, the Hebrew word *raqia'* occurs nine times in the first chapter of Genesis. The Greek translators of the Septuagint, perhaps under the influence of Greek cosmological ideas current in the second century BC, translated *raqia'* with *stereoma*. The Greek term *stereoma* typically referred to something solid (like "rock" in Pss. 18:2 and 71:3). The Latin translators made a similar decision in using *firmamentum* to translate *raqia'*, which led to the translators of the King James Version rendering the word with "firmament." More recent scholars also conclude, on different grounds, that Genesis 1 presents a picture of a solid dome separating the waters above and the waters below. Gerhard von Rad describes the meaning of the word in Genesis 1 by calling it "a gigantic hemispherical and ponderous bell . . . a separating wall between the waters beneath and above."[7] Von Rad arrived at his description surely because the verbal form of *raqia'* referred to beating out or stamping metal.[8] Since the verb referred to hammering out metal, the noun in the context of Genesis 1 must be something like a sheet of metal and shaped like a bell since it was located above the curved surface of the earth. Such an understanding of the word is reflected in the New Revised Standard Version translation "dome." John Walton assumes the same meaning and concludes that the cosmology of other ancient Near Eastern cultures influenced the author of Genesis 1 to think of the sky as solid.[9]

Both ancient and modern translators have made the mistake of translating *raqia'* as something solid because the controlling factors in their

7. Gerhard von Rad, *Genesis: A Commentary*, rev. ed., The Old Testament Library (Philadelphia: Westminster, 1972), 53.

8. See Brown, Driver, and Briggs, *The Brown-Driver-Briggs Hebrew and English Lexicon*, 955–56.

9. For Walton, the meaning of *raqia'* as something solid serves as evidence that the conception of the sky in Genesis 1 is inaccurate when judged by the standards of modern science. Therefore, we should interpret the word in a functional sense (holding back the water), not in a material sense. John H. Walton, *The Lost World of Genesis One: Ancient Cosmology and the Origins Debate* (Downers Grove, IL: InterVarsity Press, 2009), 56–58.

translations were issues other than the way the author used the word in a specific context. For some, the controlling factor in their translation is the cosmological conception of other ancient cultures. Such a suggestion, without convincing linguistic evidence, should not be taken seriously. We determine a culture's cosmology and entire theology by looking at the literature of that culture, not by looking at the literature of other cultures. More to the point, we determine the meaning of a word by the way it is used in a specific context, not by considering the ideas of neighboring cultures about related topics.[10]

For others, the controlling factor determining their translation of *raqia'* is the meaning of the verb form of the word. However, the verb form of a root and its noun form do not always carry the same connotation, especially across various contexts. The assumption that they *do* carry the same connotation is what James Barr and others call "the root fallacy." Barr defines the root fallacy as the error that "the 'root meaning' can confidently be taken to be part of the actual semantic value of any word or form which can be assigned to an identifiable root." Barr goes on to state that "the 'meaning' of a 'root' is not necessarily part of the meaning of a derived form."[11] Therefore, we should not conclude that the noun form of a Hebrew root carries the same connotations as the verb, unless contextual evidence points in that direction. In the case of *raqia'* in Genesis 1, it does not.

How is *raqia'* actually used in Genesis 1? Its location is above the earth (vv. 6, 7) in the same area that is referred to as "the heavens" (v. 8). The *raqia'* is also where the sun, moon, and stars are located (vv. 14–17) and where the birds fly (v. 20). Furthermore, verse 8 states that God calls the *raqia'* "heaven," a word that translates the Hebrew word *shamayim*, which never refers to something solid. So if we prioritize the context in which *raqia'* appears, the meaning of the word in Genesis 1 is simply

---

10. Walton makes this mistake even though elsewhere he writes: "The meaning of a word is established by the usage made of it by speakers and writers," and "in Hebrew the interpreter cannot have confidence that the words that share a common root will also share a common meaning." John Walton, "Principles for Productive Word Study," in *A Guide to Old Testament Theology and Exegesis*, ed. Willem A. VanGemeren (Grand Rapids: Zondervan, 1999), 160–61.

11. James Barr, *The Semantics of Biblical Language* (Oxford: Oxford University Press, 1961), 100–102. See also Grant R. Osborne, *The Hermeneutical Spiral*, 66–69; and D. A. Carson, *Exegetical Fallacies*, 2nd ed. (Grand Rapids: Baker, 1996), 28.

"sky," and can be translated accurately with English words like "expanse." For that reason, more recent translations typically render *raqia'* with "expanse," a word that avoids the implication that *raqia'* refers to something solid. One Hebrew scholar who has considered all the factors and prioritizes the context writes that *raqia'* in Genesis 1 is a reference to "empty space," or "the open expanse of the heavens."[12]

Why then did the author of Genesis 1 refer to the "sky" with a noun whose verb form refers to hammering out a solid surface like metal? A likely answer is that *raqia'* calls attention to God's personal involvement in making the sky, forming it as a blacksmith forms a sheet of metal. However, we should not think of the sky as a sheet of tin, or a bell, any more than we should think of humans as clay pots because God formed us out of dust (2:7). Both references are poetic, anthropomorphic language referring to God's "hands-on" creative activity.

Some interpreters may argue against this line of thinking about *raqia'* on the grounds that understanding the word as a reference to the sky, not a solid object, is not documented outside of Genesis 1. Thus, it is a new way to use the word. But most authors delight in using words in new ways, with new twists of meaning, especially poets. New usages of words occur all the time, sometimes even unintentionally. English speakers, for example, have used the word "chip" for a long time. However, only a generation ago it had no association with computers. But at some point, in one pivotal conversation or advertisement or article, someone used the word in that way and before long dictionaries had to be edited.[13] In a similar way, after Moses used *raqia'* in Genesis 1, perhaps using it in a new way, when people heard that word they looked up and thought of the sky, not a solid object.

The exercise of considering how to translate *raqia'* in Genesis 1 should help us see that when we are studying an Old Testament passage, we determine the meaning of the words in that passage not by pasting dictionary definitions into our exegesis but by studying the way(s) words are used in all the contexts in which they appear. Such a procedure

---

12. J. Barton Payne, "*raqia'*" in *Theological Wordbook of the Old Testament,* 2 vols. (Chicago: Moody, 1980), 2: 2217–18.

13. Peter J. Leithart, *Deep Exegesis: The Mystery of Reading Scripture* (Waco, TX: Baylor University Press, 2009), 83.

does not exclude the use of dictionaries and lexicons, but we use them along with a careful consideration of each context of each word. Bible translation is not as simple as matching the same English word to the same Hebrew or Greek words. Knowing a word's semantic range is important but such knowledge is just a starting point. In seeking to explain how language conveys meaning, Moisés Silva writes, "What really matters is what happens when words are combined with each other in specific contexts."[14] Context has, as we have said, a controlling influence.

A Word's History: Fascinating but Almost Worthless

I have a book in my library titled *Why Do We Say It?* It's an interesting review of the origin of many English words and phrases. For example, around AD 1247 a group of nuns founded a convent in London and named it St. Mary of Bethlehem. Soon people began referring to it as Bethlehem. Many people pronounced it so quickly though, that the name sounded like Bedlam. Some three hundred years after the founding of the convent, the facilities became "a house of detention for the insane—and the wild raving of its inmates gave 'bedlam' its present meaning."[15] Of course, when people use the word "bedlam" today they do not think of a mental health hospital, still less of a convent, and they are unaware of the origin of that word.

The history of the word is fascinating, but it doesn't help in determining what people mean when they use the word today. Similarly, the fact that "good-bye" can be traced to the expression "God be with you" does not mean that people today are invoking that blessing when they say good-bye. The study of the history of words is called etymology. Many terms have an etymology in that linguists can trace their development over the centuries. However, studying what a word meant in the *past* rarely is important in determining what it means in the *present*.

The Hebrew language is not an exception to such development over time, at least in the precise meanings of its words. As Angel Saenz-Badillos writes, Hebrew has undergone "changes that have appreciably

---

14. Moisés Silva, *God, Language, and Scripture*, 91.
15. Frank Oppel, *Why Do We Say It? The Stories Behind the Words, Expressions, and Clichés We Use* (New York: Castle, 1985), 30.

affected its vocabulary but not, on the whole, its essential morphological, phonological, or even syntactic structure."[16] Linguists refer to the study of the meanings of a word as they develop over time as diachronic study. On the other hand, they refer to the study of a word's meaning in one particular time period as synchronic study. People who teach the Bible often find it hard to resist referring to the history of a word's meaning because the stories of development are often so interesting. However, etymology can also mislead us in our attempt to determine the precise meaning of a word in a specific context.

Some theological dictionaries provide information about the etymology of Hebrew terms. Such information should be used cautiously and with the awareness that the use of a word in its context determines its meaning, not its development through time. In New Testament studies, James Barr supplies an extended critique of the *Theological Dictionary of the New Testament* because of its etymologizing tendencies, and his warnings are worthy of consideration. He writes of Bible students who "feel that in some sense the 'original,' the 'etymological meaning,' should be a guide to the usage of words, that the words are used 'properly' when they coincide in sense with the sense of the earliest known form from which their derivation can be traced." Such an approach to word meanings, though, is a tacit denial of the fact that word meanings evolve, even change radically, over time. As Barr summarizes, "The past of a word is no infallible guide to its present meaning."[17] So again, in studying individual words in an Old Testament text, context remains king.

None of this is meant to deny the validity of studying a term's etymology. In fact, such study is sometimes necessary, since a word may have been used in one sense early in its history, say, in Exodus, and in another sense late in its history in a text like Nehemiah. If we are

---

16. Angel Saenz-Badillos, *A History of the Hebrew Language*, trans. John Elwolde (New York: Cambridge, 1993), p. 50. For an excellent example of such study applied to the Hebrew of the Old Testament, see the work of Mark F. Rooker in the book of Ezekiel. To my point, Rooker offers the summarizing statement, "The Hebrew language, as it is represented in the Hebrew Bible, was subject to linguistic change over the course of time." *Biblical Hebrew in Transition: The Language of the Book of Ezekiel* (Sheffield: Sheffield Academic Press, 1990), 1.

17. Barr, *The Semantics of Biblical Language*, 107.

teaching a text in Exodus, then, we will want access to etymological information not so we can tell the interesting story of the word's history, but so we will know the meaning of the word as it is used *in Exodus*.

Language and a Culture's Way of Thinking

One Sunday when I was preaching at a church away from my home town, I visited a Bible study class that met before worship. When I walked into the room, I noticed that it was decorated with some artwork and posters featuring Hebrew words. The teacher noted that he was pleased that a Hebrew professor was in his class since he had a keen interest in Hebrew, though he had never studied the language formally. He also spoke to me and expressed why he loved Hebrew so much. "Hebrew is such a vibrant language," he stressed. "It's more concrete and expressive." I offered a friendly smile, wishing I could say something in agreement, but I could only think of ways Hebrew, as a language system, is not as expressive as, for example, Greek.

All of us are guilty, at least occasionally, of having opinions that contradict the facts, since our knowledge is lacking on so many subjects. However, when a Bible teacher has an errant opinion about the Bible or its words, as in the case of this well-meaning teacher, it can potentially harm the church if it infects his or her teaching. Unfortunately, the idea is rather common that Hebrew is somehow unique in what it is able or unable to express. In other words, the language itself somehow affects, or restricts, the mentality of those who use it. D. A. Carson names this idea as one of his "exegetical fallacies." He writes, "The heart of this fallacy is the assumption that any language so constrains the thinking processes of the people who use it that they are forced into certain patterns of thought and shielded from others."[18]

Linguists refer to the idea of a language restricting thought as linguistic relativity, or the Sapir-Whorf hypothesis, named for Benjamin Whorf, who published his work in the 1930s, and his mentor Edward Sapir.[19] A brief definition of this hypothesis is impossible, but the basic

---

18. Carson, *Exegetical Fallacies*, 44.

19. For some of Whorf's seminal essays, see Benjamin Lee Whorf, *Language, Thought, and Reality: Selected Writings of Benjamin Lee Whorf*, ed. John B. Carroll, Stephen C. Levinson, and Penny Lee (Cambridge, MA: MIT, 2012).

idea is that the structures and vocabulary of language inhibit the mind in perceiving and describing the world as it is. Different languages inhibit thought in different ways. Thus it is natural to encounter different modes of thought in different cultures since they use different languages.

In extreme forms, this idea has become linguistic determinism—a culture's language determines the way(s) the people of that culture think. That idea has been disproven in multiple ways. Contemporary linguists are more likely to acknowledge that language may *affect* the way we think, but it will not *determine* the way we think. It is also true, conversely, that a culture's way of thinking affects the development of its language and that worldview and language develop together. Perhaps it is inevitable that a culture's ideas and language parallel one another. Each culture has dominant worldview notions and the language instantiates a culture's ideas. To the degree, then, that a culture's ideas are unique, the vocabulary will also be unique. However, that fact does not mean the culture's ideas cannot be translated into another language and understood by people of other cultures.

The argument that certain ways of thinking are unique to certain languages is ultimately self-defeating. Whorf, for example, was able to describe the unique features of the Hopi language *in English*. In other words, the same concepts were communicated in another language, proving that speakers of both languages were able to communicate the ideas that were allegedly unique to the Hopi Indians.

To return to the field of biblical studies, the theological ideas of the Old Testament were understood and adopted by the authors of the New Testament, and they communicated those ideas by means of another language: Greek. New Testament authors were mostly Semitic and steeped in Hebrew thought and language. Yet they were able to communicate truth in an understandable way in the Greek language. Old Testament theology endured the transfer from one language to another, and continues to do so as the Bible's truths about God are communicated around the world in multiple languages through Bible translation and missionary advance.[20]

---

20. I am indebted to my colleague Chip Hardy for his help in thinking through and expressing issues related to linguistics.

Yet linking language and mentality persists in some circles of biblical studies. Consider the following statement, made by otherwise excellent Christian thinkers: "The Hebrew thought in pictures, and consequently his nouns are concrete and vivid. There is no such thing as neuter gender, for the Semitic everything is alive."[21] Does this mean that languages having a neuter gender are somehow less "alive"? The Greek word for "child," for example, is in the neuter gender. Is the Greek idea of child, then, somehow less "concrete and vivid" than the idea of child conveyed by the Hebrew word for child that occurs customarily in either the masculine or feminine gender? Of course not, because grammatical gender does not necessarily express physical gender, and grammatical conventions of languages do not prevent the people who use those languages from thinking in terms of physical gender.[22] In other words, people who use Greek are capable of thinking in terms of the physical gender of children even when they use a neuter word to refer to children.

James Barr provides a similar discussion about the time references of Hebrew verbs. Hebrew verbs are not in past, present, and future tenses, as strange as that seems at first to many English speakers. Barr points out that on the basis of that grammatical fact, some writers have attempted to advance the idea that the Hebrews somehow thought differently about time. Barr proves that this is not the case.[23] The peculiar forms of languages generally do not determine the way the people who use those languages think.

All of this is not to say that different cultures did not have distinctive ideas or ways of thinking. It is not difficult, for example, to find significant differences between Greek philosophy and the theology of

---

21. Norman L. Geisler and William E. Nix, *A General Introduction to the Bible* (Chicago: Moody, 1968), 219.

22. Examples of this in Hebrew are abundant. The word for "woman" (*'ishah*) has the common feminine ending, as we would expect, but the plural "women" (*n'ashim*) has a masculine plural ending. Similarly, the plural form for "fathers" (*'avoth*) has a feminine plural ending. Obviously such forms are merely irregular grammatical constructions and say nothing about the way the Hebrews thought about gender.

23. For example, he writes, "In the vast majority of cases the Hebrews were perfectly aware whether events referred to, whether as completed or as incompleted action, had already taken place . . . or would later take place; and were able to communicate accordingly." Barr, *The Semantics of Biblical Language*, 80.

the Jews, not to mention the manifest differences between the Greek pantheon and the God of Israel. The point here is that such differences should not be linked to their respective languages, as if the vocabulary and grammar available to them somehow constricted their thinking. Since the subject of this chapter is word studies, we should stress that individual words and their forms do not restrict a culture's thinking.

Selecting Words for Special Study

At the beginning of this chapter we stated that time constraints will usually prevent expositors from doing an extensive study of every word in a passage. Also, inevitably some words in a text will call for greater attention than others. Therefore, the first issue we will face in doing word studies is deciding which words we will select to study more carefully. What will guide our choice so we can study and teach the words that are most crucial in determining the meaning and application of a passage in the Old Testament? Consider five guidelines.

First, look for repeated words. Repetition of a term often signals that the author of a text is emphasizing the theme communicated by that term. Sometimes the repeated term even indicates the central theme of the entire passage. For example, in the second chapter of Ezekiel, various derivatives of the Hebrew word *marad*, or "rebel," appear seven times in God's six-verse message to his prophet. Clearly God was emphasizing to Ezekiel the theme of rebellion. When expositors give further attention to that repeated term they will learn that the verb form of *marad* is used in the Old Testament to refer to rebellion against either God or man. When it refers to rebellion against man, it typically refers more specifically to rebellion against a king, usually a foreign king. During the lifetime of Ezekiel, God had told his people not to rebel against the Babylonian king. However, they were disobeying God and rebelling. Therefore, their rebellion against Babylon was also rebellion against God, and vice versa, and perhaps that double entendre is intended to amplify the force of the message in Ezekiel 2.

When expositors look for repetition in a passage, they should sometimes consider synonyms to a main term as repetition. While synonyms are not repetitions of the same word, they likely repeat the same idea. In the first chapter of Exodus, for example, multiple terms emphasize the tremendous population growth of the Hebrews in Egypt. In verses

7–20 derivatives of the Hebrew term for "multiply" (*ravah*) occur five times. It seems clear that the author is emphasizing the multiplication of the sons of Israel. But that multiplication is further emphasized by synonyms for multiply, such as the terms translated "were fruitful," "increased greatly," and the land "was filled" with them.

Second, look for theological words. We identify a theological word by asking whether it may communicate something about God, his character, his works, or the way he relates to us. The fourth chapter of 1 Samuel records that the Philistines defeated the Israelites in battle and stole the ark of the covenant. When Eli heard the news, he fell over and died. When Eli's daughter-in-law heard the news, she went into labor. "She named the child 'Ichabod,' saying, 'The glory has departed from Israel!'" (v. 21). Expositors who teach 1 Samuel 4 will want to make sure they know what is meant by "glory." That term is important for at least three reasons. First, it must be connected to the name "Ichabod" somehow. Second, any reader of the story wants to know what exactly departed from Israel. Third, Bible readers know that glory is often connected with God in both testaments.

We do the best word studies when we consult the Hebrew word behind the English. However, if we use a concordance we can study the way the English word is used throughout the Old Testament. Using an English concordance, I once reviewed the uses of "glory" in the Bible and wrote the following while making a pastoral point in a church newsletter:

> In the Bible, sometimes the word "glory" is used as a synonym for greatness (Ps. 106:20; 1 Chron. 22:5), a synonym for praise (Luke 17:18; Rev. 4:9), or a synonym for heaven (Ps. 73:24). But primarily glory refers to the expressed, or manifest, greatness of God. When Jesus was born, the angels said, "Glory to God in the highest!" because God's greatness was being manifested in Jesus' birth. In Exodus, the glory of God is repeatedly associated with manifestations of his greatness and power. God called Israel "My glory" (Isa. 42:13), because he intended his people to be expressions of his greatness, holiness, and love. His glory is also to be manifested in the New Testament church and in individual Christians. Paul wrote to Christians, "Christ in you, the

hope of glory" (Col. 1:27). In other words, the hope that God's character and greatness will be manifested in our generation is for Christians to be filled with Christ. Christ in us is the hope of glory. That is our desire. Lord, may your holiness, greatness, power, righteousness, justice, love, and grace be manifested in this generation, and do it through us! Or, as Paul prayed, "to him be glory in the church" (Eph. 3:21).

Notice that my definition is brief, but my references to Scripture are longer. People do not remember definitions we cite from a dictionary, so why bother reading them to people? They are more likely to remember passages of Scripture that contain the word when we recite and explain the passages. In the case of "glory," that word is used in several different ways in the Bible. Since words have usages, not meanings, it is more important and more helpful to cite the way the word is used than to read a definition from a dictionary. I wrote, "Primarily 'glory' refers to the expressed, or manifest, greatness of God." That definition did not arise from a dictionary or lexicon. Instead, I looked at most of the uses of "glory" in the Bible, and my definition was an attempt to express the basic idea of the word as it occurs in the Bible. We should remember that when we define a word by citing uses of it in the Bible, we are quoting the way God uses the word. To the people we teach, citing God's use of a word is more important, more interesting, and more memorable than quoting a definition from a dictionary.

Third, look for words that are central to the main point of the passage. In the next chapter we will consider the importance of identifying the main point(s) of the passage of Scripture we are teaching or preaching. Sometimes one or two words express the essence of that idea. The theology of the passage hinges on those few words and without them the theological idea would be absent. When preaching through Leviticus, I encountered the word "atonement" in the first chapter. The subject of Leviticus 1 is the whole burnt offering, and verse 4 says the purpose of the burnt offering was "to make atonement." Obviously, then, "atonement" is an important word in Leviticus 1, and reading the remainder of Leviticus indicates that it is important throughout the book. Therefore, I knew that when I preached through Leviticus I had to define atonement rather carefully and completely or my people would not grasp a key theological idea in the book. In this case, looking at the English word was not sufficient. I read the word in the Hebrew text, made notes about the way the word is used in Leviticus and elsewhere, and read explanations of the word in commentaries on Leviticus and in Hebrew dictionaries. I arrived at the following definition:

> Verse 4 says the purpose of the burnt offering was "to make atonement." Atonement is a central theme in Leviticus. The root word translated "atone" or "atonement" occurs fifty-three times in Leviticus, and only forty-three times elsewhere in all the Old Testament. Thus, Leviticus says more about atonement than any other book in the Old Testament. . . . The English word "atonement" is formed by a combination of three words: at-one-ment. "Atonement" refers to reconciliation, two parties coming together, becoming "at one" with each other. The Hebrew word translated "atonement" refers to the beginning of that process. It denotes doing what is necessary for two parties to be reconciled. In the case of our relationship with God, it refers to the taking away of sin. God is perfectly holy. . . . Therefore, for sinners to be in the presence of God their sin must be removed, and that is the purpose of atonement. . . .
>
> After considering cognates and biblical usage, a few commentators recommend the meaning "wipe" or "purge" when referring to inanimate objects (Lev. 8:15). An atonement ritual cleansed a holy object of impurities resulting from human sin. When referring to a person, "atone" has the meaning "make a ransom payment for sin" (Lev. 17:11). The life of the sacrificial animal was given in place of the life of the worshiper and was the ransom payment for the death the worshiper's sin had earned.[24]
>
> God formalized, or symbolized, atonement for sin in the sacrificial system. In order for sin to be removed, God's righteous

---

24. See Mark L. Rooker, *Leviticus*, The New American Commentary, vol. 3a (Nashville: Broadman & Holman, 2000), 51–52; Gordon J. Wenham, *The Book of Leviticus*, The New International Commentary on the Old Testament (Grand Rapids: Eerdmans, 1979), 28.

wrath has to be satisfied; death must be the result of sin. The sacrificial system was the means of that death—the animal died because of the worshiper's sin, God's wrath was satisfied, and the worshiper could be reconciled to God. That was the reason the worshiper brought the burnt offering to God. Verse 4 says that he brought the animal "to make atonement for him." There was nothing magical about the animal or the process of killing and burning the animal. What mattered was God's command to atone for sin in that way and the worshiper's intent to obey God and to be reconciled to him by the removal of sin. It was a spiritual act; the sacrifice was physical, but its intent was spiritual. If the worshiper did not present the offering by faith, looking to the invisible God to forgive, then the visible act would mean nothing.[25]

The above definition is too lengthy and too academic sounding for many teaching contexts, so some teachers would edit or further explain it before talking to their people about the word (my definition in my sermon was shorter!). But note three key elements of the definition. First, it is based on the way the word is used in the Old Testament, and only secondarily refers to other books. Second, I attempted to explain the word with the English "at-one-ment" to make the definition easier to follow and more likely to "stick" with the hearers. Third, the definition included context-related explanation and illustration by describing the sacrificial system and its meaning. The word "atonement" deserves significant attention because of its importance to the central idea of Leviticus 1 and to the remainder of Leviticus. Many passages have such words, so faithful expositors will take the time to study and explain them so their people will understand them.

Fourth, look for words that are translated differently in the various English translations. Often when we teach or preach some of the people listening to us and following us in their Bibles are using different translations than the one we are reading. Our preparation to teach should include checking all the popular translations so we will know what

---

25. See Allan Moseley, *Exalting Jesus in Leviticus*, Christ-Centered Exposition Commentary (Nashville: Broadman & Holman, 2015), 13–14.

our people will be reading. Reading numerous translations at the same time is simple when we use a Bible software program like BibleWorks, Logos, Accordance, or a similar program. We can create an array that displays numerous translations of a verse on one page. When the English translations of a word differ from one another, that signals that the word may be difficult and/or may need explanation. At the least, it may be helpful to point out that the version we are using is different from the one others may be reading.

In Psalm 8:1, the majority of modern translations render the first line as "O LORD, our LORD, how majestic is your name" (ESV, NASB, NIV). The New King James Version, however, has, "O LORD, our LORD, how excellent is Your name." Why the difference between "majestic" and "excellent," and is the difference significant? In this case, the difference results only from the translators' choice to use different words to express the same idea. However, those two different words may evoke different ideas in the minds of the people we teach. Plus, the Hebrew word translated "majestic" or "excellent" is interesting, and an expositor could talk about the way the word is used in the Old Testament and elsewhere as a way of helping people comprehend and contemplate God's greatness.

Fifth, look for words that seem unusual in the context. If a word in the passage you are teaching raises a question in your mind, it will probably also raise a question in the minds of the people you teach. When I was preaching a series of sermons from Proverbs, I planned to refer to Proverbs 17:22. It says, "A joyful heart is good medicine."

We are accustomed to medicines in the modern world; hundreds of pharmaceutical products are available to us. However, Solomon wrote the book of Proverbs in the tenth century BC when people knew nothing about bacteria, antibiotics, or even cells. What did he mean when he wrote that joy is a "medicine"? Whatever he meant, it must have been something other than what we think of as medicine. When I looked up the Hebrew word, I learned that the verbal root refers to a healing or cure, something that sets us free from bodily affliction. So to return to Proverbs 17:22, "A joyful heart is a good healing, a cure." God said that a joyful heart frees us from that which threatens our health.

A Word Study Process to Follow

When I was a boy my father taught me to mow the lawn. The tool was the lawnmower and he began his instruction by teaching me how to start the mower. First, he showed me how to check the oil. "Don't try to start the mower without checking the oil," he said, and then he told me that running the engine without oil would ruin the engine. Next, he showed me how to add oil to the engine, how to fill the tank with gas, and how to start the engine. He taught me to follow the same process every time I mowed the lawn.

People who perform tasks more important than mowing the lawn also follow a process. Surgeons follow certain preparatory procedures and use careful techniques, and skipping steps in their process threatens the lives of their patients. This book provides a study process to follow so we can exegete Old Testament texts faithfully and accurately. More specifically, we need a process to follow when we study words to ensure that we reach accurate conclusions and teach God's Word faithfully. I suggest that we develop six habits as part of a word study routine once we have selected a word we plan to study further.

First, identify the Hebrew word. Why is knowing the Hebrew word important? If we use only an English concordance to read all the contexts where a word appears, we may look at verses where different Hebrew words are used but translators rendered the Hebrew words with the same English word. Since the Old Testament was written in Hebrew, we cannot be confident we are defining our word correctly if we look only at English definitions and usages.

When we are reading the text in Hebrew, identifying the Hebrew word is already part of our study, and expositors who read Hebrew will own and use a Hebrew lexicon and a Hebrew concordance. However, it is possible for English readers to learn something about the Hebrew words too. Several resources help Bible students identify and study Hebrew terms. When using *Strong's Exhaustive Concordance of the Bible,* the English words are numbered, and looking up the number in the back of the concordance leads to the Hebrew or Greek word that stands behind the English.[26] The definitions for the Hebrew and Greek words

---

26. James Strong, *The Exhaustive Concordance of the Bible* (Peabody, MA: Hendrickson, n.d.).

in *Strong's* are limited but often helpful. For Bible students who have not studied Hebrew, probably the best use of this concordance is the ability to look up every occurrence of English words, with the added benefit of learning whether the same Hebrew word is used in each case.

Another resource that helps English Bible students identify the Hebrew word is *Mounce's Complete Expository Dictionary of Old and New Testament Words*.[27] Word definitions in Mounce's dictionary are more extensive than Strong's concordance, and the words are also numbered according to Strong's system and according to another concordance by Goodrick and Kohlenberger.[28] When expositors select an English word to study, they can use one of the concordances to see all the uses of the English word, and they can use Mounce's dictionary to learn more about the Hebrew word. We should add the caveat that expositors who have not studied Hebrew formally run a risk of misinterpreting information about the Hebrew language and vocabulary. Such expositors should adjust their expectations from word study downward, and should pay careful attention to what experts have written about the word under consideration.

Free word study resources are also available online. Expositors can use the site blueletterbible.org as a dictionary and concordance in several translations. Like using the concordances mentioned above and Mounce's dictionary, students of the English Bible can use that website and discover the Hebrew word and look at uses and definitions of that word. Other sites like biblestudytools.com, biblegateway.com, and bibletools.org provide similar resources.

Perhaps the quickest and simplest way to study words in the Old Testament is to use Bible study software programs like BibleWorks and Logos. By placing a cursor over a word and clicking in the right place, expositors can access information from numerous resources. Readers of the English Bible can click on an English word and multiple English and Hebrew dictionaries and concordances are available immediately. Every week I use BibleWorks to look at the passage I am studying. Typically I arrange the display so that I can read each verse in Hebrew,

---

27. William D. Mounce, ed., *Mounce's Complete Expository Dictionary of Old and New Testament Words* (Grand Rapids: Zondervan, 2006).

28. Edward W. Goodrick and John R. Kohlenberger III, *The NIV Exhaustive Concordance* (Grand Rapids: Zondervan, 1990).

eight English translations (many more are available), and the Septuagint. With a few clicks I can be studying the word in a few Hebrew lexicons, and I can find every occurrence of both the Hebrew and English words. Users of other software programs like Logos can access the same information, and some of those programs provide access to many commentaries that users can import into their study. In Logos, the commentaries are word-searchable too, so users can study the way a selected word is used in the Bible and in the commentaries.

A second habit in our word study routine is to identify the grammatical form of the word and consider how the form may affect its contextual meaning. If the word is a noun, is it singular or plural? Does it have a suffix, and if so what kind of suffix? What function does it perform in the sentence—subject, direct object, object of a preposition? If the word is a verb, does it refer to action in the past, present, or future? Does the form of the verb indicate active or passive action? Is the action of the verb simple, intensive, causative, or reflexive? Is it singular or plural? Typically, the form of the Hebrew verb will provide answers to all such questions. For example, Psalm 96:1–3 is as follows:

> Oh sing to the LORD a new song
> sing to the LORD, all the earth!
> Sing to the LORD, bless his name;
> tell of his salvation from day to day.
> Declare his glory among the nations,
> his marvelous works among all the peoples!

Those three verses contain six verbs, and all of them are imperatives. Therefore, these verses constitute a compelling, sixfold command to express praise to God. English verbs have no special form that indicates whether an imperative is directed to a singular individual or to a plurality of persons. However, Hebrew imperatives can be singular or plural, and all the imperative verbs in the above verses are plural, so these commands are addressed to a congregation, or all God's people. The plural form of the verb will affect our application, for on the basis of these verses we will not exhort people to give praise to God in their personal "quiet times" with God; we exhort them to gather with God's people and express praise to him together in corporate worship. Unless we pay attention to the form of the words, our explanation and application of a text will not match what the text says.

A third habit is to explore the word's semantic range. By the time expositors reach this point, it's likely they will have already done the important work of discovering the word's semantic range—that is, reading the way the word is used in the Bible and reading dictionary entries about the word. We will probably be able to teach the text more effectively if we take brief notes as we read the various passages in which the word appears. It's likely that a few passages of Scripture will stand out to us as especially helpful to our people as we think about how to make a word meaning clear to them. We should note those passages and jot down any thoughts we have about communicating the information we are discovering. Also, checking the various English translations will help our exploration of a word's semantic range. If the translators render the Hebrew word with different terms or phrases, that likely indicates some breadth in the range of the Hebrew word. It is important to read all the verses where the word appears *before* reading definitions in dictionaries, so our impressions of the meaning of the word will be formed first and foremost by the way the word is used in the Bible. If we read the dictionary definitions first, they may prejudice our reading of the texts. Of course, the definitions have been written by competent Old Testament scholars, but the goal of our study is to be able to express the meaning of the word in our own words, not merely to recite what someone else has written.

Fourth, we look up the definitions of the word in a few dictionaries. We have already mentioned dictionaries as part of the first step. Still, this task deserves to be mentioned separately, especially since we want to stress that it follows our reading of all the Old Testament contexts in which the term appears. Four multi-volume dictionaries that provide a significant amount of information are the *Theological Wordbook of the Old Testament*,[29] the *New International Dictionary of Old Testament Theology and Exegesis*,[30] the *Theological Dictionary of the Old Testament*,[31] and the

29. R. Laird Harris, Gleason L. Archer, Jr., and Bruce K. Waltke, eds., *Theological Wordbook of the Old Testament*, 2 vols. (Chicago: Moody, 1980).

30. Willem A. VanGemeren, ed., *New International Dictionary of Old Testament Theology and Exegesis*, 5 vols. (Grand Rapids: Zondervan, 2012).

31. G. Johannes Botterweck, Heinz-Josef Fabry, and Helmer Ringgren, eds., 15 vols. (Grand Rapids: Eerdmans, 1974–2015).

Theological Lexicon of the Old Testament.[32] Bible dictionaries that use the words in the English Bible are also helpful, like the *Zondervan Illustrated Bible Dictionary*[33] or the *Holman Illustrated Bible Dictionary.*[34] If the term is significant theologically it may also be listed in a theological dictionary, like the *Evangelical Dictionary of Theology*[35] or the *Kregel Dictionary of the Bible and Theology.*[36]

Our fifth habit is to return to the text and consider the context in which the word occurs. In determining the meaning of a word, context is crucial. In the Old Testament, repetition is a means of emphasis. When a word occurs three times, it is raised to the superlative degree (e.g., Isa. 6:3). So context is not just crucial; context is crucial, crucial, crucial. The most important context is the verse in which the word occurs. How is the word used in its sentence? The second most important context is the paragraph in which the word occurs. The word we are studying fits into the message of the paragraph and contributes to it somehow. A word's meaning, then, is always contextual. The context that is third in importance is the Old Testament book. For example, Isaiah may use the word "day" as in the phrase "in that day" differently than Amos. Isaiah also seems to have a specialized meaning for "servant." Therefore, we will need to study the way the author we are reading uses the term. Next in importance is the context of genre. What does "wisdom" mean in the wisdom literature, in contrast to the way that word may be used in other parts of the Old Testament? Finally, we consider how the word is used throughout the Old Testament. The theological depth of words like "fear" and "lovingkindness"/"mercy" probably can be appreciated only after looking at the way such words are used throughout the Old Testament.

---

32. Ernst Jenni and Claus Westermann, *Theological Lexicon of the Old Testament*, 3 vols., trans. Mark E. Biddle (Peabody, MA: Hendrickson, 1997).

33. J. D. Douglas and Merrill C. Tenney, eds., *Zondervan Illustrated Bible Dictionary*, rev. ed., ed. Moisés Silva (Grand Rapids: Zondervan, 2011).

34. Chad Brand and Eric Mitchell, eds., *Holman Illustrated Bible Dictionary* (Nashville: Holman, 2015).

35. Walter A. Elwell, ed., *Evangelical Theological Dictionary*, 2nd ed. (Grand Rapids: Baker, 2001).

36. Henry W. Holloman, ed., *Kregel Dictionary of the Bible and Theology* (Grand Rapids: Kregel, 2005).

Sixth, it may be necessary or helpful to consider relevant cognate terms. A cognate term is a word in another ancient Near Eastern language that is related to the Hebrew word we are studying. If the word we are studying occurs in the Old Testament several times, consideration of cognate terms is of little or no importance because we can determine the meaning of the Hebrew word by studying the way it is used in the Old Testament. However, 1,300 Hebrew words occur in the Old Testament only once (commonly they are referred to as *hapax legomena*), and 500 words occur only twice. Often, the context in which such words occur make their meaning clear. Sometimes, however, that is not the case, so it helps to know how a related word was used in a sister language.

Imagine that out of all the books existing in the twentieth and twenty-first centuries, only a handful of books written in English survive, and in those books the English word "legume" occurs only once. A few thousand years from now, scholars could have difficulty determining the precise meaning of "legume," though from its context they could probably surmise that it referred to some kind of plant or food. Imagine also that out of the handful of books in French that survive the twentieth and twenty-first centuries, the French word "légume" occurs many times, enough to conclude with certainty that "légume" refers to a vegetable. Since French is a cognate language for English, scholars living a few millennia from now could use that information to establish a more specific meaning for the English "legume": it refers to a vegetable.

Contemporary scholars use a similar procedure to determine the meaning of Hebrew words that occur only once in the Old Testament. And since most of us do not read Ugaritic, Akkadian, Aramaic, and other ancient Near Eastern languages, we will need to rely on such scholars to help us with information about cognate terms. An example is the plant mentioned in Jonah 4:6. God appointed a plant to provide shade for Jonah. The Hebrew word refers to a specific kind of plant. What kind of plant? The King James Version has "gourd." Was the plant a gourd? The only place in the Old Testament this Hebrew word occurs is in reference to this incident in Jonah's life (4:6 [2x], 7, 9, 10). An Aramaic cognate term referred to a garden plant, usually taken to be the castor oil plant. Also, an ancient Greek writer identified a plant in Egypt as a castor oil plant, and the name of that plant was also a cognate of the term in Jonah.[37] So evidence from cognate terms helps us reach a higher level of confidence about the identity of the plant in Jonah. The castor oil plant also fits the context, since it has large leaves that provide the kind of shade described in Jonah 4.

It may be helpful to conclude this chapter with a reminder that the meaning of a word is not an inherent idea attached to the sound or symbol of that word. Instead, the sounds and symbols for what we call a "word" take on meaning only as people use that word in communication. To learn the meaning of a word, then, we study the ways people use it. For people who believe that God inspired the words in the Bible, the way a word is used in the Bible is especially important since that usage is the way God used the word, and the way God uses a word is of vital importance. What we believe about God, humanity, the universe, and how to be reconciled to God all depend on understanding the meaning of his words.

---

37. Brown, Driver, and Briggs, *The Brown-Driver-Briggs Hebrew and English Lexicon*, 884.

C h a p t e r   6

WHAT IS THE BIG IDEA?

8-STEP METHOD

STEP 1	Translating the text
STEP 2	Considering text criticism
STEP 3	Interpreting the genre
STEP 4	Exploring the context
STEP 5	Defining important words
STEP 6	**Identifying the big idea**
STEP 7	Connecting to Jesus
STEP 8	Applying the text to contemporary people

In the last chapter we focused on the fifth step in our process of exposition: identifying and defining important words in an Old Testament text. Studying the words of a text is an essential task. If we do not understand the meaning of each word in a sentence, we do not understand the sentence. Furthermore, the meaning of some sentences is impacted, or even determined, by the meaning of one word in that sentence. However, Bible study is more than word study. Words are part of sentences and meaning is conveyed in sentences, not just words. As James Barr puts it, "It is in sentences that the real theological thinking is done."[1] One might

---

1. James Barr, *The Semantics of Biblical Language* (Oxford: Oxford University Press, 1961), 234.

even legitimately ask whether it may be a misnomer to call a dictionary a *theological* dictionary. Once we begin to interpret the theology of a document, in this case the Old Testament, we move beyond considering the meaning of individual words, which is the function of a dictionary.

Theological ideas are conveyed by means of sentences, not just words. We may define "majestic" and its Hebrew equivalent accurately, but we have not said anything meaningful until we include "majestic" in a sentence like, "O LORD, our LORD, how majestic is your name in all the earth! / You have set your glory above the heavens" (Ps. 8:1; cf. v. 9). Authors combine words to ask questions, issue commands, prophesy the future, and make statements of fact. The theology of a text is expressed in the theology of such sentences, not merely in the theology of the words, if words can even be said to have a theology. Therefore, when we complete the task of studying important words, we should not consider the task of exposition finished. We take the next step of determining the main ideas of the text we are studying. But since we believe that God has inspired both the words and the ideas of the text, let us turn to him first and pray.

Pray

In *Preaching with Spiritual Vigour*, Murray Capill surveys the ministry of Richard Baxter and applies what he discovers to those who aspire to preach God's Word today. Baxter, an English Puritan in the seventeenth century, made much of the spiritual preparation of the preacher, and so does Capill. Consider, for example, the following exhortation by Capill:

> In the context of earnest prayer, our concern will not merely be to come to a right analysis of the text, but to a profound understanding of the spiritual issues in a text. We need to interact not only with the historical, grammatical and literary contexts of a text, but the spiritual concerns of it. . . . This prayerful, meditative reflection on the text ought to take priority in our preparation for preaching. If we *begin* our preparation with technical concerns (the original languages, grammar, etc.), it is quite likely we will *end* with a largely technical discourse. If, however, our preparation is borne in the context of prolonged

thought, meditation, and prayer, we are much more likely to deal, throughout our study of the passage, with the spiritual heart of the text.[2]

This chapter addresses the essential work of identifying the main theme(s) of a text in preparation to teach that text. In the process of discovering those themes, we dare not neglect what Capill calls "the spiritual heart of the text." Beyond the main theme or theological center of a text, we also give attention to the way the text confronts our own sin, the way the text challenges us to grow in holiness, and the way God uses the text to form us into the image of Jesus. If we expect our teaching to effect change in the lives of our hearers, we first allow God to use the text to change us.

Capill declares that finding "the spiritual heart" of a text begins with "earnest prayer," "prayerful, meditative reflection," and "prolonged thought, meditation, and prayer." All of us who teach God's Word should take his exhortation to heart. However, we have to reckon with the fact that our culture, even our church culture, does not encourage "prayerful, meditative reflection." Electronic devices clamor for our attention. While we are using computer resources to study the biblical text, our computer alerts us to the arrival of new emails and news feeds. We are not prayerful and meditative, we are distracted. And where is the time for "prolonged thought, meditation, and prayer" when our days are filled with so many other activities? Even most Christians have no idea of the enormous amount of time that is necessary to prepare the heart and mind of the Bible teacher to feed the sheep. Many hearers seem to think that their pastor or teacher picked up all the knowledge necessary to teach the Bible sometime in the past, such as during seminary years. They would be surprised to learn that the content of teaching is the result of many hours of weekly study, and the godly disposition of the teacher is the product of multiple hours in earnest prayer each week. So, since we live in an environment that competes with prayer, and since we serve people who are unaware of the great necessity of prayer for those who teach, we who teach the Bible will need

---

2. Murray A. Capill, *Preaching with Spiritual Vigour: Including Lessons from the Life and Practice of Richard Baxter* (Fearn, Scotland: Christian Focus, 2003), 193.

to strengthen our resolve to keep our appointment with God in prayer. Without it, we will never teach God's Word as we ought.

What Do We Mean by "Big Idea"?

In the last chapter, we cited Psalm 96:1–3 and called attention to the imperative verbs that exhort readers to praise the Lord. Consider those verses again.

> Oh sing to the LORD a new song;
>   sing to the LORD, all the earth!
> Sing to the LORD, bless his name;
>   tell of his salvation from day to day.
> Declare his glory among the nations,
>   his marvelous works among all the peoples!

Who can read that passage of Scripture and fail to conclude that the main idea is the imperative to express praise to God in song? Those verses also include subordinate, or supplementary, ideas. For example, the psalmist is exhorting *the entire creation* to praise God ("all the earth"), he is calling people to praise God's *name*, to praise God *daily* ("from day to day"), and to praise God *as a witness* of his greatness to people who don't know God ("among the nations" and "among all the peoples").

With the notable exception of chapters 10–31 in Proverbs, most paragraphs in the Old Testament include one primary idea and other supplementary ideas. Authors of books on exposition refer to the main idea with various nomenclature, such as the "central proposition of the text,"[3] the "main idea of the text,"[4] the "big idea,"[5] or the "essence of the text."[6] Sidney Greidanus calls the main idea the "theme." He

---

3. Ramesh Richard, *Preparing Expository Sermons: A Seven-Step Method for Biblical Preaching* (Grand Rapids: Baker, 2001), 65-70.

4. Daniel L. Akin, William J. Curtis, and Stephen Rummage, *Engaging Exposition: A 3-D Approach to Preaching* (Nashville: Broadman & Holman, 2011), 34, 38–39.

5. Keith Willhite, "A Bullet versus Buckshot: What Makes the Big Idea Work?" in *The Big Idea of Biblical Preaching: Connecting the Bible to People*, ed. Keith Willhite and Scott M. Gibson (Grand Rapids: Baker, 1998), 13–19.

6. Harold T. Bryson and James C. Taylor, *Building Sermons to Meet People's Needs* (Nashville: Broadman, 1980), 54.

defines the theme as "the central message, the unifying thought, the major idea, the point of the text. . . . A theme, we can say, is a summary statement of the unifying thought of the text . . . the dominant idea that encompasses all others . . . the text's primary affirmation."[7]

Faithful exposition of Old Testament texts will include discovering and stating the main theme of the text. Also, we will discover and state the supplementary ideas, which are also important. Haddon Robinson refers to the big idea and supplementary ideas as the subject and the complement. He writes, "We do not understand a passage until we can state its subject and complement exactly." Therefore, as we read a passage in the Old Testament, the questions we ask are, "What precisely is the author talking about?" and "What is the author saying about what he is talking about?"[8] The answer to the first question is the main idea. The answers to the second question are the supplementary ideas.

One of the most important tasks in the preparation to teach or preach from the Old Testament is to ensure that our main point is the main point of the text and our supplementary points are the supplementary points of the text. First, we determine the subject of the text, then we make the subject of our message the same as the text. Following that order is the only way we will be assured that our message will be expository, truly based on what the biblical text says. If we determine our subject and then select a text that mentions that subject, our method is not expository. The subject of our message arises from our study of the text. Only after we determine the main theme of the passage of Scripture can we know the main theme of our message, since the latter arises from the former.

Some teachers of expository preaching stress that a message from a biblical text should include only one big idea. As Donald Miller puts it, "Ideally, any single sermon should have just one major idea. . . . Two or three or four points which are not parts of one great idea do not make a sermon—they are two or three or four sermons all preached on one occasion."[9] If we are writing a technical commentary on a passage

---

7. Sidney Greidanus, *The Modern Preacher and the Ancient Text: Interpreting and Preaching Biblical Literature* (Grand Rapids: Eerdmans, 1988), 131, 134.

8. Haddon W. Robinson, *Biblical Preaching: The Development and Delivery of Expository Messages*, 3rd ed. (Grand Rapids: Baker, 2014), 23.

9. Donald G. Miller, *The Way to Biblical Preaching* (Nashville: Abingdon, 1957), 53.

in the Old Testament, we have the freedom and the responsibility to explore every possible idea raised by the text and discuss the meaning and implications of each idea. However, when we are addressing hearers in a Bible study or sermon, the situation demands that we find the primary proposition of the text and emphasize it until we are sure that our hearers understand it. To teach that proposition, we also use the supplementary data that are in the biblical text, that is, the secondary ideas that support the main idea.

One Sunday a little boy's mom was not feeling well so she stayed home from church. When the boy and his dad returned from worship, the mom asked her son, "What was the preacher's sermon about?" The little boy replied, "He never said." Unfortunately more than a few sermon listeners have had that experience, and some of them have it frequently. They listen to a lesson from the Bible, and the preacher makes some excellent statements, but what is the big take-away? They don't know. A sermon should have a big idea that no one can miss. The same is true for a Bible lesson in contexts other than preaching. We could compare a lesson's big idea to a flashing red light on a highway. It's a clear, compelling message. A better analogy is a roadblock—we are required to stop, lower our car window, and show our license to an officer of the law before he allows us to proceed. The main point of a sermon or lesson should command that much attention. If it does not, it is unlikely that listeners will remember it. We also work to make sure our main point matches the main point of the text; if it doesn't, it's not worth remembering.

David Buttrick raises a legitimate question about finding a theme, or main proposition for each text. Can a rational, propositional method of interpreting and teaching a text do justice to biblical language that is so often poetic or narrative? Isn't something lost in the process of converting a poem or story into a list of theological propositions? As Buttrick expresses it, "What has been ignored? The composition of the 'picture,' the narrative structure, the movement of the story, the whole question of what in fact the *passage* may want to preach."[10] But Buttrick answers the question as he asks it. If in

---

10. David G. Buttrick, "Interpretation and Preaching," *Interpretation*, 35, no. 1 (1981): 49.

fact the passage wants to preach something, the teacher's job is to discover that and preach it so that the teacher is making the same point as the text.

Ellen Davis raises Buttrick's question through quoting an essay by novelist Flannery O'Connor:

> People have a habit of saying, "What is the theme of your story?" and they expect you to give them a statement: "The theme of my story is the economic pressure of the machine on the middle class"—or some such absurdity. And when they've got a statement like that, they go off happy and feel it is no longer necessary to read the story. Some people have the notion that you read the story and then climb out of it into the meaning, but for the fiction writer himself the whole story is the meaning, because it is an experience, not an abstraction.[11]

O'Connor helps us appreciate the novel as an art form and the experience of reading it as an end in itself. But is it appropriate to apply the same kind of literary analysis to both novels and biblical stories? The stories in the Old Testament are not fiction, and the fact that they are non-fiction has enormous implications for our approach to interpretation. We do not read non-fiction and interpret it as fiction. Such an effort would be like looking at a black object and asking, "How should I go about describing a white object?"

The stories in the Old Testament are literature but they are not *mere* literature. They describe the real acts of God in space and time. They would not be placed in the entertainment section of a newspaper but in the news section. Second, the stories are news but they are always news with a point. God inspired the authors of the Bible's narratives to write stories that reveal something about him. That revelatory goal is fundamentally different than the goals of authors who write fiction. Third, we hope the result of our exposition of an Old Testament text will be

---

11. Flannery O'Connor, "The Nature and Aim of Fiction," in *Mystery and Manners*, ed. Sally Fitzgerald and Robert Fitzgerald (New York: Farrar, Straus & Giroux, 1969), 73, quoted in Ellen F. Davis, *Wondrous Depth: Preaching the Old Testament* (Louisville: Westminster John Knox, 2005), 9.

"an experience," but it will not be an experience without theological content.

For example, texts that either assume or argue for monotheism are ubiquitous in the Old Testament. So whatever we may experience as we read such texts, it will not be the experience of receiving permission to worship other gods. To the contrary, our experience will have something to do with being challenged to worship the one true God in all his glorious, mysterious attributes. Why else would orthodox Yahwists throughout the Old Testament rail against the worship of false gods?

Something is at stake here beyond mere experience, and that something is the truth upon which our experience is based. O'Connor's restriction to two choices—"experience" or "abstraction"—is reductionist. Mere experience and mere abstraction are both inadequate consequences of reading the Bible. When we read an Old Testament narrative, we encounter a moving account of events that actually happened. When we read a poem, proverb, or prophecy, the artistic form delights our senses, but something more happens. The text instructs our minds, stirs our hearts, challenges our choices, and as God's word it even transforms our souls. Something happens beyond our appreciation of the art of a poem, our enjoyment of a good story, or our delight in a "word fitly spoken" of a proverb (Prov. 25:11). Is the Old Testament literature? Yes, and we do not understand it fully if we do not adequately consider its literary qualities, but the Bible is more. It is a repository of truth. The goal of exposition is to discover the main truth and supplementary truths of each text and teach those truths.

A Commitment and a Lifestyle

Finding the big ideas is not automatic, nor is the ability to do so. Identifying what is central or most significant in a text is an acquired skill, and most people have not acquired it. Furthermore, most people will not acquire it with their current lifestyle. In *Why Johnny Can't Preach*, David Gordon maintains that most pastors do not preach well because they have not learned to read texts well and Western culture generally does not encourage the ability to do so. He calls attention to the distinction between reading for information and reading texts. He summarizes,

Culturally, then, we are no longer careful, close readers of texts, sacred or secular. We scan for information, but we do not appreciate literary craftsmanship. Exposition is therefore virtually a lost art. We don't really read texts to enter the world of the author and perceive reality through his vantage point; we read texts to see how they confirm what we already believe about reality.[12]

For a long time Western culture has been heading away from the textual and toward the technological. We are constantly bombarded with media images on our phones, our computers, and our televisions. Our brains are conditioned to process images and headlines that come to us almost simultaneously from multiple sources. We are *not* conditioned to contemplate the meaning of an ancient text, ruminating on its contents until insights begin to dawn on us. It's not that Western culture is not dealing with weighty philosophical and ethical issues. We face such issues, but people don't stop to think about them much. Virtually daily an event somewhere in the world calls for a decision based on right and wrong, life and death, but when we read about the event in the media or hear about it in the news, commentators offer only a citation of someone's zinger, a quote from someone's poster in a picket line, or a blog of extemporaneous thoughts. The underlying philosophical issues are not explored; we rarely hear someone offer a sustained argument for one position or another.

How does the sensory nature and vacuity of the secular media relate to our exposition of the Old Testament? The issue is the way we gather and evaluate information, and even the way our minds work. The droning media train us to think in sound bites, not to reflect on underlying principles, assess their relative importance, and apply them judiciously to issues at hand. Yet this latter way of thinking is precisely what is needed to read a text, identify its main ideas, and weigh which idea is central and which ideas are supplementary. Such skills are simply not being developed by most people in contemporary Western culture. Bible expositors, however, *must* develop the skill of reading a biblical

---

12. T. David Gordon, *Why Johnny Can't Preach: The Media Have Shaped the Messengers* (Phillipsburg, NJ: P&R, 2009), 49.

text and thinking about its theology. What is at stake is representing or misrepresenting God's communication to humanity.

All of this means that Old Testament expositors will need to make a commitment. Exposition is a process that requires extended time, solitude, and separation from the sights and sounds of the visual media. If preachers and teachers aspire to excellence in exposition, they will commit the time and the effort. Also, identifying the main and supplementary ideas takes practice. Our commitment will be tested week after week, so to become skilled at exposition we will keep our commitment every week.

Of course, the media provide us with an alternative. Instead of studying a passage using a process like the one described in this book—meditating on the grammar, genre, and words of a text; contemplating what it says about God, the gospel, and the human condition; identifying the primary ideas; praying it into our souls; struggling with its application; and living its truths—we can use the media to skip that effort and access a study another teacher has already provided. Such an approach was publicly recommended in an editorial in *Christianity Today*:

> We in the church still suffer from the romantic illusion (a result of the European Enlightenment and American rugged individualism) that the sermon is the creative, prophetic effort of the lonely individual who wrestles with the text in a closed study and emerges with a revelation from God. This is silly. . . . If a pastor reads a dynamite sermon that fits a congregation's needs, we see no reason not to say, "I found this wonderful sermon by Max Lucado that I thought you should hear. Let me preach it to you as best I can."[13]

That is not the approach commended in this book. I am not arguing that Bible teachers should refuse to access technology or that they should not learn from the sermons or Bible studies of other teachers. The point I am attempting to make is that if we use the media to take shortcuts in our thinking we compromise our growth in the ability to read and interpret the Old Testament well. Each week we either step

---

13. "When Pastors Plagiarize," *Christianity Today* (Dec. 9, 2002), 29.

forward or back in becoming the kind of person who can meditate on God's Word to find its truth so we can teach it accurately. I am recommending that we make a commitment and follow a lifestyle. If we do so, we will establish a habit and that habit will become a trajectory of life. The trajectory of careful exposition will lead us to become a different kind of person than who we would become if we limited ourselves to consumption of media images and reading for information. The habit of careful exposition will also be challenged every week. The way we respond to those challenges will determine whether we advance or retreat in our gradual growth as expositors.

Following a Process

This book is about a process that involves eight steps. In this sixth step of identifying and outlining the big ideas, habitually using a process will help. Consider regularly practicing the disciplines that are described below.

First, jot down ideas as you read the text. Some expositors use a separate blank page for each verse they are studying. So they write on the top of a blank page "verse 1," and the number of pages they use is the same as the number of verses they are studying. The exception to the page-per-verse technique is a study of a narrative, in which case it is doubtful that a page will be necessary for every verse. Personally, regardless of the number of verses I am studying I use only one blank sheet of paper, though sometimes the back of that page and a second page are required. As I read the text, I write down all the ideas that come to me: grammatical data, relevant translation issues, textual variants, theological ideas, application ideas, parallel passages of Scripture, questions I need to answer, ideas and questions about the meaning of words, and even life-related stories that may illustrate the ideas in the text.

All our discussions about exposition in this book will come to bear here, so we will spend most of our time in this stage. We will translate the passage from Hebrew, defining words and noting grammar and syntax in the process. We will find any relevant textual variants, and we will define the genre and determine its relevance. We will research the historical and literary context, and we will study words that appear essential to understanding the meaning of the passage. As we do all that work, we will be asking about the big idea: "What is the main point in this passage of Scripture?"

In the process of making notes, it's likely that most expositors will choose to use a computer or tablet rather than paper. Regardless of the tool, expositors can practice the same discipline. One benefit of using a computer in this stage of study is that the notes page(s) eventually can become the manuscript for the sermon or Bible study. Ideas typed as notes can be converted into sentences in the final document.

As an example, consider Malachi 1:6–14. For this exercise, read the text in English without doing further background research. As you read the text, write all the ideas that come to mind.

> [6] "A son honors his father, and a servant his master. If then I am a father, where is my honor? And if I am a master, where is my fear? says the LORD of hosts to you, O priests, who despise my name. But you say, 'How have we despised your name?' [7] By offering polluted food upon my altar. But you say, 'How have we polluted you?' By saying that the Lord's table may be despised. [8] When you offer blind animals in sacrifice, is that not evil? And when you offer those that are lame or sick, is that not evil? Present that to your governor; will he accept you or show you favor? says the LORD of hosts. [9] And now entreat the favor of God, that he may be gracious to us. With such a gift from your hand, will he show favor to any of you? says the LORD of hosts. [10] Oh that there were one among you who would shut the doors, that you might not kindle fire on my altar in vain! I have no pleasure in you, says the LORD of hosts, and I will not accept an offering from your hand. [11] For from the rising of the sun to its setting my name will be great among the nations, and in every place incense will be offered to my name, and a pure offering. For my name will be great among the nations, says the LORD of hosts. [12] But you profane it when you say that the Lord's table is polluted, and its fruit, that is, its food may be despised. [13] But you say, 'What a weariness this is,' and you snort at it, says the LORD of hosts. You bring what has been taken by violence or is lame or sick, and this you bring as your offering! Shall I accept that from your hand? says the

Lord. [14] Cursed be the cheat who has a male in his flock, and vows it, and yet sacrifices to the Lord what is blemished. For I am a great King, says the LORD of hosts, and my name will be feared among the nations."

First, we cannot miss the fact that this passage is in the form of a dialogue, whether real or rhetorical. In verse 6, God addresses priests specifically, so the conversation is between God and the priests who lived during Malachi's lifetime. It's clear that God was displeased with the way the priests were worshiping, since they were offering substandard sacrifices. However, people who are not priests are also complicit in the substandard worship, since they were bringing the unworthy sacrifices to the priests. We make a note here to look up God's commands in the law concerning what constituted an acceptable sacrifice to him.

In verses 6–8 we see three analogies for God's relationship with his people: father and son, master and servant, and governor and citizen. God uses all three analogies to impress on the people the fact that their worship was unacceptable. We also note the repetition of "despised"— four times in verses 6, 7, and 12. We jot down a question about the meaning of that word: Could it really mean "hate," which is what we normally mean when we use that word? Surely they didn't have feelings of hatred for God (v. 6), the place of worship (v. 7), and the sacrifices (v. 12).

We are already reaching the conclusion that this passage is primarily negative. So far, God has accused them of the sins of offering substandard sacrifices and even despising God, the place of worship, and the sacrifices. We can add to that list their failure to give God the honor he deserves (v. 6), and boredom with worship, since they called it "weariness" (v. 13). This passage also includes God's response to their worship. Most of the passage is in the form of confrontation: God named their worship sins. Also, God flatly stated that he would not accept their worship, and because their worship was a sham he would not show favor to them (vv. 9–10). He even shockingly exhorted them to shut the doors of the temple, presumably putting an end to their worship altogether.

We also make a note that in this passage about wrong worship God interrupts his confrontation of his people to state that people all over the world *will* worship him (vv. 11, 14). The international nature of this worship is emphasized by the threefold repetition of "among the nations" (vv. 11, 14), and by the phrase "in every place" (v. 11). The context of this prophecy about God's greatness inspiring worldwide worship sets four truths in bold relief. First, God is truly great, whether his people see it or not. Second, God is *so* great that he is worthy of the worship of all peoples, not just the Jewish people. Third, God sees a time in the future when people outside Judaism will offer him worthy worship. Fourth, people who only observe meaningless rituals will miss participation in the glorious praise offered to God by people all over the world.

A second discipline in the process of identifying the big ideas is to look over your notes and read the passage again, asking the question, "What is the main idea here?" In the first step, we wrote down thoughts as they occurred to us, in no particular order or priority. Next, we want to ask which thought stands out as the big idea, the central theme of the entire passage. We are looking for the main idea, and "the main idea of the text is the single unit of thought that binds together and gives meaning to all the particulars of a text."[14] As we look through all the thoughts we recorded about Malachi 1:6–14, one idea keeps surfacing: worship! When we study some passages, we will want to check several commentaries to make sure we are not off the mark in our thinking about the main theme. But in the case of Malachi 1:6–14, the big idea is virtually impossible to miss.

Consider also Jeremiah 42:1–43:7, a passage that will require more time and effort to determine the main idea. Though this passage is set in a prophetic book, its genre is narrative. Read the passage, taking note of all the issues that occur to you, but especially asking our question about the main idea.

> [42:1] Then all the commanders of the forces, and Johanan the son of Kareah and Jezaniah the son of Hoshaiah, and all the people from the least to the greatest, came near [2] and said to Jeremiah the prophet, "Let our plea for mercy come before you, and pray to the LORD your God for us, for all this remnant—because we are left with but a few, as your eyes see us—[3] that the

---

14. Daniel L. Akin, in Akin, Curtis, and Rummage, *Engaging Exposition*, 130.

LORD your God may show us the way we should go, and the thing that we should do." [4] Jeremiah the prophet said to them, "I have heard you. Behold, I will pray to the LORD your God according to your request, and whatever the LORD answers you I will tell you. I will keep nothing back from you." [5] Then they said to Jeremiah, "May the LORD be a true and faithful witness against us if we do not act according to all the word with which the LORD your God sends you to us. [6] Whether it is good or bad, we will obey the voice of the LORD our God to whom we are sending you, that it may be well with us when we obey the voice of the Lord our God."

[7] At the end of ten days the word of the LORD came to Jeremiah. [8] Then he summoned Johanan the son of Kareah and all the commanders of the forces who were with him, and all the people from the least to the greatest, [9] and said to them, "Thus says the LORD, the God of Israel, to whom you sent me to present your plea for mercy before him: [10] If you will remain in this land, then I will build you up and not pull you down; I will plant you, and not pluck you up; for I relent of the disaster that I did to you. [11] Do not fear the king of Babylon, of whom you are afraid. Do not fear him, declares the LORD, for I am with you, to save you and to deliver you from his hand. [12] I will grant you mercy, that he may have mercy on you and let you remain in your own land.[13] But if you say, 'We will not remain in this land,' disobeying the voice of the LORD your God [14] and saying, 'No, we will go to the land of Egypt, where we shall not see war or hear the sound of the trumpet or be hungry for bread, and we will dwell there,'[15] then hear the word of the LORD, O remnant of Judah. Thus says the LORD of hosts, the God of Israel: If you set your faces to enter Egypt and go to live there, [16] then the sword that you fear shall overtake you there in the land of Egypt, and the famine of which you are afraid shall follow close after you to Egypt, and there you shall die. [17] All the men who set their faces to go to Egypt to live there shall die by the sword, by famine, and by pestilence. They shall have no remnant or survivor from the disaster that I will bring upon them.

[18] "For thus says the LORD of hosts, the God of Israel: As my anger and my wrath were poured out on the inhabitants of Jerusalem, so my wrath will be poured out on you when you go to Egypt. You shall become an execration, a horror, a curse, and a taunt. You shall see this place no more. [19] The Lord has said to you, O remnant of Judah, 'Do not go to Egypt.' Know for a certainty that I have warned you this day [20] that you have gone astray at the cost of your lives. For you sent me to the LORD your God, saying, 'Pray for us to the LORD our God, and whatever the LORD our God says declare to us and we will do it.' [21] And I have this day declared it to you, but you have not obeyed the voice of the LORD your God in anything that he sent me to tell you. [22] Now therefore know for a certainty that you shall die by the sword, by famine, and by pestilence in the place where you desire to go to live."

[43:1] When Jeremiah finished speaking to all the people all these words of the LORD their God, with which the LORD their God had sent him to them, [2] Azariah the son of Hoshaiah and Johanan the son of Kareah and all the insolent men said to Jeremiah, "You are telling a lie. The LORD our God did not send you to say, 'Do not go to Egypt to live there,' [3] but Baruch the son of Neriah has set you against us, to deliver us into the hand of the Chaldeans, that they may kill us or take us into exile in Babylon." [4] So Johanan the son of Kareah and all the commanders of the forces and all the people did not obey the voice of the LORD, to remain in the land of Judah. [5] But Johanan the son of Kareah and all the commanders of the forces took all the remnant of Judah who had returned to live in the land of Judah from all the nations to which they had been driven—

[6] the men, the women, the children, the princesses, and every person whom Nebuzaradan the captain of the guard had left with Gedaliah the son of Ahikam, son of Shaphan; also Jeremiah the prophet and Baruch the son of Neriah. [7] And they came into the land of Egypt, for they did not obey the voice of the Lord. And they arrived at Tahpanhes.

To address the question, What is the main idea of this passage? the following answers could be offered as possible central themes:

A. The actions of Judeans after the destruction of Judah by Babylon
B. Biographical information about the period of Jeremiah's life after the destruction of Judah by Babylon
C. The relationship of post-destruction Judeans to the prophet Jeremiah
D. How to distinguish false prophecy from true prophecy
E. Believing a true word from God and rejecting ideas that contrast with his word
F. Discovering and following God's will

Answers A and B are too general and would leave us asking *which* actions of the post-destruction Judeans or *what* biographical facts about Jeremiah are addressed in the passage? More importantly, answers A and B give us no information about God and his ways with people, and the consistent witness of the church and scholarship has been that the prophetic book of Jeremiah does not exist merely for the purpose of conveying historical or biographical information. Surely a message about God and his ways is present in this text. Answer C is more specific, but not specific enough, and it does not relate the passage to God. Further, it shows little promise for contemporary application, since Jeremiah is no longer living. At first glance, answer D seems possible, since Jeremiah gave the people God's word that came to him and the people claimed Jeremiah's prophetic word was false. However, the book of Jeremiah firmly establishes Jeremiah as a true prophet in contrast with the false prophets of the day and in contrast with the general populace (Jer. 14:10–18; 23:1–40; 29:8). Therefore, when we read chapter 42 in the context of the entire book, we conclude that Jeremiah 42 does not contain ambiguity about who is the real prophet delivering a true word from God. Answer E identifies an issue that is present in Jeremiah 42. The people of Judah should have believed Jeremiah's prophetic word, but they did not. However, the theme of the chapter is more broad, not only about belief and unbelief but about obedience and disobedience. Answer F seems to encompass the primary thrust of the passage. The people who approached Jeremiah ostensibly wanted to know God's will in the matter of whether to go to Egypt or not. Jeremiah told them what God revealed to him regarding his will, they rejected what God said through Jeremiah, and God announced his judgment for their disobedience to his revealed will.

In the effort to identify the big idea of a passage, a third discipline is to write one sentence that expresses the main idea of the text. We never use only a word, phrase, or clause to state the main idea of a text. Therefore, "worship" will not suffice as a statement of the main idea of Malachi 1:6–14, and none of the clauses listed (answers A-F) qualify as a final statement of the main idea of Jeremiah 42. A word does not make a statement, and a clause is not extensive or specific enough. Our statement of the main idea of a passage should state the central subject and what the passage says about the subject. Ramesh Richard writes of the importance of identifying and stating the main idea of the text, and he argues that the central proposition of a text "is *always* in the form of a full grammatical sentence. If it is less than a sentence, it is not a proposition."[15]

Worship is the main theme of our passage in Malachi, but we also ask what the text states about the main theme. In the case of Malachi 1:6–14, God confronted the Jewish people of Malachi's day with their inadequate worship, so the main idea of the text is negative, not positive. The subject of the passage is wrong worship, not right worship.

Having defined the big idea of the passage generally, our goal is to state the big idea in one declarative sentence. Taking into consideration all the notes we made regarding Malachi 1, our efforts to express the big idea of this passage in one sentence could yield a statement like, "God does not accept worship that disobeys his word and dishonors his greatness." Notice that the subject of the sentence is God. It would also be possible to express the main idea of the text in a sentence with people as the subject. A sentence like, "Our worship is wrong when we are not obedient to God's word and when we dishonor God's greatness" still expresses the main idea of the passage. Perhaps the primary benefit of the latter sentence is that it builds application into the central proposition. It is already oriented toward our response to the truth of the passage since it has to do with "our" worship and what "we" do.

---

15. Richard, *Preparing Expository Sermons*, 67.

As for Jeremiah 42:1–43:7, we stated that the big idea is discovering and following God's will. Now we ask further what this passage asserts about that big idea. The Judeans were at a crossroad in their lives, essentially asking what they were going to do and where they were going to live in their post-destruction lives. They asked Jeremiah what God wanted them to do. We want to ask why they did not ask God for themselves instead of asking an intermediary, but the text does not answer that question. When they asked Jeremiah, he did not give a hasty answer. He waited ten days until he knew he had the "word of the Lord" (42:7). When he gave that word to the people, however, it was not what they wanted to hear. Instead of submitting to God's command, they accused Jeremiah of lying and even of collusion with the Babylonians. God said through Jeremiah, "Do not go to Egypt" (42:19), but "they came into the land of Egypt" (43:7). In an ironic twist, they even took Jeremiah with them, perhaps hoping he would be a magic talisman and protect them from the judgment God had announced on them through Jeremiah. Obviously, the Judeans asked for God's will but didn't follow it.

Our one sentence statement of the big idea of this story could be, "When considering a new stage of life, God reveals his will and we follow his will." Again, if we wanted to make people the subject of the sentence instead of God, the sentence could be, "When considering a new stage of life, we seek and follow God's will." In our exposition we would have to address the means of God's revelation at some point. In the case of the Judeans, God revealed his will through an authoritative prophet, but most people would view such a means today as exceptional, not normative. Still we have a sentence that expresses the primary subject of the passage, and we can expand on it by exploring and stating further what the text says about that subject.

Notice three facts about our big idea sentences. First, the verbs are in the present tense. Some teachers of preaching recommend that expositors first write a sentence with past tense verbs to do justice to the historical nature of the exposition. In the case of Malachi, such a sentence would be, "God did not accept the worship of his people because they were disobeying his Word and dishonoring his greatness." Certainly such a sentence ties the exposition to its biblical/historical context. However, I recommend referring to Malachi and his context throughout the exposition, but writing our big idea sentence in the present tense to build contemporary application into the heart of the exposition from the first.

Second, the verbs in our big idea sentences are active, not passive, and not forms of the verb "to be." "Worship is unacceptable when it is disobedient and does not honor God's greatness" uses a form of the verb "to be" twice, and therefore it is a weaker and less precise sentence and it removes God from the action.

Third, in our big idea sentence for Jeremiah 42, we used first person plural pronouns. If our only goal was to describe the historical circumstances of the text, we would use past tense verbs and third person pronouns. So the big idea sentence for Jeremiah 42 would be, "When the Judeans were considering a new stage of life after the destruction of Jerusalem, God revealed his will but they did not follow his will." However, our goal is not to provide a history lesson about "them," but to apply the Word of God to "us," the people we teach and ourselves.

A fourth discipline to cultivate related to identifying the big ideas of our passage is to return to the text and your notes and ask, "What does this Scripture say about the main point?" The result of answering that question should be an outline that mirrors the contents of the passage we are teaching or preaching. The big idea of our passage in Malachi is worship, and our big idea sentence is "God does not accept worship that disobeys his word and dishonors his greatness." Both the big idea and the big idea sentence arose from the contents of Malachi 1:6–14. Now we ask, "What more does that passage of Scripture state about the big idea?" Here we will refer to all the notes we recorded in the first step of discovering the big idea, and we will re-read the text and allow the inspired sentences to answer our question.

Returning to the first chapter of Malachi, we have noted that God's message in the passage is negative in that God was expressing his disapproval of the Judeans' worship. God's first observation about their worship was that they were not showing him honor. In the language of the text, they were despising his name (vv. 6–7). Second, they were bringing substandard sacrifices to be offered on the altar (vv. 7–9, 13–14). Third, God declared that their worship was unacceptable but that his name is great (vv. 10–11). Fourth, the people stated that worship was boring ("weariness"), and God reiterated his greatness (vv. 13–14).

When I preached through the book of Malachi, the ideas about wrong worship in Malachi 1:6–14 yielded the following outline:

1. Our worship is wrong when it is unworthy of the name of God (vv. 6–8, 11, 14).
2. Our worship is wrong when we're unwilling to sacrifice for God (vv. 8, 14).
3. Our worship is wrong when it is unwelcome to the people of God (v. 13).
4. When our worship is wrong, it is unacceptable in the sight of God (vv. 10–11).

The outline above could be stronger if we replaced some of the uses of "is" with action verbs. For example, the first two points could be stated, "We worship wrong when we don't honor God's name" and "We worship wrong when we don't sacrifice anything for God."

We expressed the big idea of Jeremiah 42:1–43:7 with this sentence: "When considering a new stage of life, God reveals his will and we follow his will." Now we ask, what does the passage say about that big idea? When I preached from these verses, I stated that in this passage God gives a negative model of following his will and a positive model. The Judeans who came to Jeremiah to ask his counsel serve as a negative model. Jeremiah serves as a positive model. I wrote the following outline to summarize the main ideas about seeking and following God's will in Jeremiah 42:1–43:7. Some explanatory remarks are included to indicate the textual basis for each statement.

1. The model of the Judeans teaches us to reject wrong motivations. (42:11 mentions their fear.)
2. The model of the Judeans teaches us to reject rebellion. (42:20 says they had "gone astray," or deceived themselves, and in the end they did the opposite of what God told them to do.)
3. The model of the Judeans teaches us to reject religious pretention. (In 41:17; 42:3, 5–6; 44:15–18 they claimed they wanted to follow God's will, but they were also practicing idolatry and already preparing to go to Egypt.)
4. The model of Jeremiah teaches us that following God's will can

involve adversity. (Jeremiah followed God's will, but the book records that authorities arrested and beat him.)

5. The model of Jeremiah teaches us that following God's will can lead people from rejection to respect. (The Judeans had persecuted Jeremiah, but when they wanted to know God's will they came to him for guidance.)

6. The model of Jeremiah teaches us that following God's will can lead people from unbelief to belief. (In 40:1–3 the captain of the Babylonian army confessed that Yahweh had caused the destruction of Judah because Yahweh's people sinned against him. The mention of moving from unbelief to belief also opens the door to call people to believe in the gospel.)

Note the active verbs in the present tense in each statement. We are summarizing the contents of the text, but simultaneously making application. A sentence like "the Judeans' request for God's will seemed sincere, but it was not" states a fact, but it also sounds like a history lesson. Why not use the primary statements in our outline to show our hearers that the passage of Scripture relates to their lives in some way? Building application into the big idea statements of the sermon or Bible study will help hearers remain engaged as we explain the details of the text.

The imperative in our efforts to outline a text is ensuring that every statement in the outline arises from a clear truth in the text. Some expositors will first choose to state each main idea in the text (and therefore in the outline), then show hearers what the text says about that main idea. Other expositors will prefer to explain what the text says first, then state the main idea as they begin to apply the text. Either way, if we are practicing exposition that is faithful to the Bible, our big idea statements will match affirmations in the biblical text. And the life of a faithful expositor includes devotion to the exciting task of meditating on a new text every week to discover, organize, and communicate its truth to people who need that truth.

Chapter 7

WHAT IS THE CONNECTION TO JESUS?

8-STEP METHOD

STEP 1	Translating the text
STEP 2	Considering text criticism
STEP 3	Interpreting the genre
STEP 4	Exploring the context
STEP 5	Defining important words
STEP 6	Identifying the big idea
STEP 7	**Connecting to Jesus**
STEP 8	Applying the text to contemporary people

"Where is Jesus?" My mother did not intend for that question to rebuke me, but it did. I was in the seminary apartment where my wife and I lived and my parents were visiting. I had recently purchased a multi-volume theological dictionary and was showing it (off) to my mom, who is a devoted Christian. As I pointed out some of the sentences in German, Hebrew, and Greek, her expressions seemed to shift between perplexed and vacant. I read a few lines here and there, and when I saw the word "Jesus" in Greek I said matter of factly, "And there's Jesus." Instantly my mother's interest roused and her eyes transfixed on the page. "Where is Jesus?" she asked eagerly. I felt a surge of embarrassment that I attempted to conceal. I realized that my mother was excited about Jesus, not the academic study of texts, and at that moment my excitement was in the other direction. I felt a stinging rebuke, not from my mom but from my own conscience and from God. In that moment (and in countless moments since then) I have had to ask myself my mom's question: "In all the study you are doing, where is Jesus?" All teachers and preachers of the Bible should ask themselves something like that: "In my exposition, what is my goal? Am I pursuing the accumulation and dissemination of information, or am I pointing people to Jesus?" It's an important question, maybe our most important question.

At several points we have mentioned the importance of moving from Old Testament texts to Jesus and his gospel. At this point we will devote our full attention to that important subject. Every sermon or Bible study from the Old Testament should include leading hearers to Jesus. Without mentioning Jesus we can provide information about the Old Testament text and its context. We can talk about God and even the way he saved people before Jesus. But if we do not speak about Jesus we will not show people today how they can be reconciled to God and find new and eternal life. In Dennis Johnson's *Him We Proclaim* he writes, "The Christian preacher must never preach an Old Testament text . . . in such a way that his sermon could have been acceptable in a synagogue whose members do not recognize that Jesus is the Messiah."[1]

To understand the meaning of an ancient document like the Old Testament, anyone, whether Christian or not, will translate the text accurately, identify and interpret the genre properly, explore the contribution of the context to the text's meaning, define any terms that are particularly important or unusual, and identify the main ideas in the passage. However, when Christians teach Old Testament texts, they will also point their hearers to Jesus. One of the fundamental beliefs of Christians is that the Old Testament is not complete without the New Testament. The old covenant leads to and is fulfilled by the new covenant, and the new covenant is about Jesus. If we do not refer to Jesus in our exposition of Old Testament texts, we risk giving the impression that the old covenant is adequate or that we are adequate without Jesus.

---

1. Dennis Johnson, *Him We Proclaim: Preaching Christ from All the Scriptures* (Phillipsburg, NJ: P&R, 2007), 51.

A sermon that is not Christ-centered may arise from godly impulses in the preacher, such as the desire to speak against the rampant evils of our time. However, if the sermon does not point to the Savior who can give new life, then we have only described the problem without giving a solution. Even worse, such a sermon implies that the solution is that we improve our behavior on our own, which is the antithesis of the gospel.

If such a statement sounds shocking, I can sympathize. I remember when I first encountered the idea that every sermon should include the gospel and that we should not preach "do better" sermons. I thought, "What's wrong with preaching to people to do better? Isn't moral exhortation legitimate? If Christian preachers don't challenge people to stop committing sin, who will do it?" I was missing the point. Certainly it is legitimate to exhort people to obey God. When we preach, for example, on the eighth commandment—"You shall not steal"—we should feel free to say, "Don't steal! Stealing is sin!" But we cannot stop with that exhortation. If we do, we leave our hearers with no hope other than their own best efforts and that is not the gospel. In fact, it is a gospel of works, which is contrary to the gospel of grace (Gal. 2:15–20). If we want to lead people to access God's grace and power, we will point them to Jesus, "whom God made our wisdom and our righteousness and sanctification and redemption" (1 Cor. 1:30).

Pointing people to Jesus in every exposition does not necessarily mean that every part of the exposition will be about him. To the contrary, the exposition is about the contents of the Old Testament text we are teaching. Also, as we stated above, we can feel free to include parenesis, or moral admonition. When Paul referred to the Israelites' idolatry, sexual immorality, and grumbling in the wilderness, he proceeded to exhort the Christians in Corinth not to commit idolatry, not to commit sexual immorality, and not to grumble like the Israelites did (1 Cor. 10:5–11). When James referred to Elijah, his purpose was to exhort Christians to pray like Elijah prayed (James 5:16–18). In the same way, we can call contemporary people to right behavior based on the contents of the text we are teaching. Teaching in that way is not moralism, it is teaching the Old Testament in the way the apostles taught. However, we cannot stop there, since "do better" is "a different gospel" (Gal. 1:6). We exhort people to right behavior, and we show them that we can be right with God and behave in a godly way only through Jesus. Our union with Jesus is the only means of salvation and the only means of obedience. If we neglect to lead people to Jesus in the exposition, we will preach what Bryan Chapell calls a "well-intended but ill-conceived legalism."[2] We aim to preach the gospel, not legalism. But first we must pray.

Pray

Years ago I heard someone speak on the topic of personal illustrations in preaching. He called attention to the fact that those of us who preach tend to tell personal stories in which we are the heroes. When preaching about temptation, we relate an incident when we depended on God's strength and he enabled us to overcome the devil's fiery darts. In a sermon on evangelism, we tell a story about sharing the gospel with someone who received the gospel favorably or even put their faith in Jesus as Savior. When preaching about intimacy with God, we gush about a time alone with God in which we enjoyed an unforgettable worship experience. We could argue that such stories are necessary in order to let people know that we practice what we preach. But a little of that goes a long way. The fact is that *some*one will be the hero of our sermon or Bible study: Do we want the hero to be us or Jesus?

As we prepare to preach and teach about Jesus from the Old Testament, we begin by acknowledging that Jesus will not be the center of our speaking if the teacher is the center, and Jesus will not replace the teacher as the center until we pray ourselves out of the way. As Edmund Clowney puts it, "Self-consciousness always threatens our presenting Christ."[3] In our preparation and presentation, it is difficult if not impossible to think of ourselves and at the same time glorify Jesus. In teaching God's Word, ultimately what matters is not what people think of us, but what people think of Jesus. Part of our preparation to teach, then, should be to wrestle in prayer over the issue of our own self-interest.

---

2. Bryan Chapell, *Christ-Centered Preaching: Redeeming the Expository Sermon*, 2nd ed. (Grand Rapids: Baker, 2005), 20.

3. Edmund Clowney, *Preaching Christ in All of Scripture* (Wheaton, IL: Crossway, 2003), 58.

Such wrestling requires searching our hearts, confessing our pride, and asking God to use us to point people to Jesus, not to us.

Paul's motto was, "What we proclaim is not ourselves, but Jesus Christ as Lord, with ourselves as your servants for Jesus' sake" (2 Cor. 4:5). In our preparation to preach or teach, in prayer we make a commitment to make that motto our own. Fulfilling such a commitment requires that we confess our penchant to think about ourselves and talk about ourselves. After our confession, we ask God to forgive us for our self-centeredness and empower us to glorify only Jesus. Prayer is necessary so that we will put the self-life to death (Gal. 2:20) and ask God to use our words to lift up Jesus. May we always make Jesus the hero of our teaching and preaching. We can do that when teaching from any text in the Old Testament.

Detective Novels and the *Sensus Plenior*

Christians believe that the Old Testament was fulfilled in the person and work of Jesus Christ. In this chapter we aim to demonstrate why that is a reasonable belief and how to make a connection to Jesus from every Old Testament text. Connecting the testaments in this way inevitably entails a certain way of reading the Old Testament, and we believe it is the only way to read the Old Testament correctly.

David Steinmetz provides a compelling illustration of how to read the Bible as a Christian: like a detective novel. Steinmetz explains that detective novels have two narratives.[4] The first narrative is the sequential unfolding of the main plot of the book. The second narrative is the solution to the crime. This second narrative appears near the end of the book and unveils what the detective has been searching for throughout the first narrative. Of the second narrative, Steinmetz writes:

---

4. David C. Steinmetz, "Uncovering a Second Narrative: Detective Fiction and the Construction of Historical Method," in *The Art of Reading Scripture*, ed. Ellen F. Davis and Richard B. Hays (Grand Rapids: Eerdmans, 2003). This analogy is also suggested by Alec Motyer in *Look to the Rock: An Old Testament Background to Our Understanding of Christ* (Downers Grove: IL, InterVarsity Press, 1996), 19–20. R. W. L. Moberly also cites this illustration from Steinmetz in his "Preaching Christ from the Old Testament," in *Reclaiming the Old Testament for Christian Preaching*, ed. Grenville J. R. Kent, Paul J. Kissling, and Laurence A. Turner (Downers Grove, IL: InterVarsity Press, 2010), 236–38.

This narrative is crisp and clear and explains in considerable detail what was really occurring while the larger narrative was unfolding. The cogency of this narrative is not in the least undermined by the fact that none of the characters except the perpetrator of the crime and, until the very end of the story, the principal investigator himself or herself had any clear notion what the story was really about. . . .

It is important to understand that this second narrative is not a subplot, even though it is short. It is the disclosure of the architectonic structure of the whole story. Therefore, the second narrative quickly overpowers the first in the mind of the reader, who can no longer read the story as though ignorant of its plot and form. The second narrative is identical in substance to the first and therefore replaces it, not as an extraneous addition superimposed on the story or read back into it, but as a compelling and persuasive disclosure of what the story was about all along. . . .

Traditional Christian exegesis reads the Bible very much in this way. . . . The long, ramshackle narrative of Israel . . . is retold and reevaluated in the light of what early Christians regarded as the concluding chapter God had written in Jesus Christ.[5]

Three points in this illustration seem especially relevant. First, the second narrative explains what was really happening in the first narrative, or discloses "what the story was about all along." That is the case with the New Testament's disclosure of the meaning of the Old Testament. All along, the story of God's interactions with humanity in general and more specifically with Israel was leading to Jesus. Reading the Old Testament without considering the New Testament, we can see that the Old Testament is leading to something. But only after reading the New Testament can we give a name to that something.

Second, most if not all the characters in the first narrative did not have "any clear notion what the story was really about." The Old Testament contains numerous prophecies about the coming of Jesus the Messiah

---

5. Steinmetz, "Uncovering a Second Narrative," 55–56.

(more about that below). Therefore, numerous Old Testament authors knew part of God's plan of fulfillment. However, no one had the full story in mind except for God himself, the narrator. He reveals that full story in the New Testament.

Third, Steinmetz affirms that once readers of a detective novel have read the second narrative, they can no longer read the first narrative as though ignorant of the outcome of the plot. This is an essential point in interpreting and teaching the Old Testament. We know how the story ends. We do not want to teach the Old Testament as if the story has not reached its zenith. It has. And that zenith, the ending of the story, is the key to the happiness and eternal salvation of every person. Therefore, it is not desirable to teach the Old Testament as if the New Testament does not exist.[6]

Steinmetz's "second narrative" is similar to an interpretive principle referred to by many writers as the *sensus plenior*. That phrase was likely coined in the late 1920s,[7] but it expresses a way of interpreting Scripture that reaches as far back as the Old Testament period.[8] The phrase means "fuller sense," or "fuller meaning." The sensus plenior generally refers

---

6. With due respect to Walter Kaiser, his argument for the "analogy of antecedent Scripture" is confusing on this point. On the one hand, he emphasizes that the Old Testament leads to Jesus. See *Preaching and Teaching from the Old Testament: A Guide for the Church* (Grand Rapids: Baker, 2003), 20–23. On the other hand, Kaiser argues that proper exegesis of the Old Testament does not allow the exegete to consider any later revelation, including the New Testament, but only antecedent Scripture. One is left to wonder how Old Testament exegetes may show that the Old Testament is fulfilled in Jesus if they are not allowed to refer to him, since Jesus came later than every Old Testament passage. Further, the New Testament often quotes or alludes to Old Testament passages, and to disallow such New Testament passages as part of Old Testament exegesis deprives the exegete of authoritative/canonical interpretations of Old Testament passages. Kaiser makes the important point that Old Testament texts must be exegeted in their own contexts. We have made the same point in this book, but we also argue that Christian exegesis does not end there. See also Walter C. Kaiser Jr., *Toward an Exegetical Theology: Biblical Exegesis for Preaching and Teaching* (Grand Rapids: Baker, 1981), 140, 161.

7. Raymond E. Brown, *The Sensus Plenior of Sacred Scripture* (1955; reprint, Eugene, OR: Wipf & Stock, 2008), xiii. Roman Catholic theologians, like Brown, regard the official doctrines of Catholicism as authoritative and definitive for the sensus plenior, but we will limit the "fuller sense" to the development of theological themes within the Bible.

8. See, for example, Michael Fishbane, *Biblical Interpretation in Ancient Israel* (Oxford: Oxford University Press, 1985).

to a deeper, extended meaning, usually unseen by the human author but intended by God and made explicit in New Testament revelation. Regarding the relation between the testaments, David Baker writes that the sensus plenior "implies that the Old Testament has a deeper meaning of which the human authors were unaware but which becomes clear in the light of the New Testament."[9]

It is important to note the limited scope of this definition of sensus plenior. When we hear "fuller meaning," we may think of allegorizing, or what Charles Spurgeon called "spiritualizing."[10] An example of the latter that Spurgeon approved was spiritualizing God's command to Moses to take the serpent by the tail (Exod. 4:4) and preaching that "there is a way of taking everything." We take hold of our afflictions and we see God turn them into something positive (as God turned the snake back into a rod), we take hold of right doctrine and God uses it for good in our lives, and so on. The difference between such spiritualizing and allegorizing seems negligible, and Spurgeon himself acknowledged that such interpretation arises from the preacher's "imagination," or "sanctified ingenuity."[11]

Sensus plenior as we are using it refers only to the fuller meaning of Old Testament texts revealed by the New Testament, even when such full meaning is not explicit in the Old Testament text itself and may not have been anticipated by the author. Such a fuller sense is possible for those who believe the Bible is divinely inspired. Whether the human author saw the completion of the story or not, the divine Author saw the way everything in the Old Testament would be fulfilled in Jesus.

> The fact that the Bible is not just a collection of individual writings, but a unified literary work, behind which lies a divine authorial intent, suggests that grammatical-historical exegesis by itself is not enough. . . . If God is the author of the entire Bible, and if that Bible is a coherent communication

---

9. David L. Baker, *Two Testaments, One Bible: The Theological Relationship between the Old and New Testaments*, 3rd ed. (Downers Grove, IL: InterVarsity Press, 2010), 184–85.

10. Charles H. Spurgeon, *Lectures to My Students* (1889; reprint, Peabody, MA: Hendrickson, 2010), 100–13.

11. Ibid., 106, 108.

from God, then his earlier statements will have some relationship to his later statements, and thus mean more than would
have been perceived by the human authors of those earlier
statements.[12]

Such a way of reading the Bible is not novel. The church has always
viewed the Old Testament as fulfilled in Jesus. Christians have done
so with good reason, since Jesus himself taught that he is the consummation of the Old Testament. His reading of the Old Testament was
Christocentric. When Jesus read from the book of Isaiah in the synagogue in Nazareth, he concluded by saying, "Today this Scripture has
been fulfilled in your hearing" (Luke 4:21). Jesus was stating that in
that moment, as the words of Isaiah fell on the ears of the people in the
synagogue, that Old Testament passage was being realized in his own
person and ministry.

If that point is not clear to some modern interpreters, it was certainly
clear to the Jewish people who heard him. At first it seems they did not
comprehend the radical nature of his claim. But when they got it, they
didn't like it. "All in the synagogue were filled with wrath. And they
rose up and drove him out of the town and brought him to the brow of
the hill on which their town was built, so that they could throw him
down the cliff. But passing through their midst, he went away" (Luke
4:28–29). To those Jewish people in Nazareth that day, Jesus' claim that
the Old Testament was fulfilled in him was heresy. But to those who
followed him, and later to his church, his words became the key to understanding the Old Testament.

On another occasion Jesus was speaking to Jewish leaders. He said,
"You search the Scriptures because you think that in them you have
eternal life; and it is they that bear witness about me" (John 5:39). The
"Scriptures" that the Jewish leaders were searching were the texts of the
Old Testament. Jesus said those Scriptures bear witness to him. Then
Jesus added, "Yet you refuse to come to me that you may have life" (v.
40). They were studying the Old Testament but missing the point of
the Old Testament, or rather they were missing the One to whom the

---

12. Dan McCartney and Charles Clayton, *Let the Reader Understand: A Guide to Interpreting and Applying the Bible*, 2nd ed. (Phillipsburg, NJ: P&R, 2002), 160.

Old Testament points: Jesus. Life is not found in mere knowledge of the Scriptures or even in compliance with its commands. The Scriptures point to Jesus and life is found in him. Jesus taught the Old Testament in that way. People who follow him should also follow his way of interpreting the Scriptures.

Why Allegorical Interpretation Is Not a Good Idea

Once I heard a sermon from 1 Samuel 18, which describes the friendship between Jonathan the son of King Saul, and David the future king of Israel. Verses 3 and 4 refer to the establishment of a covenant between Jonathan and David, and to formalize the covenant Jonathan gave to David his robe, armor, sword, bow, and belt.

On the human level, such a covenant seems like the opposite from what we might expect. Jonathan was the son of the king and the presumptive heir to the throne. We might expect David to give gifts to him, but instead Jonathan gave gifts to David. Such an act was an indication that God's eternal plan was playing out in history. God had already announced his choice of a replacement for Saul who would be a man after His own heart (1 Sam. 13:14), and God had identified David as that man (16:12–13). David is God's chosen leader, and the narrator emphasizes that fact by recording the unlikely but real circumstance of the king's son supporting David, even though Jonathan would never be king if he supported David.

The story of Jonathan's deference to David is also a way of highlighting that Saul was not fit to be king. Even Saul's son was willing to submit to God's plan and God's chosen king, but Saul was not willing. Still, God's plan moved inexorably forward, and his plan would ultimately lead to the descendant of David who is the eternal King. The friendship of David and Jonathan was one way God chose to exalt David to his future throne and Jesus to his eternal throne.

The sermon I heard, however, highlighted none of these sovereign acts of God in salvation history. Instead, the preacher said that when Jonathan gave his robe to David, it represented giving our position to Jesus. The giving of Jonathan's clothes represented giving our possessions to Jesus. The act of giving his sword to David represented giving our protection to Jesus, and giving his bow represented giving our prowess to Jesus. Thus the preacher made an allegorical connection between the details of the text and Jesus. The theology and application of the sermon did not rise from what Jonathan gave to David but from what we are to give to Jesus.

John Phillips, who preached the sermon referenced above, has written to defend the legitimacy of the allegorical method of interpretation:

> This, then, is the value of an allegorical interpretation of a passage of Scripture. It can be used to illustrate a clear teaching of Scripture, a teaching that is well supported elsewhere in the Bible: plain doctrinal statements. . . . We can most certainly dig down beneath the surface of a passage of Scripture for deeper meanings. . . . We can know when we have discovered such a hidden allegory because "things fit." The emerging illustration is not artificial . . . it is satisfyingly complete.[13]

So how do we know the allegorical meaning of a specific passage of Scripture? According to Phillips, we have at least two guidelines. First, the allegorical meaning must be well supported by "plain doctrinal statements" that are elsewhere in the Bible. Such "plain passages," of course, are not interpreted allegorically. Ironically, to use allegory properly requires using a method of interpretation other than allegory to understand the plain passages. Further, by what criteria do we determine which passages are "plain"? What is plain to one interpreter may not be plain to another. Also, we miss the theological message of the passage we are studying, because allegory imports theology from other passages that seem more plain.

According to Phillips, the second way we know the allegorical meaning of a passage of Scripture is that "things fit" and the allegorical connection "is satisfyingly complete." That criterion seems even more subjective than the first, since the individual interpreter is the arbiter of whether "things fit" or not. As an exegete studies a passage of Scripture and arrives at certain allegorical connections with New Testament

---

13. John Phillips, *Bible Explorer's Guide: How to Understand and Interpret the Bible* (Grand Rapids: Kregel, 1987), 55–56.

theology, where does he get the idea that "things fit" between the Old Testament text and his allegory? He gets that idea from his own mind.[14]

Inevitably, allegory as a method of interpreting the Old Testament derives theology from a truncated canon, since it abandons the effort to discover the theological ideas of allegorized passages and instead uses such passages as emblems of New Testament theology. Moreover, the allegorical connections, and hence the alleged meaning of the passage, arises in the mind of the reader, not the text.

Thus far I have referred to the allegorical method only in its more contemporary expressions. We cannot consider this subject, however, without noting that this method was prominent as an interpretive approach for 1,500 years of church history. How can we say that allegory is not a good idea when generation after generation of Christian teachers used this method and considered it a good idea? Surely the church did not go astray in its biblical interpretation for that long. We dare not commit the sin of chronological arrogance, thinking that our modern way of interpretation is superior because our era is more advanced and therefore we are more intelligent.

Origen, perhaps the best known of the early allegorists (third century), was demonstrably brilliant and well educated. He was an able scholar of the Hebrew text of the Old Testament and of all the Greek documents of the early church. He did not overlook the literal meaning or historical context of Old Testament passages, but still he used allegory freely.

Origen stated that allegory was often preferable because many prophecies concerning the Messiah were not fulfilled by Jesus. Hence, they are symbolic and their meaning can be discovered by allegory. Contemporary evangelicals interpret such passages as still to be fulfilled in Jesus' future reign. Also, for Origen some divine deeds in the Old Testament were morally unacceptable, such as God's command to conquer Canaan and kill the Canaanites. He avoided the moral dilemma by writing about the spiritual warfare between Christ-followers and our opposition. In addition, many texts are obscure if interpreted only

---

14. Spurgeon also provides "limits and boundaries" for allegory, but his criteria for acceptable "spiritualizing" are just as subjective. Spurgeon, *Lectures to My Students*, 101–13.

literally, and they can find meaning through an allegorical connection to New Testament theology.[15]

Fundamental to understanding the legitimacy of allegory in the early church is grasping their combination of Greek philosophical ideas and the divine inspiration of the Scriptures. It would be inaccurate to claim that Origen was a follower of Plato or that he was a Platonist. However, students of church history and hermeneutics have long seen that he was influenced by some of Plato's philosophical ideas. Simply stated, for Plato all *things* in the visible world represent higher *ideas* that exist in the spiritual world. The things are the shadows; the ideas are reality.

When such a conception is applied to a document, the words on the page are shadows that represent higher ideas. Words become symbols that denote deeper spiritual truths. Taken this way, the word "Canaan" does not merely denote the geographical, political, and ethnic entity west of the Jordan River and east of the Mediterranean Sea. It also denotes something deeper: the spiritual enemies of Christ and his church. The allegorists among the church fathers believed that they did not *invent* such hidden, deeper meanings, they *discovered* them, because God himself built such connections into the text. It is likely accurate to say that for Origen and others the words of Scripture were Platonic symbols, but it is also accurate to say that they believed that those symbols are divinely inspired. The words bear meaning beyond their natural, linguistic, or historical sense, precisely because the Holy Spirit inspired them. When the same Spirit works in interpreters who are spiritually mature, he reveals the deeper meaning. Through such a spiritual process, allegory becomes an acceptable method, and the table of bread in the tabernacle becomes human emotions and the incense altar becomes the human will.

The notion that all the words in Scripture are divinely inspired and replete with divine meaning and power beyond their natural sense is a compelling idea. Such a view of inspiration is likely the reason the allegorical method endured in the church. If every word of Scripture is invested with divine meaning that is fulfilled in Christ and the spiritually

---

15. For a more complete review of the hermeneutics of Origen and other church fathers, see David S. Dockery, *Biblical Interpretation Then and Now: Contemporary Hermeneutics in the Light of the Early Church* (Grand Rapids: Baker, 1992).

enlightened can see such meaning, then to argue against such an idea may have seemed like arguing against divine inspiration, or at least arguing that the Scriptures are less inspired than claimed by the allegorists.

After the Renaissance, in many circles human reason became the arbiter of meaning and the Bible lost its privileged status as a divine book. Rationalism argued that the Bible is only a human book with *no* divine inspiration. According to this way of thinking, the Bible should be interpreted as any other book, according to the ordinary rules of human language. The believing church responded by continuing to argue for the inspiration of Scripture while acknowledging its human authorship. Rationalism pressed upon the church the question of whether the words of Scripture are subject to the rules of grammar and syntax of the language in which it was written. The answer of the church was affirmative, but believers also insisted that the words of Scripture carried divine truth inspired by God. One consequence of such intellectual developments was that the human author and his context came back into view, as did authorial intent. The believing church still viewed every word as inspired, but the human author combined the words to communicate a point. The goal of exegesis became determining the point intended by the author, not to see the words as emblems representing something extraneous to the text.

What is the point of this brief review of allegorical interpretation? We cannot dismiss a method used by so many fathers of the faith without considering why they used it.[16] We have to consider the possibility that perhaps they were right and we are wrong. In my view, their high view of the inspiration of the Scriptures was correct and commendable. However, their combination of such a view with a Platonic understanding of reality resulted in a method of reading texts that is regrettable. At best, the allegorical method prevents interpreters from grasping the meaning of Old Testament texts. At worst, it opens the door to egregious errors in both theology and practice. We can respect the reasons allegory endured for centuries, but we can also decline to use it as a way

---

16. This is one primary theme in Moisés Silva, *Has the Church Misread the Bible? The History of Interpretation in the Light of Current Issues* (Grand Rapids: Zondervan, 1987). Silva offers no definitive answer to the question in the title, but he wisely explores the question and provides helpful guidance for contemporary interpretation and application of the Scriptures.

of reading the Old Testament. Allegory does not match the way we think God inspired the Old Testament, and it does not match the way the New Testament uses the Old Testament.[17]

How the Old Testament Leads to Jesus

After Jesus' resurrection, he was speaking with two of his disciples on the road to Emmaus. Luke records that "beginning with Moses and all the Prophets, he interpreted to them in all the Scriptures the things concerning himself" (Luke 24:27). Then Luke quotes Jesus as saying, "These are my words that I spoke to you while I was still with you, that everything written about me in the Law of Moses and the Prophets and the Psalms must be fulfilled" (v. 44). Jesus referred to all three divisions of the Old Testament canon (the Torah, the Prophets, and the Writings) and he said that all of it is about him and all of it will be fulfilled. Since Jesus was so clear about the fact that the Old Testament was fulfilled in him, we do not ask *whether* the Old Testament leads to Jesus; we need only ask *how*.

First, the Old Testament is a book of history. Comparing the Old Testament to the first narrative of a detective novel, as we did earlier, can help us understand certain properties of the Old Testament. However, all such analogies are incomplete, since no other book is completely like the Bible. One way the Old Testament contrasts with a detective novel is that the Old Testament is not fiction. It is a book of history in that it contains narratives of historical events that occurred in space and time. Those narratives also combine to form a metanarrative that stretches from before the creation of the universe to about 425 BC when the Jews were living in Judah again after their return from exile. If we include the references to the future in the Old Testament, its metanarrative reaches all the way to the consummation of the age and the eternal reign of Christ, since some of the prophets referred to such events.[18] A few books, like Proverbs, Ecclesiastes, and Song of Songs, are essentially ahistorical, but they were written at specific moments

---

17. With the exception of Galatians 4:21–31, where Paul uses the Greek term *allegoroumena*. However, "although this is indeed an allegorical interpretation, it does not violate the overall contextual intent of the original story in Genesis" (McCartney and Clayton, *Let the Reader Understand*, 166–67).

18. For example, see Isaiah 9:5–7; 11:4–10; Joel 2:30–32; Micah 4:1–7.

within the history of Israel. They exist only because of God's covenant relationship with Israel, and they are set in particular eras in the history of that relationship.

This historical character of the Old Testament distinguishes it from other books. The Old Testament consists of numerous books written over a period of a thousand years by various authors in several different genres. However, it is not merely an anthology of individual books. All the books in the Old Testament fit within the history narrated in the Old Testament. Even in the psalms, which are for the most part individual and corporate worship texts, readers encounter constant echoes of events and persons in Israel's history. For those who ask how the New Testament connects to the Old Testament, the historical nature of the Old Testament cannot be overemphasized. The two testaments connect because their histories connect: the old covenant to the new covenant, Israel to the church, the coming One to Jesus who came.[19]

Second, the history of the Old Testament is linear and purposeful. Humanity is far from agreement over the nature of history. Eastern religions generally represent history as cyclical. History has no beginning and no end; it is a never-ending cycle. We live either an infinite number of lives or the same life an infinite number of times. Philosophies like nihilism and existentialism assert that both life and history are absurd, meaningless. Naturalism portrays history as a linear stream of events but driven only by random cause and effect, without purpose.

The Bible clearly presents history as moving forward in one direction, not in a cycle. Certain events are cyclical, like the alternation of seasons, and birth and death,[20] but all such things are part of a history that is marching forward from the present into the future. In other words, history is progressing along a timeline, so it is linear. Throughout that history, God is present and active. At the beginning of the universe, he already existed. At the end, he will still be present. God is also guiding

---

19. James Orr contrasted the Bible with the Koran and Zoroastrian and Buddhist Scriptures at just this point. The former is "a miscellany of disjointed pieces," and the latter two "collections of heterogeneous materials, loosely placed together." The Bible, however, "has one connected story to tell from beginning to end; we see something growing before our eyes." James Orr, *The Problem of the Old Testament* (New York: Charles Scribner's Sons, 1907), 31–32.

20. The author of Ecclesiastes wrote about such phenomena (see 1:4–10; 3:14–15).

history. At the beginning, he created the physical universe, including the reality of time, as the heavenly bodies are "for signs and for seasons, and for days and years" (Gen. 1:14). At the end of the Bible, God is still present and is superintending the transition from this age to the next.

Our friends in systematic theology call such linear, purposeful history "teleological." The word comes from the Greek *telos*, or "end." The fact that history is teleological means that it is moving toward a known and intended end. God knows every plot turn in the story, he knows how everything will end, and he knows when the credits are going to roll. Not only does he know all of that, he planned it. He created time to be linear and time's purpose is his purpose. As God was announcing through Isaiah his future judgment on Babylon and Assyria, he declared, "As I have planned, so shall it be, and as I have purposed, so shall it stand" (Isa. 14:24). What happens on the plane of history is God's plan. Regarding his own life, Job affirmed concerning God, "What he desires, that he does. For he will complete what he appoints for me" (Job 23:13–14). So God is in control of the direction of the history of the world and the history of our lives and his purpose cannot be thwarted (cf. Dan. 4:34–35).

As God's plan for history moved forward through time, later revelations built on former revelations. Seminal ideas unfolded over time, clearly demonstrating the unity of God's work throughout history and the unity of his revelation of that work. Walter Kaiser uses the biological term "epigenetic" to describe the purposeful development or gradual growth of God's revelation over time. Later revelations did not contradict former revelations; they built upon them, amplifying them. This too was part of God's purposeful guidance of history.[21]

Third, the One who is guiding history knew the end from the beginning. If history is teleological (and it is), then history has an end. The prophets regularly prophesied of that end. God knows what will happen tomorrow and how history will end, and he knew it all from the beginning. An oracle from God in Isaiah addresses his rule over history: "I am God, and there is none like me, declaring the end from

---

21. Kaiser refers to God's purposeful guidance of history as his "promise-plan." See Walter C. Kaiser Jr., *The Messiah in the Old Testament* (Grand Rapids: Zondervan, 1995), 24–29.

the beginning and from ancient times things not yet done, saying, 'My counsel shall stand, and I will accomplish all my purpose,'. . . I have spoken, and I will bring it to pass; I have purposed, and I will do it" (Isa. 46:9–11). God predetermined the course of world history. God also knows about all the days of our lives as individuals before we were born. Though we believe that humans possess free will and make real choices, we also believe that God rules time and that those two realities are reconcilable in his mind. The psalmist said to God, "In your book were written, every one of them, the days that were formed for me, when as yet there were none of them" (Ps. 139:16).

The implications of the fact that God has planned history and knows the end from the beginning are far-reaching. It means that the Bible (if we believe in its divine inspiration) comes from the mind of the God who guides history and knows where it is going. This fact also affects the way we interpret and teach every passage in the Old Testament. We can place every passage somewhere on a time line, and we can know that God was managing that point, and every point, on that time line. We can also know that God was guiding forward the events of that time in his salvation history that would culminate in Jesus.

Fourth, in the Old Testament, the end time has both a beginning and an end. Another way of saying this is that from the perspective of the Old Testament, some prophesies address the future and some prophesies address the distant future. In New Testament terms, some prophesies address the first coming of Jesus, and some prophesies address the final rule of Jesus. For example, the Old Testament refers to the birth of Jesus (Isa. 7:14; Micah 5:2), Jesus' triumphal entry into Jerusalem (Zech. 9:9), the sacrificial death of Jesus (Isa. 52:13–53:12), and the resurrection of Jesus (Ps. 16:10; Isa. 53:10–12), to mention a few of the prophesies regarding Jesus' first coming.

The Old Testament also looks beyond the first coming of Jesus to a future consummation. Isaiah refers to Jesus reigning from the throne of David forever (9:7), and a return to the idyllic pre-fall state of creation (11:6–10). Joel describes catastrophes on a cosmic scale that will occur at the consummation (2:30–31). Zechariah prophesies the Lord will appear on the Mount of Olives for an international battle at Jerusalem, which the Lord will win and subsequently he will reign over the entire world (14:1–9).

Distinguishing the beginning of the messianic age from the end of the age is significant for understanding and teaching the Old Testament. When we connect texts to Jesus, we will want to determine which part of Jesus' salvation work to emphasize. Does the text anticipate the coming salvation accomplished by the Messiah or the coming consummation also accomplished by the Messiah? To answer such a question, we will have to know the passage we are teaching, the contents of the Old Testament, and the contents of the New Testament.

Fifth, both the beginning and the end of the telos feature one central Person. This fact is implied in number four, but it bears special mention. To continue the discussion above, the beginning of the end features Jesus: his lineage, birth, life, sacrificial death, and resurrection. The end of the end time also features Jesus: his return, his final battle with evil, his reign from the throne of David, and his establishment of a new creation. Thus when we place Old Testament texts in the context of salvation history, we are not merely connecting them with events. We are connecting texts to the person who is the star of all salvation events: Jesus. This is crucial, since people need more than knowledge about how the Old Testament connects to the end. People even need more than the assurance that God is in control of the end. People need Jesus, because only he can save, sanctify, and eternally glorify people. Therefore, we point to him from every text.

Sixth, the central person anticipated in the Old Testament is prophesied explicitly. Peter wrote plainly about this phenomenon in his first letter. After describing salvation in Jesus, he wrote, "Concerning this salvation, the prophets who prophesied about the grace that was to be yours searched and inquired carefully, inquiring what person or time the Spirit of Christ in them was indicating when he predicted the sufferings of Christ and the subsequent glories" (1 Peter 1:10–11). That is, the prophets prophesied about the grace that has come to us in Christ, and the Holy Spirit revealed to them and predicted through them Christ's suffering and resurrection. Peter further wrote, "It was revealed to them that they were serving not themselves but you, in the things that have now been announced to you through those who preached the good news to you by the Holy Spirit" (v. 12). Anyone who doubts the relevance of the Old Testament for the church should meditate on that verse. The prophets were serving not themselves but us, the New

Testament church. By "the things that have now been announced to you," Peter surely meant the fulfillment of the prophets' messages that had been accomplished in Christ and announced by the early preachers of the gospel.[22]

The Old Testament contains many specific prophecies that Christ fulfilled. As an example, consider the cluster of detailed prophecies in Isaiah 49:1–9 concerning the one Isaiah refers to as the servant. First, in verses 1 and 6, the Messiah's ministry is said to be to "peoples from afar" and to "the nations." In other words, his salvation would be offered to all people in the world. That prophecy was fulfilled in Jesus. On the night Jesus was born, the angel said that his birth was good news of great joy "for all the people" (Luke 2:10). Jesus told his followers to "make disciples of all nations" (Matt. 28:19). And the book of Revelation refers to the Messiah's future rule over all nations (Rev. 15:3–4; 19:15).

Second, also in verse 1 of Isaiah 49, the Messiah says that God gave him his name from the womb. That too came to pass in Jesus. Luke 1 says that an angel told Mary before the birth of Jesus that she was to name him "Jesus" (v. 31). The Gospel of Matthew says that an angel told Joseph the same thing: "You shall call his name Jesus, for he will save his people from their sins" (1:21). God named Jesus from his mother's womb.

Third, verse 2 of Isaiah 49 says that the Messiah's mouth would be like a sharp sword. This is poetic language pointing to the fact that the words the Messiah would speak would be powerful. Jesus' words were powerful. That is attested numerous times in the New Testament, and in the book of Revelation Jesus is portrayed as returning to earth with a sword protruding from his mouth (1:16; 2:16; 19:15, 21).

Fourth, verse 2 says the Messiah would be a polished arrow. In other words, he would be a weapon. Jesus was a weapon, since he attacked the forces of evil, cast out demons, defeated the devil in his crucifixion and resurrection, and he sends to eternal condemnation those who oppose him. Fifth, verses 3 and 5 of Isaiah 49 state that the Messiah would be a servant, and Jesus said that he came not to be served but to serve (Mark 10:45). The sixth prophecy is in verse 4, which refers to the rejection of

---

22. Karen H. Jobes, *1 Peter*, Baker Exegetical Commentary on the New Testament (Grand Rapids: Baker, 2005), 103.

the Messiah; he says, "I have labored in vain." Jesus was rejected; John 1:11 says that "he came to his own, but his own people did not receive him." The seventh messianic prophecy in Isaiah 49 is in verse 7; it says that kings will rise in honor of the Messiah and princes will bow before him. The 45th chapter of Isaiah has the same truth; in verse 23 the Lord says, "To me every knee shall bow, every tongue shall swear allegiance." Philippians 2:10–11 says the same thing about Jesus: "Every knee should bow, in heaven and on earth and under the earth, and every tongue confess that Jesus Christ is Lord." That refers to Jesus' eternal and universal reign in the millennium and beyond.

Eighth, in verse 8 God says to the Messiah, "I will keep you and give you as a covenant to the people." Did Jesus come bringing a covenant? Yes, Jesus established the new covenant, about which Jeremiah wrote and to which Jesus referred during his last supper with his disciples when he said, "This cup that is poured out for you is the new covenant in my blood" (Luke 22:20; cf. Jer. 31:31, 34). Jesus' covenant is the better covenant of Hebrews 7:22 and 8:6. Jesus was given as a covenant for the people, just as Isaiah prophesied.

Ninth, Isaiah 49:9 says the Messiah will say to prisoners, "Come out." The Messiah sets prisoners free. In John 8 Jesus said, "If you abide in my word, you are truly my disciples, and you will know the truth, and the truth will set you free" (vv. 31–32). Jesus also said of himself, "If the Son sets you free, you will be free indeed" (v. 36).

The tenth messianic prophecy in Isaiah 49 is also in verse 9; it says that the Messiah will bring people who are in darkness into the light. In John 8:12 Jesus said, "I am the light of the world. Whoever follows me will not walk in darkness, but will have the light of life."

It is difficult to see how the connection between the Old Testament and Jesus could not be more explicit or specific. Isaiah 49 is just one example. The Old Testament contains numerous explicit prophecies.[23] Expositors should be ready to encounter them and to show the connection to Jesus. The danger of looking at such individual prophecies is that

---

23. The fulfillment of so many specific prophecies in one person is impossible without the divine inspiration of the prophecies and God's guidance of history, a fact that has contemporary apologetic value. See Josh McDowell, *The New Evidence That Demands a Verdict* (Nashville: Thomas Nelson, 1999), 164–202.

expositors will miss the larger story, the development of the main plot of the Old Testament, which is also fulfilled in Jesus. Expositors should adopt a "both-and" approach, acknowledging that both the main story line and individual prophecies are fulfilled in Jesus.

Seventh, numerous Old Testament texts are cited or alluded to in the New Testament where the writers demonstrate fulfillment in Jesus and the church. Roger Nicole writes that a conservative count of separate references to the Old Testament in the New Testament is 295, spread over 352 verses in the New Testament. If clear allusions are added to that number, the count goes up by hundreds, with the result that over 10 percent of the New Testament consists of citations or direct allusions to the Old Testament.[24] The most common reason New Testament writers refer to Old Testament texts is to show how they are fulfilled in Jesus. For example, "All four canonical Gospels declare that the Torah and the Prophets and the Psalms mysteriously prefigure Jesus."[25]

Beyond the Gospels, much of the preaching and writing of the apostle Paul was exposition of the Old Testament, and Paul's use of the Old Testament was Christocentric. For example, when Paul preached in the synagogue in Pisidian Antioch, he gave a brief review of the history of Israel, beginning with God's election of the Jews. He concluded with David and quoted 1 Samuel 13:14 that states David was a man after God's heart. Then Paul said, "Of this man's offspring God has brought to Israel a Savior, Jesus, as he promised" (Acts 13:23). The people in the synagogue could not have missed Paul's point: the history of God's dealings with the Jews, salvation history, culminated in Jesus.

Also, one does not fully understand who Jesus is unless one sees that he is the descendant of David as prophesied in the Old Testament. Paul continued to show the connection with David by quoting the second Psalm as a messianic psalm: "You are my Son, today I have begotten you" (v. 33). Paul said those words refer to Jesus. Acts 13 states that Paul used Isaiah 55:3 to further demonstrate that Jesus is the fulfillment of

---

24. Roger Nicole, "New Testament Use of the Old Testament," in *Revelation and the Bible*, ed. Carl F. H. Henry (Grand Rapids: Baker, 1958), 137–38.

25. Richard B. Hays, *Reading Backwards: Figural Christology and the Fourfold Gospel Witness* (Waco, TX: Baylor University Press, 2014), 3.

the prophecies concerning a coming Messiah who would be Davidic: "I will give you the holy and sure blessings of David" (Acts 13:34). Paul went on to cite other Old Testament passages in the same sermon.

Paul's purpose in his sermon in Pisidian Antioch was the same as can be demonstrated elsewhere in the New Testament: to explain the person and work of Jesus by referring to the Old Testament. For example, to address the question of why we need salvation in Jesus, Paul referred to the fall described in Genesis 3. "Sin came into the world through one man, and death through sin" (Rom. 5:12), and "in Adam all die" (1 Cor. 15:22). We need the salvation Jesus offers because of the sin that entered the human race through Adam and that remains in us. And what is necessary to be freed from the curse of our sin? The answer is faith, and the early church explained that answer by referring to the Old Testament. Paul used the example of Abraham: "Abraham 'believed God, and it was counted to him as righteousness.'" Then Paul applied Abraham's example by writing, "It is those of faith who are the sons of Abraham" (Gal. 3:6–7). Paul used a line from Habakkuk (2:4) to make the same point: "The righteous shall live by faith" (Gal. 3:11; Rom. 1:17). And we do not need generic faith: faith "in something bigger than ourselves," or "faith in God as we understand him," as people are apt to say these days. We need faith in Jesus, because "a person is not justified by works of the law but through faith in Jesus Christ" (Gal. 2:16). The strategy of using the Old Testament to explain new covenant truth is pervasive in the New Testament.[26]

Getting from the Old Testament to Jesus by Asking the Right Questions

The seven points above provide a brief introduction to the ways the Old Testament leads inexorably to the New Testament and is incomplete without it. But how do we go about connecting specific Old Testament texts to Jesus when we teach? Is there a practical method to follow in weekly exposition? The section below offers help to expositors by

---

26. For a thorough consideration of the New Testament on this point, see G. K. Beale and D. A. Carson, eds., *Commentary on the New Testament Use of the Old Testament* (Grand Rapids: Baker, 2007); G. K. Beale, *Handbook on the New Testament Use of the Old Testament: Exegesis and Interpretation* (Grand Rapids: Baker, 2012).

showing how asking certain questions will open the door to the pathway to Jesus and the gospel.

1. Is the passage repeated or reflected in the New Testament?

This is likely the most obvious path to teach about Jesus from the Old Testament. In this case, the door has already been opened by the New Testament itself. Sometimes the reference to the Old Testament is only a passing allusion. Matthew, for example, refers to the fact that Joseph settled in Nazareth and raised Jesus there "that what was spoken by the prophets might be fulfilled" (2:23). We are familiar with the prophetic announcement that the Messiah would be born in Bethlehem (Micah 5:2; Matt. 2:4–5), but where in the prophetic books is a statement that the Messiah would be from Nazareth? Most likely, Matthew was referring to Isaiah 11:1, where the prophet referred to the coming Messiah as a "branch."[27] The Hebrew word for branch is *nezer*, a word that can be seen in the name Nazareth. Nazareth was "branch town," a pun that Matthew did not miss. In an exposition of Isaiah 11, we would not want to miss it either, especially since it has been pointed out for us by the Gospel writer.

In other places the New Testament comments on an Old Testament passage more extensively. Habakkuk 2:4, for example, is quoted in the New Testament three times (Rom. 1:17; Gal. 3:11; Heb. 10:38). It states, "The righteous shall live by his faith." The writer of Hebrews cited the verse to make the point that we endure trials by faith. Paul quoted the verse as part of his argument that we are saved by faith, not by works. When I preached from Habakkuk, I made both points, since the New Testament applies the verse in both ways. I stated:

> Habakkuk 2:4 says, "The righteous shall live by his faith." The writer of Hebrews quoted that, and to paraphrase what he wrote to Christians like us, he wrote, in the midst of trials "You have need of endurance." Jesus is coming again and he'll set everything right, but in the meantime we have to live by faith. When you encounter difficulties or face persecution, or have questions, don't shrink back. "The righteous shall live

---

27. The same idea is in Isaiah 53:2, though the term *nezer* is not used there.

by his faith" (Heb. 10:36–38). When we don't understand our circumstances, we can't live by understanding; we have to live by faith. . . .

Also, the apostle Paul quoted Habakkuk 2:4 to make the point that we are saved by faith. We have eternal life, reconciliation with God, by faith, not by works. Habakkuk wrote, "The righteous shall live by his faith," and in Romans 1:17 and Galatians 3:11 Paul wrote that we have spiritual life, eternal life by faith, not by works. We're saved not by works of the law but by faith. In Galatians 3:6 Paul also quoted Genesis 15:6, which says, Abraham "believed the Lord, and he counted it to him as righteousness." That word "believed" is the same word Habakkuk used that's translated "faith." Abraham had faith, and God counted it to him as righteousness. Abraham could not be made right with God by works of the law, since at that point God had not even given the law. Paul's point is that we are made righteous by Christ in the same way Abraham was counted righteous: by faith, not by works of the law.

Decades ago I preached a sermon from Habakkuk in which I did not mention the passages in Romans, Galatians, and Hebrews. I cannot imagine such an oversight now. In an exposition of an Old Testament passage, why would we skip the authoritative interpretation that God inspired for us in the New Testament? If our passage is repeated or reflected in the New Testament, we teach what the New Testament states about it.

2. Does the passage address a theological theme that is also addressed in the New Testament?

This question is similar to the first, but it does not require quotation or allusion, just a revelation about the same theme. For example, numerous passages in the Old Testament relate to the old covenant sacrificial system—narratives about the construction of the tabernacle in Exodus, descriptions of the sacrifices in Leviticus and Numbers, allusions to sacrifice in Psalms and elsewhere, and prophetic denunciations of liturgical abuses. How does a new covenant believer teach the sacrificial system? Thankfully, we have numerous references to the sacrificial system in the New Testament that provide theological commentary for us, and the book of Hebrews provides a lengthy explanation of how the coming of Jesus has altered the way we view the sacrificial system. Consider the 16th chapter of Leviticus, which describes the observance of the Day of Atonement. When I preached from Leviticus 16, I said the following:

> The ninth and tenth chapters of the book of Hebrews describe in detail how Jesus' death on the cross supersedes both the Day of Atonement and all the old covenant sacrifices. Hebrews says that on the Day of Atonement the high priest offered the blood of animals; Jesus offered his own blood, and since he is eternal his atonement for our sins is eternal (Heb. 9:12). The high priest entered an earthly tent; Jesus offered his sacrifice in the presence of God himself (9:24). The high priest offered sacrifices for his own sins (Lev. 16:6, 11, 17; Heb. 9:7); Jesus had no sin so he was the perfect high priest and the perfect sacrifice (7:26–27). The high priest had to offer sacrifices repeatedly; Jesus offered himself as a sacrifice once for all eternity (9:25–26; 10:11–12). The writer of Hebrews concluded that the old covenant sacrifices were "a shadow of the good things to come" (10:1), and Jesus has abolished the old covenant and established the new covenant in his sacrifice on the cross (8:13; 10:9). Jesus is God's offer of atonement and removal of sin. That's the teaching of the New Testament and it's the gospel that the church has always preached.[28]

That part of the sermon was merely a review of Hebrews' commentary on the sacrificial system. In such cases, connecting the Old Testament text to Jesus is simple, since the New Testament does it for us. The same could be said for Old Testament passages related to Adam, Abraham, etc., since the New Testament explication of the gospel includes references to such persons: Jesus is the new Adam, and our salvation is through faith as was Abraham's. All the passages in the Old

---

28. See also Allan Moseley, *Exalting Jesus in Leviticus* (Nashville: Broadman & Holman, 2015), 211.

Testament that relate to giving praise to God lead us to Hebrews 13:15, which also addresses the theme of praise and states that we offer praise through Jesus. We will not miss such references as long as we remember to ask the question, "Does this passage address a theological theme that is also addressed in the New Testament?"

3. Does the passage reveal something about the human problem?

The human problem is sin and the alienation from God caused by sin. It has been traditional for Protestants to emphasize that the Old Testament law serves to call attention to human sin, to demonstrate our fallen condition so we may see our need to be rescued spiritually by the Savior. While that is indeed a special function of the law, we may also see some reminder of human sinfulness in every passage in the Bible. In every Bible study or sermon we show how the biblical text before us highlights a human need that results from our fallen condition, and then we show how God meets that need. If we do that, we will include in every sermon or Bible study the central theme of Scripture and the only hope of humanity: our sin and God's salvation, our enslavement and God's redemption, our brokenness and God's healing. Such an approach will lead naturally to speak of Jesus, since salvation is in him.

Bryan Chapell refers to highlighting our sin and need for a Savior as the "fallen condition focus." He defines this concept as "the mutual human condition that contemporary believers share with those to or about whom the text was written that requires the grace of the passage for God's people to glorify and enjoy him. . . . All Scripture has a Fallen Condition Focus."[29] So we identify the sin in every passage and remind our hearers that all people today are sinners. Once we have accomplished that, we have three alternatives. We can point out the sinfulness of our hearers but provide no solution, we can tell them to try harder and do better, or we can explain that Jesus offers salvation from sin and sanctification. Only the final alternative is the gospel.

How do we highlight the human problem in our exposition? The passage we are studying includes a reference to a human being at some

---

29. Chapell, *Christ-Centered Preaching,* 50.

point, and that person was a sinner in need of a Savior. Calling attention to that fact provides an opportunity to declare that all people today are also sinners in need of a Savior. When teaching from the Pentateuch, all the patriarchs committed sins. When teaching from any of the historical books, all the judges and kings fell short, even David. The wisdom books assert that foolishness leads to sin, and the prophets preached against sin. Even when a character's behavior was exemplary, like Elijah standing against the prophets of Baal on Mt. Carmel, still we teach that ultimately we do not want to be like Elijah. We want to be like Jesus, and we want to be like Elijah to the extent that he was like Jesus. The only way we can be like Jesus is through his presence and power in us. Only Jesus solves the human problem.

4. Where is the passage located in salvation history?

Every passage in the Old Testament is located on a timeline that stretches from creation into the Persian period. Since part of our exposition will be to explore the historical context of the passage, we will identify the location of the passage on the timeline. That timeline is not just history; it is *salvation* history—the history of God's gracious acts to redeem humanity. Further, that salvation history culminates in the coming of Jesus the Savior, and one day he will consummate history as we know it and inaugurate a new order. No matter where our passage is located on the timeline of salvation history, we can point out to our hearers that God's plan progressed from that point and reached its denouement in Jesus. Then we explain the gospel as the fulfillment God intended all along. Sidney Greidanus includes this approach as one of his seven ways of preaching Jesus from the Old Testament, and he calls it "the way of redemptive-historical progression."[30]

When I preached a sermon from the twenty-one verses of Obadiah, I connected Obadiah's message to the New Testament and Jesus by describing Obadiah's message as one moment in the long history of redemption that led to Jesus. Consider a few paragraphs from that sermon as an example:

---

30. Sidney Greidanus, *Preaching Christ from the Old Testament: A Contemporary Hermeneutical Method* (Grand Rapids: Eerdmans, 1999), 203–206, 234–40.

Verse 18 says, "There shall be no survivor for the house of Esau, for the LORD has spoken." That prophesy about Edom came to pass. The nation of Edom is no more. The Edomites have been absorbed into the Arab peoples, and the territory of Edom is now occupied by the country of Jordan.

God is glorified by the fulfillment of his word. But God would be glorified in an even greater way. The history of the world has involved and will involve many wars. But the history of the world involves one war that transcends all others. That war lasts from the beginning of history to the end. It's the war between God and those who oppose him, led by our adversary the devil. In every age God has moved history toward his redemption plan, and in every age the devil has opposed God's work. The book of Obadiah describes one more battle in the long war between the serpent the devil and God's plan to bring redemption to all people. Ultimately the conflict between Edom and Israel was not a sibling conflict or even a national conflict; it was a spiritual conflict. Obadiah records just the next chapter in that story—the war story that began with creation and will end in the consummation of the age. And it wasn't the last chapter that involved the Edomites.

Fast forward almost six hundred years to the birth of Jesus. When Jesus was born, wise men from the East informed King Herod that a king had been born in that area. King Herod ordered the deaths of all male babies so he would be sure to kill that one baby, the baby Jesus. King Herod, otherwise known as Herod the Great, was an Idumean. In that word "Idumean" you can hear the word "Edom." The word "Idumean" was a Hellenized version of the word "Edomite." Herod was an Edomite. Jesus, God's Messiah, escaped Herod's plan to murder him, Herod died, Jesus manifested himself as the Messiah, died on the cross for the sins of humanity, rose from the dead, today his gospel is spread worldwide by his church, one day he will return and reign over all, and when he returns he will come to Mt. Zion and the book of Revelation says his saints will rule with him from there. So when verse 21 says, "Saviors shall go up to Mount Zion to rule Mount Esau, and the kingdom shall

be the LORD's," that's referring to something more than the
Jews returning from exile and occupying their ancestral land.
Obadiah was writing about a coming kingdom that would be
universal, beginning with the coming of Jesus, the going of
his church to preach his gospel, and ending with the return of
Jesus to reign over all. When all the kingdoms that were going
to last forever have passed off the scene, when every nation that
thought it would rule the world has been destroyed, Jesus will
be on the throne. God will be glorified.[31]

The New Testament records that the earliest Christian preachers referred to salvation history in retrospect (e.g., Acts 7:2–52; 13:16–41).
Similarly, when we preach or teach from the Old Testament we can refer
to salvation history in prospect. Either way, Jesus is the center of history.

5. Does the passage raise a question that is answered by Jesus or the New Testament?

In Psalm 73 the psalmist raised the age-old question of the prosperity of
the wicked (v. 3) and the suffering of the righteous. It's a difficult question about God's justice that at times can rock us to our spiritual core.
However, before Psalm 73 is finished, the psalmist wrote about how he
arrived at an answer for his questions. In worship he viewed the inequities of life from the perspective of eternity. From that vantage point he
could see the end: judgment for the wicked and reward for the righteous.

Not all passages in the Old Testament raise theological questions
and then answer them. Occasionally we encounter issues that are not
answered. Theological tensions raised by the text are not resolved in
any final way. Such passages are more common in books like Job and
Ecclesiastes. Yet those books are part of a canon of Scripture that does
contain answers for their questions, and all our questions find their answers ultimately in Jesus. G. Campbell Morgan's *The Answers of Jesus to
Job* is an illustration of that fact. It's a brilliant little book that matches
Job's plaintive words with statements Jesus made, the latter supplying

---

31. For a summary of the historical information, see Carl E. Armerding,
"Obadiah," in *The Expositor's Bible Commentary*, ed. Frank E. Gaebelein (Grand
Rapids: Zondervan, 1985), 7: 354–55.

gospel truth to the former. For example, Job wanted to find God, so he said, "Oh, that I knew where I might find him" (Job 23:3). Jesus said, "Whoever has seen me has seen the Father" (John 14:9).[32] What Job was looking for, Jesus provides. Every person today needs the same answers to Job's questions.

In the matrix of Solomon's backsliding from God and philosophical quest, he wrote some rather unorthodox ideas. Ecclesiastes 3:19–4:6 is a case in point.[33] When I preached from that passage, I gave the sermon a title that I took from one of Tennyson's poems: "An Infant Crying for the Light." Solomon was crying for the light and what he cried for, Jesus gives. I attempted to make that clear in my sermon, which included the following words:

> Like Solomon, Jesus observed injustice, but he was never a passive observer. When he saw the crooked money-changers in the temple, he threw them out. Jesus also grieved over oppression as Solomon did. Matthew 9:36 says that when Jesus "saw the crowds, he had compassion for them, because they were harassed and helpless, like sheep without a shepherd." But unlike Solomon, Jesus did more than grieve; he healed the sick, cast out demons, defended the helpless, and when he died he took the sins of all people on himself, taking our penalty for sin so we can be reconciled to God and live forever in his presence. He rose from the dead, he's alive today, and he gives life to all people who put their faith in him. Unlike Solomon, Jesus was not confused about our eternal destiny. In Matthew 25, Jesus said that a day of judgment is coming. . . . Right now, like Solomon, we don't understand a lot of things. We see injustice, and we don't understand why God doesn't bring his judgment immediately. We see the oppression of the innocent, and we don't understand why God allows people to suffer. But we are going to be with him forever and we will understand one day.

---

32. G. Campbell Morgan, *The Answers of Jesus to Job* (1935; reprint, Eugene, OR: Wipf & Stock, 2013).

33. I am taking the position that Solomon wrote Ecclesiastes, which is by no means a unanimous position.

. . . Right now, to some extent we're all infants crying for the light—so much we don't understand. But thank God we know the One who *does* understand and who is in charge. One day we'll be with him forever. We'll understand it better then, and we'll tell the story how we've overcome.

Those few words represent one attempt to apply a gospel truth to a dilemma raised but not answered in an Old Testament passage. Whenever we encounter questions raised by an Old Testament text, in our teaching we do not leave them unanswered. Instead, we provide the answers provided by the gospel of Jesus.

6. Does the passage reveal an attribute or activity of God?

When we encounter in the Old Testament a description of God's presence or his work, or a testimony as to his character, we are encountering a description of Jesus. Jesus said, "I and the Father are one" (John 10:30), and "Whoever has seen me has seen the Father" (John 14:9). Christians believe that Jesus is the one, true, eternal God because that's what Jesus said. The Jewish leaders of Jesus' lifetime understood him, and that's the reason they wanted to kill him (John 5:18). The early Christians also understood him, and they believed him. Colossians 1:15 says of Jesus, "He is the image of the invisible God," and verse 19 adds, "In him all the fullness of God was pleased to dwell." As the Nicene Creed expresses it, Jesus is "very God of very God."[34]

In Tremper Longman's *Making Sense of the Old Testament*, one of the "crucial questions" he explores is, "Is the God of the Old Testament also the God of the New Testament?" Longman surveys theological themes in both testaments, and his answer to the question is an emphatic yes.[35] Longman is interested in the way God is portrayed in each testament, and he concludes that the two testaments' portrayals of God are more alike than popularly imagined. My interest here is to state that not only do the portrayals match, but God is the same person in

---

34. See Philip Schaff's description of the Council of Nicaea and its results in *History of the Christian Church*, 5th ed., vol. 3 (Grand Rapids: Eerdmans, 1910), 622–83.

35. Tremper Longman III, *Making Sense of the Old Testament: Three Crucial Questions* (Grand Rapids: Baker, 1998), 55–101.

both testaments: one God acting, being the same. That fact is simply an entailment of adopting an orthodox view of the Trinity. So when the New Testament describes Jesus' works and words, it is describing the works and words of God the Father: the one, true, eternal God of the universe. When the Old Testament describes the works and words of God the Father, it is describing the works and words of God the Son: the one, true, eternal God of the universe. That is precisely the belief of the writers of the New Testament. Paul, for example, was fully aware that Genesis 1:1 affirms, "In the beginning, God created the heavens and the earth" when he wrote of Jesus, "By him all things were created" (Col. 1:16; cf. John 1:3). The prophets repeatedly asserted that they were preaching God's message, and Peter affirmed that they prophesied by "the Spirit of Christ in them" (1 Peter 1:11). Writing such statements created no conflict for Paul or Peter, since they believed that Jesus is the same person as the God of the Old Testament.

To return to our question above, if the Old Testament passage we are studying refers to an activity or attribute of God, that is also an activity or attribute of Jesus. Grasping that truth has enormous implications for our exposition of the Old Testament. When we read a description of God in the Old Testament, we may apply that description to Jesus.[36] Whatever the Old Testament shows God doing is something that Jesus does. Again, that was Paul's theological assumption when he exhorted the Christians in Corinth to be different from the Israelites who tested God in the wilderness. Instead of writing "God," Paul wrote "Christ" in the sentence "we must not put Christ to the test, as some of them did and were destroyed by serpents" (1 Cor. 10:9). When the Israelites tested God, they were testing Christ. Paul was reading the presence of Jesus back into the Old Testament. We may do the same and thus connect the Old Testament text to Jesus.

7. Is the idea of covenant in the passage—in the foreground or in the background?

The reality of a covenant between God and his creation, including humanity, is one of the most important realities in the Old Testament.

---

36. Edmund Clowney also makes this point in *Preaching Christ in All of Scripture*, 11–15.

God relates to people through covenants he establishes by his grace. Some have even seen the idea of covenant as the central concept that binds all the Old Testament together. In some sense, every passage in the Old Testament relates to the covenants God made with his people in some way.[37] That fact relates directly to Jesus because he too established a covenant in fulfillment of all God had done throughout history. Through Jeremiah God promised his old covenant people that he would make a new covenant (Jer. 31:31–33). Jesus inaugurated that new covenant when he told his disciples in the upper room, "This cup that is poured out for you is the new covenant in my blood" (Luke 22:20). Therefore, when we encounter the idea of covenant in the Old Testament, to complete the history of God's covenant-making work we refer to the new covenant in Jesus.

What is the nature of the new covenant in Jesus? In Jesus we have a new priesthood (Heb. 7:1–28), a new sacrifice (Heb. 8:1–10:18), a new nation/people (Eph. 2:11–22), and a new perspective toward the law (Rom. 8:3-4; 10:4; Gal. 3:9-26; 5:1-6; Heb. 10:1-29). Since God has inaugurated a new era through a new covenant in Jesus, when we encounter references to a covenant with God in the Old Testament, we remember that we now have a new covenant in Jesus. Because God offers his covenant through him, we also invite people to put their faith in him.

8. Does the passage contain a promise that is fulfilled in the New Testament?

This question is more complicated than it may first appear. First, in some sense virtually all the Old Testament is a promise. As we noted earlier, every passage is on a teleological timeline that culminates in Jesus. Every moment in salvation history in some way carries forward God's eternal plan to incarnate himself in flesh as our Savior. Thus,

---

37. The idea of a covenant first appears in Genesis 6:18 with reference to God's covenant with Noah, so no explicit covenant exists before Noah. However, many Reformed theologians refer to an Adamic covenant. For discussions of this issue, see Peter J. Gentry and Stephen J. Wellum, *Kingdom through Covenant: A Biblical-Theological Understanding of the Covenants* (Wheaton, IL: Crossway, 2012), 60–61, 177–221; Paul R. Williamson, *Sealed with an Oath: Covenant in God's Unfolding Purpose* (Downers Grove, IL: InterVarsity Press, 2007), 52–58, 69–76.

every Old Testament passage is promissory in that it anticipates the fulfillment of God's promise. However, John Sailhamer points out that "the OT itself does not have a word or expression for the NT idea of 'promise.'"[38] Therefore, he prefers to define promise in terms of future covenant blessing and the coming seed of Abraham. Further, he writes that the identification of the seed of Abraham as a future individual is an important key to the theology of the entire Pentateuch and is even part of its compositional strategy.[39] So "promise" is not necessarily limited to the prophetic predictions we typically associate with the idea of promise. It includes numerous ways the Old Testament anticipates the fulfillment of God's salvation plan.

Second, we must define "fulfilled." Jesus said that he came to fulfill the law and the prophets (Matt. 5:17), but his fulfillment of some laws meant that he was abolishing and superseding them. The word "fulfill" often appears in Matthew, but evidently Matthew had a rather broad definition of the word. He wrote that Jesus' escape from Egypt "was to fulfill" Hosea 11:1 (Matt. 2:15). But Hosea 11:1 is a statement about something in Hosea's past, not a prediction about the future. Therefore, Matthew used "fulfill" here and elsewhere in the sense of historical correspondence—that is, God delivered his people from slavery by leading them out of Egypt, and God provided salvation in Jesus by leading him out of Egypt.[40] Matthew saw that as fulfillment and so should we. In Jesus, God did something new. In another sense, God did what he has always done: he graciously acted to offer reconciliation to himself. Therefore, the work of God in Jesus is parallel to much that God did in the past and that is recorded in the Old Testament. In a sense, such parallels are also promissory.

Though we should keep such complications in mind, the point I am making here has to do with promise in the more narrow sense, what is popularly referred to as a prophetic prediction. For example, consider the following partial list of messianic prophecies, with partial descriptions of each prophecy:

---

38. John H. Sailhamer, *The Meaning of the Pentateuch: Revelation, Composition, and Interpretation* (Downers Grove, IL: InterVarsity Press, 2009), 421.

39. Ibid., 419–59.

40. Craig L. Blomberg, "Matthew," in *Commentary on the New Testament Use of the Old Testament*, ed. G. K. Beale and D. A. Carson (Grand Rapids: Baker, 2007), 7–8.

Genesis 3:15: The seed of the woman will prevail over the seed of the serpent.

Genesis 12:1–3: Abraham and his progeny/seed will bless the world.

Genesis 49:10: The Messiah will come from the tribe of Judah.

Numbers 24:17–19: One shall rise from Israel to bring victory and to rule.

Deuteronomy 18:15, 18: A prophet like Moses will come.

2 Samuel 7:9–16: A descendant of David and will reign forever.

Job 19:25: Job anticipates a living redeemer who will "stand upon the earth."

Psalm 16:10: The Messiah will be resurrected (cf. Acts 2:27; 13:35).

Psalm 22: The Messiah will be mocked and tortured.

Isaiah 7:14: The Messiah will be born to a virgin.

Isaiah 9:1–7: The Messiah will be the "mighty God" and will reign forever.

Isaiah 52:13–53:12: The Messiah will suffer vicariously for the sins of others.

Daniel 7:13–14: The Messiah will be the "son of man" and will rule forever.

Micah 5:2: The Messiah is the eternal Ruler and will be born in Bethlehem.

More specific prophecies are in the Old Testament, and many of them are repeated in the New Testament as having been fulfilled in Jesus. When our exposition includes an Old Testament passage that is fulfilled in Jesus in some way, we have a canonical connection to Jesus. We should draw attention to such promises and show that Jesus is the promised Messiah of the Old Testament.

9. Does the New Testament contrast or supersede the passage in some way?[41]

In numerous New Testament passages, the writers state explicitly that the new covenant in Jesus contrasts with the old covenant. While it is true that from the beginning God has sought sinners in love and grace, it is also true that in Jesus God was doing something new. The new covenant in Jesus is "better," Jesus' ministry is "more excellent," and his work has made the old covenant "obsolete" (Heb. 8:6, 13). Ceremonies, days, and dietary codes that were sacred in the old covenant were the shadow, but the substance is Jesus (Col. 2:16–23; Heb. 8:3–6; 10:1).

Jesus himself drew contrasts between the Old Testament and his own teaching. In the Sermon on the Mount, Jesus cited Old Testament moral codes and proceeded to say, "But I say to you" (Matt. 5:22, 28, 32, 34, 39, 44). In doing so, he was claiming that he has the authority to amend earlier divine revelation. He did the same when he said that his authority transcends laws about the Sabbath (Mark 2:23–28). Jesus also broke down the barrier wall between Jews and Gentiles (Eph. 2:11–22), and the mission Jesus gives to his church includes the Gentiles. Whereas the Old Testament contains God's command to eliminate the Canaanites, Jesus sent his followers to all nations to make disciples (Matt. 28:18–20). Whereas the Old Testament declares that the unclean defiles the clean (Hag. 2:10–14), when Jesus touched a leper Jesus was not defiled but the leper was cleansed (Matt. 8:2–3).

In teaching the Old Testament, expositors will often encounter passages that contrast with Jesus and his new covenant. We should always highlight such contrasts as a way of holding forth Jesus as the Savior we need. In doing so, we should be careful not to give the impression that

---

41. In Greidanus' ways to preach Christ from the Old Testament, this is his "way of contrast." See Greidanus, *Preaching Christ from the Old Testament,* 224–25, 271–77.

the Old Testament describes a different God or that there is no continuity between the testaments. Jesus is God and the New Testament is a continuation of the Old Testament precisely because it is a continuation of his work. My point here is that we do not hesitate to extol Jesus as the New Testament does, for without him we are not preaching the gospel.

10. Does the passage refer to something or someone that is a type of Jesus?

Before we consider how to make typological connections from the Old Testament to Jesus, it is necessary to define typology since it is defined and practiced in a variety of ways. Since typology can refer to "fanciful kinds of biblical interpretation closely related to allegory," then "the place of typology in the Christian use of the Old Testament depends entirely . . . on what is meant by the word."[42] Our purpose here is not to provide a word study of the Greek *tupos* or review and assess the various ways interpreters have defined and used typology.[43] These are important issues, but the goal here is more modest. We merely aim at stating what we mean by typology and describing briefly how it can be used as a valid method of connecting the Old Testament to Jesus.

Stated most simply, typology is identifying an activity or work of God that is typical of the way he works. "Its basis is in the Old Testament understanding of the unchanging nature of God and his unchanging covenant and principles of dealing with men."[44] Since in Old Testament history God established that he acts in particular ways, we can expect him to act in those ways in the future. Usually the expositor using typology proceeds to show how the typical activity of God is also true of Jesus. The Old Testament action or item is the *type*, and Jesus is the *antitype*.

---

42. David L. Baker, "Typology and the Christian Use of the Old Testament," *Scottish Journal of Theology* 29 (1976): 137.

43. For an examination of the use of the term *tupos* in the New Testament, see Leonhard Goppelt, *Typos: The Typological Use of the Old Testament in the New* (Grand Rapids: Eerdmans, 1982).

44. Francis Foulkes, "The Acts of God: A Study of the Basis of Typology in the Old Testament," in *The Right Doctrine from the Wrong Texts? Essays on the Use of the Old Testament in the New*, ed. G. K. Beale (Grand Rapids: Baker, 1994), 371.

Far from divorcing the text from its literary and historical context, the text's context is the starting point for any typological considerations. In other words, a typological method should not read into an Old Testament text a different or higher meaning, but draw from the text a different or higher Christological application of the same meaning.[45] In addition, to justify a typological connection between an Old Testament passage and Jesus, expositors should be able to point to factors such as linguistic correspondence between the type and antitype, and they should note how both are related similarly to God's plan of redemption. Plus, as we move from type to antitype we look for escalation. That is, the antitype is greater in nature and/or scope than the type. This final criterion will necessarily be fulfilled if we follow the rule to limit typology to those types that find their antitype in Jesus.[46]

To see how typology works, consider how we might teach the Old Testament tabernacle as a type of Jesus. In its Old Testament context, the tabernacle represented the presence of God among his people. God said to Moses, "There I will meet with you" and "I will meet there with the sons of Israel" (Exod. 25:22; 29:43). In describing the work of the priests in the tabernacle, God repeatedly referred to their service as "before the LORD" (e.g., 28:29, 30, 35, 38; 29:23, 24, 25, 26, 42). So serving in the tabernacle was serving in the presence of God. The account of the building of the tabernacle concludes with the report that "the glory of the LORD filled the tabernacle" (40:34).

How, then, is the tabernacle a type of Jesus? In Jesus, God came to meet with us. Still today, we meet God in Jesus. We are not alone in making such an affirmation. The Gospel of Matthew states that the birth of Jesus was a fulfillment of Isaiah 7:14, which states that the coming Messiah would be called Immanuel, "God with us" (Matt. 1:23). John 1:14 says, "The Word became flesh and dwelt among us." The Greek word

---

45. Benjamin J. Ribbens, "Typology of Types: Typology in Dialogue," *Journal of Theological Interpretation* 5 (2011): 89.

46. For discussions of methodological controls on typology that serve to subdue interpreters who are apt to flee the constraints of context and shared terminology, see David Dockery, "Typological Exegesis: Moving Beyond Abuse and Neglect," in *Reclaiming the Prophetic Mantle: Preaching the Old Testament Faithfully*, ed. George Klein (Nashville: Broadman, 1992), 161–78; David Schrock, "What Designates a Valid Type?: A Christotelic, Covenantal Proposal," *Southeastern Theological Review* 5 (2014): 3–26.

translated "dwelt" is the verb form of the noun used in the Septuagint to refer to the tabernacle. Translating John 1:14 literally, we could say that Jesus "tabernacled" among us or he "pitched his tent" among us. Also, the New Testament refers to Christians as the temple of the Holy Spirit, meaning that God lives with/in people who know Jesus (1 Cor. 3:16–17; 6:19; 2 Cor. 6:16). Thus the tabernacle "represents" Jesus in that this work of God is typical of the way God works throughout history and in Jesus.

Typology is not the same as allegory. If we applied allegory, or some sort of allegorical abuse of typology, to our study of the tabernacle, we would claim that the tripartite structure of the tabernacle represents the Trinity, the making of the incense represents the study habits of the church's leaders as they prepare to teach, and the ephod the priest wore represents "putting on Christ," and so on as far as our imagination could take us. Because of such abuses of allegory, and because typology has sometimes degenerated into allegory, perhaps we could use words like "analogy," "paradigm," or "correspondence" instead of "typology" to refer to this way of connecting Old Testament texts to Jesus. Still, it is a valid method when it is controlled by focusing on the immediate context and limiting the application of the method to the typical ways God has acted in salvation history as demonstrated in the Bible.

To conclude consideration of this method and of the importance of connecting the Old Testament to Jesus, let us heed the following words of Francis Foulkes:

> We should not look back to this part of the Bible just for the history of the Jewish religion, nor just for moral examples, nor just for its messianic prophecy, nor to see the excellence of the faith of Israel in contrast to the religious faith and understanding of other nations of antiquity. In actual fact Israel was often faithless, and it is God seeking to show himself to man, rather than man searching after God, that we need most to see. We look to the Old Testament to see God in his grace revealing himself in the history of Israel in preparation for the sending of his Son, the Incarnate Word and the Savior of the world.[47]

---

47. Foulkes, "The Acts of God: A Study of the Basis of Typology in the Old Testament," 370–71.

When we read the Old Testament through a Christological lens, we can see Jesus everywhere in the Old Testament. When we read that God provided for his people, we remember that God provided himself for his people in his incarnation as Jesus of Nazareth. When we read an example of obeying God, we recall that Jesus obeyed God perfectly and he empowers us to obey. When we read an example of victory for God's people, we consider how we can be victorious only with Jesus' deliverance and help. When we read about God's judgment of sin, we think of how Jesus is going to return and initiate final judgment. Examples of sin in the Old Testament remind us that all of us are sinners in need of Jesus the Savior. When we read about God working in the life of a Gentile, we think of how the gospel of Jesus brings Jews and Gentiles together in the church. As Jesus said of the Old Testament Scriptures, "they . . . bear witness about me" (John 5:39). As we teach and preach the Old Testament, may we also bear witness to him.

Chapter 8

HOW DO WE APPLY THE OLD TESTAMENT TO CONTEMPORARY PEOPLE?

8-STEP METHOD

STEP 1	Translating the text
STEP 2	Considering text criticism
STEP 3	Interpreting the genre
STEP 4	Exploring the context
STEP 5	Defining important words
STEP 6	Identifying the big idea
STEP 7	Connecting to Jesus
STEP 8	Applying the text to contemporary people

We have reached the final step in our 8-step process of exposition. If we stop short of this step, though, all our former work will have been futile. Please don't misunderstand. Following the previous steps in this volume is essential if we are to understand the Old Testament. But understanding is an insufficient goal. If we study a text and its context carefully, outline the main points clearly, and even see the connection to Jesus, yet fail to apply the truth of the text to the lives of people, what have we accomplished? Not much. As Daniel Doriani writes, "The goal of biblical exposition is Christian living, not merely

Christian thinking."[1] It is possible to give people knowledge about a text with no challenge to put the truth to work. It's not just possible; it happens all the time.

Doriani also identifies a few reasons why some expositors resist working at applying a text to the lives of contemporary people. On the one hand, some preachers and teachers think practical application of a text is so easy that it is not necessary to work on it or prepare for it. Points of application will merely occur to teachers as they teach, or to hearers as they hear. On the other extreme are expositors who see application as impossible for Bible teachers to do adequately, so they can do nothing but rely completely on the Holy Spirit to apply the text to the lives of hearers. Doriani sees both of these approaches as errors and he summarizes, "Application is not so easy that it can be left to the listener, nor so problematic that it must be left to God. Rather, it is a challenge that demands sustained effort."[2]

The effort about which Doriani and others have written is important work. Knowing the truth but not doing the truth is nothing less than a spiritual tragedy. James 1:22 has the imperative, "Be doers of the word, and not hearers only, deceiving yourselves." Later in his letter he wrote, "Whoever knows the right thing to do and fails to do it, for him it is sin" (4:17). So hearing God's Word and knowing God's Word are not sufficient. We must do God's Word, and if we fail to do it our failure is sin. Even partial obedience is still disobedience. Samuel told King Saul to destroy the Amalekites, and Saul obeyed—almost. Saul spared Agag the Amalekite king and some animals to offer as sacrifices. Samuel confronted Saul with his partial obedience and said, "To obey is better than sacrifice" (1 Sam. 15:22). Simple obedience to God's word trumps observance of religious rituals, and no ritual can compensate for disobedience. Disobedience is doing what we want to do instead of what God tells us to do. And when we do what we want to do, we are directing our own lives and we are our own lords. At such times we should hear Jesus' question, "Why do you call me 'Lord, Lord,' and not do what I tell you?" (Luke 6:46). It's a sobering question: Do we even have the

---

1. Daniel M. Doriani, *Getting the Message: A Plan for Interpreting and Applying the Bible* (Phillipsburg, NJ: P&R, 1996), 128.
2. Ibid., 134.

right to call Jesus our Lord if we know his word but do not obey it? Obedience is imperative. Therefore, teachers and preachers of the Old Testament have not completed their work until they call for such obedience. Challenging hearers to obey, to live the truth, is the work of application. As Doriani reminds us, such application requires sustained effort. In such effort we need God's help, so we had better pray.

Pray

Richard Baxter wrote *The Reformed Pastor* in 1656. Throughout that book, Baxter repeatedly challenged pastors to give themselves fully and fervently to the work of teaching every church member and evangelizing every person in the community. It is an understatement to say that Baxter believed in and practiced the application of the Scriptures to the lives of people. He was deadly serious about catechizing every believer home by home, he worked tirelessly to do so, and he challenged other pastors to do the same.

However, the first chapter in *The Reformed Pastor* addresses the subject of "the oversight of ourselves." Baxter emphatically maintained that before ministers are ready to apply the Scriptures to others, they must prepare themselves spiritually to do so by applying the Scriptures to themselves. Consider a few excerpts from Baxter's plea.

> Content not yourselves with being in a state of grace, but be also careful that your graces are kept in vigorous and lively exercise, and that you preach to yourselves the sermons which you study, before you preach them to others. . . . They will likely feel when you have been much with God. . . . When I let my heart grow cold, my preaching is cold. . . . When I have grown cold in preaching, they have grown cold too. . . . We are the nurses of Christ's little ones. If we forbear taking food ourselves, we shall famish them. . . . O brethren, watch therefore over your own hearts: keep out lusts and passions, and worldly inclinations; keep up the life of faith, and love, and zeal; be much at home, and be much with God. If it be not your daily business to study your own hearts, and to subdue corruption, and to walk with God . . . all will go wrong, and you will starve your hearers. . . . Above all, be much in secret prayer

and meditation. . . . Prayer must carry on our work as well as preaching: he preacheth not heartily to his people, that prayeth not earnestly for them.[3]

Baxter's exhortation is worthy of our humble meditation and application. Baxter was directing his words to the preaching of pastors, but his words could apply more generally to all Bible teachers.

He pointed to two ways our prayer is dynamically connected to our preaching and teaching. First, our prayer affects the results of our teaching. Lack of prayer inevitably results in cold preaching, and cold preaching will produce cold hearers. Second, our prayer will affect the fervency of our preaching. When we do not pray earnestly for the people we teach, we will not preach heartily or fervently to them. They will not sense the spiritual passion in our hearts, because if we have not spent much time in prayer it is not likely that we will possess much spiritual passion.

Baxter's theme of "the oversight of ourselves" belongs at the head of a chapter addressing the application of the Scriptures. Before we apply the Bible's truth to the lives of other people, we apply it to our own lives. If we have not seen to our own obedience, are we ready or worthy to challenge other people to obey? The apostle Paul wrote that he sacrificed and disciplined himself "lest after preaching to others I myself should be disqualified" (1 Cor. 9:27). Paul also counseled the elders in the church in Ephesus, "Pay careful attention to yourselves" (Acts 20:28), and he wrote to Timothy, "Keep a close watch on yourself" (1 Tim. 4:16). When Paul directed believers in Galatia to restore Christians who were caught in sin, he also told them, "Keep watch on yourself, lest you too be tempted" (Gal. 6:1). Richard Baxter's priority on the oversight of ourselves is also a priority in the Scriptures.

After we have studied a passage of Scripture, we will likely begin to see some ways the passage can be applied in the lives of contemporary believers. At that point, before we consider how we will challenge other people to apply the text to their lives, we fall to our knees and pray about the application of the text to our own lives. We ask God to help

---

3. Richard Baxter, *The Reformed Pastor* (1656; reprint, Carlisle, PA: Banner of Truth, 1974), 61–62, 122.

us to be brutal in our assessment of our own obedience. We ask God to show us where we have sinned. When he shows us, we confess our failure to live out all that is required by the text before us. When we have confessed our negligence in obeying God's Word, we receive God's forgiveness and cleansing by faith (1 John 1:19). Without such cleansing we will not be "useful to the master" (2 Tim. 2:20–21). After God cleanses us by his grace, we ask him to empower us to obey his word in the future. We will not be able to live his way without his power in us enabling us (Phil. 2:12–13; Col. 1:29). And we will not be able to effect change in the lives of other people through teaching God's Word unless we have allowed God to change us first. Let us go to him in prayer, asking for such change, and asking him to use us as his agents of change in the lives of other people.

The Inadequacy of Knowledge

As the senior editor of the *Life Application Study Bible*, Dave Veerman guided the editors in writing the application notes. He began with a working definition of application; it was "confronting people with the right questions and then motivating them to action."[4] In *How to Apply the Bible*, he explains and illustrates what the right questions are and how to motivate people to action. At one point he writes, "Gathering facts is an important first step, but it is not enough. . . . Many people understand biblical truths without changing their lives. . . . Satan has a good understanding of the Bible."[5] He's right. James 2:19 says, "The demons believe and shudder." The demons have knowledge and belief but not obedience. Knowledge is inadequate.

King David knew God's standards of right and wrong. After he committed adultery with Bathsheba, Nathan the prophet confronted him with his sin indirectly. He told David a story about a wealthy man stealing the property of a poor man. David was outraged and demanded the punishment of the wealthy man (2 Sam. 11:1–12:14). David knew that stealing what belongs to another person is wrong, and he knew that someone guilty of such a crime should be punished. He had a keen sense

---

4. Dave Veerman, *How to Apply the Bible: Discover the Truths of Scripture and Put Them into Practice* (Wheaton, IL: Livingstone, 2009), 126.
5. Ibid., 21.

of morality and justice. David's problem was not lack of knowledge; it was lack of application, and for years he suffered the consequences of his disobedience.

I tell my students that one reason studying is commendable is that knowledge is preferable to ignorance. Knowing is better than not knowing. Education, therefore, is virtuous. However, we humans can corrupt even the best things and knowledge is no exception. When we know information that others do not know, we are tempted to be proud of ourselves. Self-exaltation, in fact, is one motive for gaining more knowledge. First Corinthians 8:1 says that mere "knowledge puffs up." Knowledge can be dangerous; it can lead us to commit the sin of pride. Of course, that's no excuse for not studying, since not studying is lazy and laziness is also sin.

"Knowledge puffs up"—it makes us feel like we're big. Some people have a lot of money and it makes them arrogant—"Look at how big I am; you're not as important as me because you don't have as much money." People do the same thing with knowledge—"You're not as important as me because I know facts that you don't know."

Intellectual pride is common in the world but it has no place in the church. In the church, we are servants of Jesus and of one another, and the greatest person is not the person who knows the most, but the person who serves the most (Matt. 20:25–27). In 1 Corinthians 8:1, Paul also wrote, "All of us possess knowledge." Knowledge is universal. When we know something, we should not flatter ourselves that we're better than other people. They have knowledge too—knowledge about different subjects. My sister sent a note to me asking about clothes sizes for my grandsons, like I would know that information. I forwarded the note to my wife, who knows so much about clothes sizes that she should be awarded a PhD. Everybody possesses knowledge, but different knowledge. If someone like me ran the world, everybody would know and love Hebrew but our clothes wouldn't fit. Possessing knowledge is no good reason for pride.

When I was in seminary, I was spending a lot of time learning to read the New Testament in Greek and the Old Testament in Hebrew, plus attempting to learn some church history, theology, etc. I was gaining a lot of new information. Then one day when I was reading the Bible devotionally I read what Paul wrote to Timothy in 1 Timothy 1:5:

"The aim of our charge is love that issues from a pure heart and a good conscience and a sincere faith." Paul had encyclopedic knowledge of the Old Testament and he was a compelling teacher. But what was the end game of his knowledge and instruction? His goal was to produce more love, purity, and faith. After I read 1 Timothy 1:5, for days I read no further in the Bible. I meditated on that verse and asked God to help me to think and live like that, that is, "The aim of our charge is love." I did not want to gain information and fail to grow in godliness. Learning information is easy for most of us; expressing love to people is hard for most of us. Information is a means to an end, and the end is love. So do you know who Mephibosheth is? How about Melchizedek, Methuselah, Malchus, or Micaiah? If you know them, that's wonderful. But this year are you better at loving people than last year? "All of us possess knowledge. This knowledge puffs up, but love builds up" (1 Cor. 8:1). Knowledge is inadequate.

Guidelines for Application

Howard and William Hendricks caution that the application of scriptural truth will vary for each person. They do not mean that we can apply Scripture any way we choose, nor do they mean that we can select certain Scriptures to obey while neglecting the passages that do not appeal to us. They mean that each person is different and each person's circumstances are different, so the way we apply the Bible will be rather customized. As they put it, "The specific way in which you grow and mature will probably look a bit different than the way I grow and mature. That difference has to do with our unique, God-given design."[6] Obedience is not optional, but everyone's obedience may not involve precisely the same behaviors. For example, Ephesians 5:25 says, "Husbands, love your wives." All followers of Jesus who are husbands are under obligation to obey God's command to love their wives. However, since all husbands and wives are different, the way each husband expresses love will be different.

As teachers and preachers of the Bible apply its truths to hearers, it will be wise to keep in mind God's unique design of each person and

---

6. Howard G. Hendricks and William D. Hendricks, *Living by the Book: The Art and Science of Reading the Bible*, rev. ed. (Chicago: Moody, 2007), 329–30.

each person's unique circumstances. Such mindfulness will prevent us from attempting to force everyone into the same mold, since uniformity does not seem to be God's intention. With such diversity in mind, we can learn certain guidelines that will help us apply the Scriptures to the lives of the people we teach.

First, the application must match the exposition. Bible teachers should regard this as an inviolable rule. What the text says and what it means drives our application. We apply what *the text* says, not what we want to say. I once heard a pastor preach on the account of Jesus healing the woman with a discharge of blood. He referred to the fact that she had gone to many physicians prior to going to Jesus but her condition only grew worse. His application was that people should not delay in coming to Jesus. "Come to Jesus now," he said, "Don't wait as this woman did." The problem with that application is that the text never says that the woman delayed in coming to Jesus. Instead, the text gives the impression that she went to physicians prior to hearing about Jesus. Also, the text states, "She had heard the reports about Jesus and came up behind him in the crowd and touched his garment" (Mark 5:27), implying that she went to Jesus soon after she heard about him. The pastor's plea was commendable: people should not delay in coming to Jesus. But in grafting that application onto that text, he forced the text to say something it does not say. His application drove his exposition, and that order must be reversed: the exposition drives the application. One application that would fit that text is a challenge to take the good news about Jesus' power to all people, because without him they have only what the world offers, which is not sufficient. That application fits the text, since the woman in the text looked for help from the world to no avail, but when she heard about Jesus she went to him and he healed her. Before we determine our application to our hearers, we remind ourselves of what the text says. What are the main ideas? That is what we will apply.

Second, remember that Jesus is the answer for every sin problem. As we stated in the last chapter, we do not call people merely to try to do better or be better. Attempts at obedience in the flesh will fall short and they are not the gospel. In every application we will include Jesus and his power to save and sanctify. Only he can effect lasting change in us. Therefore, we will not merely say, "Look at how Elijah stood alone against the prophets of Baal on Mt. Carmel. Let's be willing to stand alone too!" Instead, we will say, "Look at the power God displayed on Mt. Carmel in answer to Elijah's prayer. Let's seek God's power to help us fulfill his will, even when we have to stand alone against a great number of people. He can do great things with us, just as he did on Mt. Carmel, when we obey him instead of conforming to the crowd." If we do not include God's offer of salvation and sanctification in Jesus, we are offering people no answer to their sin problem and ultimately offering no hope.

Third, do not assume your hearers are good at application. Many people are not. Therefore, we have a responsibility to be clear about what the text says, what it means, what it means to us, and what we should do in light of what the text says. Tell the people what to do. Fill in the blanks for them. Be specific and help them to see exactly what to do to apply God's Word. To apply the account of Elijah's encounter with the prophets of Baal on Mt. Carmel, we could ask questions like, "When you are at school, do you ever feel like you are alone and surrounded by people who have completely different priorities? At the office or in your neighborhood, do you feel like a fish swimming upstream? When someone tells a dirty story, what are you going to do? When someone asks you why you bother with church on Sundays, what are you going to say?" We would not stop with asking questions. We would proceed with describing how it might look to stand alone in God's power in each of those circumstances.

How might we apply Deuteronomy 6:5? It says, "You shall love the LORD your God with all your heart and with all your soul and with all your might." It is not sufficient for us to say, "We should love God more. Do we love God as we ought?" We apply specifically. We could ask, "If we love God with all our hearts, won't we behave toward God like we behave toward other people we love? We'll really enjoy spending time with him and we'll look forward to it. Are you spending time with God, speaking to him in prayer and listening to him speak to you from the Scriptures? When we love people with all our hearts, we'll also want to please them. Do you want to please God? Is there something in your life that doesn't please him? Ask God to help you get that out of your life, and ask him today." That's an effort to apply specifically. In preparation to apply a passage of Scripture, we ask ourselves,

"In light of what this text says, what do I want these people to do?" We are not ready to teach the Bible until we have asked and answered that question.

Fourth, live the truth before you teach it. People who teach communication often refer to Aristotle's three categories of rhetoric: logos, pathos, and ethos. The *logos* ("word") is the content of rhetoric. It includes the proofs or argumentation for the message we are communicating. The *pathos* ("feeling") is the emotion with which we deliver the content of our communication, and the emotional reaction we seek to elicit in the hearers. The *ethos* ("custom" or "standard") is the personal character of the speaker, that is, his or her competence and credibility. Aristotle wrote that all three rudiments are necessary to persuade an audience.

If people in secular society require speakers to be competent and credible in order to be persuaded by their messages, how much more will God's people require the same of their teachers and preachers? Before we ask people to do something, we should first ask if we have the right to ask. It is pointless to ask people to do something we are not doing. They will not do it, and we have not earned the right to ask them to do it. For example, how can an expositor tell people they should give generous offerings to God in worship when he or she is not giving generously? How can a teacher challenge people to share the gospel when he or she is not doing so? Therefore, our preparation to teach Scripture includes asking questions like, "If this passage of Scripture contains a command, am I obeying it? If the text describes a lifestyle, am I living it?" William Perkins, a pastor in England in the late sixteenth century, put it succinctly: "The people can hardly be sanctified by the ministry of an unsanctified man."[7]

Fifth, make the entire exposition understandable. In order to apply the truth, people have to understand the truth. Application of a message they do not fully understand will be ineffective. I once heard a sermon in which the preacher used the word "inclusio" twice without defining it. We should usually keep shop talk in the shop.

I don't know a lot about computers. I know enough to do my work and that's all. Occasionally, therefore, I require the assistance of people

---

7. William Perkins, *The Art of Prophesying and the Calling of the Ministry* (1592; reprint, Carlisle, PA: Banner of Truth, 1996), 88.

who know a lot more about computers. Once I was having a conversation with a computer expert who was training me to perform a new task. He began talking to me as if I possess his level of knowledge. Since I don't, I had no idea what he was saying. Eventually we were able to communicate with one another but not without some starts and stops. At one point I was tempted to say, "Let's press pause and take a break while I step out and study computer science for a few years. Then I'll come back and we can finish this conversation." In teaching the Bible, we can be just as unclear. The apostle Paul asked the Christians in Colossae to pray for him as he preached the gospel: "that I may make it clear, which is how I ought to speak" (Col. 4:4). We too ought to speak God's Word clearly.

When we say that our entire exposition should be "understandable," what is understandable depends on who is listening. We will explain the Scriptures differently to graduate students than we will if we are teaching children. But what if both types of people are among our listeners? It is challenging but possible to teach so as to challenge mature Bible students while being understood by children. In my view, we should aim at being understood by children, and then perhaps even the adults will understand! And understanding is essential, because we cannot expect people to put into practice some principle that they do not fully comprehend.

Sixth, remember that the Scripture has one meaning but many applications. As we explain and apply the Scripture, it is imperative to avoid giving people the impression that the Scripture may mean something different to them than it does to us, that the meaning of the text is dependent on the perspective of the interpreter. It is not. The meaning of the text is absolute, not relative; it is eternal, not malleable. The meaning is not dependent on human opinion; it is divine revelation. Of course, emphasizing that the text has one meaning is not the same as saying that every text's meaning is easy to determine or to understand. Sometimes we struggle to arrive at a text's meaning. Also, sometimes interpreters disagree with one another, but one interpretation is correct and the others are incorrect, though we may be uncertain which is correct.

Communicating to people our uncertainty about the meaning of a text is perfectly acceptable, but it is not acceptable to communicate that arriving at the text's one meaning doesn't matter. Likewise, it is not acceptable to say that "this text may have one meaning to you and another meaning to me." The text has one meaning. But the way we put the meaning into practice, the way we apply the meaning to our lives, will likely be different.[8] The distinction between meaning and application is significant, even more so in light of the prominence of postmodern or reader-response ways of reading texts in the wider culture.[9] Especially if we speak of the meaning of a text and its application to our lives in close proximity to one another, we will want to make the distinction between meaning and application crystal clear.

Seventh, pay attention to any factors in the text that may delimit application. For example, in the first verse of Malachi God addresses Israel as a whole. Then, in verse 6 God says he is addressing "you, O priests." So should application be limited to vocational ministers? Hold the phone. Verse 8 mentions offering substandard sacrifices. Only priests placed sacrifices on the altar, but other people "offered" sacrifices in that they brought them to the priests. Furthermore, verse 13 mentions the animals "you bring," and verse 14 refers to animals in the flock. These latter allusions point to activities performed by all worshipers. So it seems that while priests are singled out for special condemnation, all worshipers are implicated in this divine denunciation of worthless worship. That fact is important in guiding contemporary application, and it may also be important to point out to people who listen to our exposition since they may read "you, O priests" and conclude that nothing in the passage relates to them.

The book of Proverbs repeatedly addresses young men. For example, in warnings against adultery the writer exhorts readers to avoid "the forbidden woman," "the evil woman," and "the adulteress" (e.g., 5:3; 6:24), not the forbidden man, the evil man, and the adulterer. The reason for such forms is that the book of Proverbs consists of wisdom that was used, at least in part, to train young men for leadership. In a patriarchal society, women were not prepared for leadership in the same way,

---

8. See Daniel Akin's explanation in Daniel L. Akin et al., *Engaging Exposition* (Nashville: B&H, 2011), 172, 181.

9. For further information see N. Allan Moseley, *Thinking against the Grain: Developing a Biblical Worldview in a Culture of Myths* (Grand Rapids: Kregel, 2003), 56–73.

and Proverbs reflects that historical reality. However, Proverbs contains no suggestion that women should not be wise and ethical, or that men are never adulterers. Furthermore, Proverbs is part of a canon of Scripture that refers to women in countless ways, including calls to be wise and holy. Since today women serve in many leadership roles in society (something not prohibited by Scripture), it is perfectly legitimate to apply Proverbs to both males and females. In some contexts it may be important to make that point when encountering masculine forms of address in Proverbs. We should not delimit our application unless we have ample scriptural warrant to do so.

Eighth, be open to listen to the way other people apply the text. Just as part of the process of exegesis is consulting what other interpreters have written in commentaries, part of the process of application can be listening to how other people apply a text to their lives. In the church where I am a member, our small groups spend time in sermon-based application. After we hear the pastor's biblical exposition and application, we talk about further ways we should apply the passage of Scripture in our lives. For ten years I was the pastor of our church, and for the final year we had that small group ministry. I was in a small group, so after I preached the sermon on Sunday, on Tuesday nights I was part of a group of people who talked about further ways to apply the sermon and Scripture to their lives. On most Tuesday nights, as I listened to the ways people in our small group applied the Scripture to their lives, I thought, "Why didn't I think of that?" Again, Scripture has one meaning but many applications. Before teaching a passage publicly, consider listening to the ways a few other people apply that passage in their lives. It may strengthen the public application.

Ninth, consider the life situations of your hearers. While this kind of consideration may seem basic, it is often overlooked. Many expositors live in a different world than the people who listen to them. Pastors, for example, live in the context of the church. They work at the church and they think about the church all the time. It's their world. It's not the world of the people who listen to them preach. Church members spend their days working as homemakers, salesmen, teachers, attorneys, students, clerks, health care workers, mechanics, etc. Before we are ready to teach a passage of Scripture to such people, we should spend some time thinking about the ways the passage applies to contexts outside church life. Many pastors limit almost all of their application to "our church," or "what we are doing as a church." That subject is very important, but the Bible also applies to all the situations people face at work, school, and home—that is, outside the context of the church. To show such application, we need to spend some time thinking outside our life context and thinking about theirs.

Tenth, love the people you teach. Scripture repeatedly commands us to love one another (John 13:34–35; 15:12, 17; Rom. 12:10; Gal. 5:13; 1 Thess. 3:12; 4:9; 1 Peter 1:22; 4:8; 1 John 3:11, 23; 4:7; 2 John 5). If an expositor does not love a brother or sister in Christ, he or she is under obligation to God to confess and repent immediately. But beyond our obligations as followers of Jesus, we bear certain obligations as teachers of the Bible. One of those obligations is to teach in love. In doing so we are showing the people we teach how to love. Also, and this is why this point belongs in a chapter on application, our love for the people we teach will affect the way we teach. When we love the people we teach, we will not fail to apply the truth to their lives because we want them to prosper and to experience God's blessing. Of course, our motive in application is to glorify God, but another motive is to help the people live godly lives, not merely to point out their sins. Inevitably, the motive of love will affect our content, our tone, and even our countenance. We will not "talk down" to the people; we will implore them to be faithful as we would implore a beloved member of our family.

When I served as a pastor full time, every day I asked God to help me love the people I pastored. How can a shepherd lead the sheep well if he is not genuinely concerned for their welfare? How will he be motivated to do what is best for them if he does not love them? Loving the people we teach will affect our communication with them, but love is more than a communication technique. We cannot fake love. People can sense whether we love them or not. Furthermore, we should express our love. If our hearers know we love them, they will be more willing to listen sympathetically to our teaching and more likely to put into practice our application of the Bible.

Eleventh, include yourself in the application. When applying the Scripture to a group of people, every time we use "you," we should consider changing it to "we." Saying "You need to apply this to your life," "You should repent," or "You will experience joy if you obey

God's Word" may or may not reflect an arrogant heart but it sounds arrogant. As William Perkins put it, "Whenever possible the minister should include himself in his reproofs. In this way his preaching, teaching, and counseling will be expressed in a mild and gentle spirit."[10] In contrast, including only others in reproofs, or in application, puts the speaker on a pedestal above the hearers. If saying "you" instead of "we" reflects the way the teacher thinks, his or her teaching is an exercise in self-deception. All of us should apply the text to our lives, repent, obey, because we too are sinners in need of sanctification. To think otherwise is spiritually unhealthy.

Of course, there are exceptions to our use of "we" in application. Sometimes it will help people more when we attempt to drive the truth home to them by saying, "Are you living like this?" Also, sometimes we may have to say "you" because the application does not fit us. Proverbs 31:10–31 describes a virtuous woman. When a man teaches those verses, it will not fit for him to say, "Ladies, when we, by God's grace, pattern our lives after this description, our husbands will praise us." Such exceptions aside, generally we should identify with the people we teach. We too need to hear and heed God's Word, even as we teach it.

Twelfth, use life-related illustrations to help people to see the truth in action. Telling stories serves multiple functions in Bible teaching. Stories grab people's attention. People remember stories. When we teach we capitalize on the power of stories and use them to explain and apply the contents of the Bible.

When some people think of illustrations, they think of object lessons, the kind ministers used commonly a few decades ago in "children's sermons." The idea behind such object lessons is that spiritual truth is difficult to understand, so we explain it with something that is visible and easy to understand. That makes sense, as far as it goes, but showing people a plant and talking about how God created plants does not show them how to worship the Creator. How much better to tell a story about someone who observed the creation, decided to worship God who created it all, and was completely changed by a relationship with the Creator. Concrete illustrations are good, but they fall short of

---

10. Perkins, *The Art of Prophesying*, 62.

life-related illustrations. For example, I have read and used the following illustration about faith. It is concrete, but not life-related.

> A man was walking in an unfamiliar forest in the winter. He
> came upon a small river that was covered with ice. Was the
> ice thick enough to support his weight? He didn't know, so he
> slowly crept out on the edge of the ice on his hands and knees.
> Ever so slowly, he moved his hands forward, gradually increas-
> ing the weight on them until they supported his weight and he
> could move a few more inches forward. After he had moved
> only a few feet like that, he heard the jingle of bells. He looked
> up and saw a sleigh coming down the middle of the river pulled
> by two horses. Obviously the ice was strong enough to support
> him. Aren't we all like that when we are tentative about trust-
> ing God? We should never doubt his ability to support us. He is
> infinitely worthy of our trust.

That is not a bad illustration, in my opinion. However, contrast it
with the following illustration. I was preaching on Proverbs 3:5–6 and
talking about trusting God, not money, not ourselves, and not other
people, but God. I began with some conceptual illustrations and then
offered a real-life illustration of trusting God, or not trusting God:

> We should trust God, not people. It's not that no one is worthy
> of our trust. We can trust the banker to keep our money safe.
> We can trust the grocer to sell sanitary food. And we all know
> we can trust politicians to keep all their campaign promises.
> We know that some people have earned our trust and there's no
> rational reason not to trust them. But we should *not* trust people
> to do something that they're not capable of doing. If you asked
> me to translate Hebrew for you, you can trust me to do that.
> But if you asked me to wire the electricity in your house and I
> come over to do it, get your family away from the house as soon
> as possible. I can't be trusted to do that.
>   Here's the important point: No person on earth can take
> God's place, so we shouldn't trust them to do that. No person
> can give us eternal life, only God can do that. . . . There are

many things only God can do for us, and we have to learn to trust him, not people. And trusting people instead of God, putting people in the place of God, leads to disastrous consequences.

That's the story of a lady we'll call Mary. I met Mary not long after her husband died. We'll call him Bob. Mary and Bob had been married for years. They had shared a wonderful life together. But after Bob died, Mary not only grieved his death, she also went into deep depression for a long time. She didn't know what to do with her time, how to live, or even how to feel. Her entire life had been wrapped up in Bob—her schedule, her thoughts, and her feelings had all revolved around him. After his death, she found herself at a loss and didn't know where to turn. Her depression was so dark and intractable that she began frequenting the office of a psychiatrist and he gave her medication to dull the emotional pain. One day, she went to the drug store to fill the prescription for her medication and on a lark she bought some earrings. She had no idea why she had done it. She didn't need earrings; she had stopped going anywhere in public. But for some reason, as she looked at her new earrings the thought came to her that she could wear them if she went to church. So the next Sunday, for the first time in a long time, she went to church.

She wasn't prepared for what happened there. She had gone only because she thought that dressing up and getting out would make her feel better. She hadn't planned on meeting God. But during the experience of singing praise, listening to people pray, and hearing God's Word, she came to realize that God was there and that she should turn to him for help. Mary did that, and over a period of months I had the joy of hearing her talk about how God was healing her heart. And the main lesson God taught her was about trust. God showed her that she had looked to Bob for everything. All of life had revolved around him. She had looked to her husband to do things only God can do. And when he died, it was as if *her* life had ended too. She learned that trusting people *instead of* God is idolatry and it leads to disastrous consequences. There are some things no person can do; only God can do them.

I hope that story (which is true) helped to demonstrate to people how to apply the truth of Proverbs 3:5–6: "Trust in the LORD with all your heart, and do not lean on your own understanding. In all your ways acknowledge him, and he will make straight your paths." That is the purpose of such stories: to show people what it looks like to apply the Scriptures to their lives.

Thirteenth, be a student of the culture in which you teach. When missionaries move to a new culture, they learn enough about that culture to be able to relate to the people who live there. The more they know about the culture, the fewer barriers between them and the people will exist. Missiologists refer to this phenomenon as "contextualization." All of us live and minister in a context. To communicate well with people in our context, we will need to know about the context in which they live.

Of course, no culture is monolithic. American culture, for example, consists of a mixture of sports, media, religion, art, politics, literature, professional life, etc. Some people live in the country, others live in the city, and others live in the suburbs. Each of those locations are in some ways different niches of our culture. Think about the people who will hear you teach. In what part of the culture do they live? It seems best to relate most to that part of the culture. So if only a few of the people you teach care about sports, telling lots of sports stories will probably not be the best approach to apply biblical truth in that context. Learning the context of the people we teach is simply part of loving them and caring about their lives. Such sensitivity to people will also help us apply the Scriptures to their lives.

Fourteenth, show passion for the lives of the people you teach. First, *possess* passion for the people you teach—for their salvation, their ho-liness, their unity with the whole church, their witness, and their joy in Christ. Such passion is the inevitable result of love—love for people and love for God. When we love people we will fervently desire them to prosper in every way. When we love God we will fervently desire him to be glorified in the lives of the people we teach. Consider the following challenge by Richard Baxter. Though he wrote almost four hundred years ago, his exhortation still applies:

How plainly, how closely, how earnestly, should we deliver a message of such moment as ours, when the everlasting life or everlasting death of our fellow-men is involved in it! . . . What! Speak coldly for God, and for men's salvation? Can we believe that our people must be converted or condemned, and yet speak in a drowsy tone? In the name of God, brethren, labour to waken your own hearts . . . that you may be fit to awaken the hearts of sinners. . . .Whatever you do, let the people see that you are in good earnest. . . . You cannot break men's hearts by jesting with them, or telling them a smooth tale. . . . Men will not cast away their dearest pleasures at the drowsy request of one that seemeth not to mean as he speaks. . . . With the most of our hearers, the very pronunciation and tone of speech is a great point. The best matter will scarcely move them, if it be not movingly delivered. . . . Let us, therefore, rouse up ourselves to the work of the Lord, and speak to our people as for their lives.[11]

Baxter exhorts us to care for the salvation and sanctification of people and then to *show* that we care. A teacher's manner of showing passion may differ according to the personality of the teacher and the hearers, but somehow we who teach ought to communicate that the application of the Scriptures to their lives matters to us. Such passion will help motivate them to holiness by seeing someone who feels its urgency.

Fifteenth, communicate realistic expectations. The sixth chapter of Daniel says that Daniel prayed three times per day, even after a decree was issued that prohibited petitions to any person or god except for Darius the king (vv. 1–10). Clearly Daniel was committed to pray. In teaching or preaching from Daniel 6, in our application we will challenge people to commit themselves to pray. We should also be as specific as possible in our application. So exactly what are we going to ask our hearers to do? If we ask them to commit to pray every day for one hour, we are likely being unrealistic. Some people may make the commitment and honor it for years to come. However, the people who make the commitment and fail to follow through at some point are headed for disappointment. The people who are not willing to commit

---

11. Baxter, *The Reformed Pastor*, 147–49.

to praying one hour per day may feel that they don't measure up as godly people like Daniel.

Why not ask the people to commit to do something that is more attainable, something at which they are more likely to be successful? For example, we could ask, "Would you be willing to make a commitment to never let a day go by without spending at least five minutes talking to God in prayer? I hope all of us will have many times of prayer that go far beyond five minutes, but surely we can commit to pray at least five minutes every day, and I think devoting at least some time for prayer every single day will make a great difference in our lives." Hopefully such an application would have two positive results. First, more believers would be willing to make this more modest commitment. Second, more people would follow through with the commitment so they would be encouraged in their prayer life instead of discouraged.

A Concluding Note

In Daniel Doriani's book on applying the Bible, he wisely points out that the tasks of exegesis and application are not always easily separable. In actual practice, "teachers begin to detect relevance before they finish interpretation. Interpretation and application coalesce and propel each other forward. . . . We do not exclude all thoughts of relevance until we complete our exegesis."[12] In texts that are more difficult to understand, our explanation of a text may stand alone, while we reserve application until we think we and our hearers understand the meaning of the text adequately. However, sometimes the meaning of a text is clear. Therefore, early (both in our process of study and in our preaching or teaching) we see the application and we see how we will challenge people to put the truth into action.

We also ask God to help us. We need his help to apply his truth to our lives, and we need his help to challenge other people to apply his truth. And as we think about our need for God's help in putting his truth into action, we conclude our consideration of the process of exposition where we began: with the prayer for God to open our eyes. When he does that spiritual work in us, something more happens than

---

12. Daniel M. Doriani, *Putting the Truth to Work: The Theory and Practice of Biblical Application* (Phillipsburg, NJ: P&R, 2001), 20, 22.

understanding an ancient text and its relevance for today. In the process of interpretation, the Bible begins interpreting us. We sense God calling us to fall on him and his grace so he can help us live the challenge of the text; we hear him drawing us to live as he created us to live.

All eight of the steps of exposition described in this book are important, but biblical exposition is more than following steps. It is meeting God and hearing God speak in his Word. In the process of exegesis, as we give our best to understand the text so we can be faithful in teaching it, we also depend on God's Spirit to flood our minds with insight and our hearts with conviction. May we always pray, "Open my eyes, that I may behold wondrous things out of your law" (Ps. 119:18).

Printed and bound by CPI Group (UK) Ltd, Croydon, CR0 4YY

13/04/2025

14656542-0005